T0345195

Deeper Learning

Integrating brain science, cognitive psychology, education and information technology, the books studies how technology has promoted deeper learning on mathematics in Chinese primary schools.

After introducing the theoretical basis, connotation and mechanism of deeper learning, the author fully explains its practice, including the composition of deeper learning teaching content, the development of digital resources, classroom teaching technology and teachers' professional development of deeper learning. He especially adopts multiple and interdisciplinary research methods, such as deeper learning "triangle evidence" paradigm, learning brain observation, education big data analysis, artificial intelligence education analysis, education action, and qualitative and quantitative research.

On one hand, the book will give researchers of learning theory and pedagogy an in-depth understanding of what deeper learning is and why it provides a systematic theoretical system; on the other hand, it will also provide school practitioners with operational methods and cases to learn from.

Hang Hu is an associate professor at Southwest University, Chongqing, China. He focuses on "deeper learning" and has published over 30 academic papers in SCI, SSCI and CSSCI journals. The research result "Empirical Study on Technology for Deeper Learning in Primary Mathematics" won the National Award for Outstanding Achievements in Educational Science Research (2018).

China Perspectives

The *China Perspectives* series focuses on translating and publishing works by leading Chinese scholars, writing about both global topics and China-related themes. It covers Humanities & Social Sciences, Education, Media and Psychology, as well as many interdisciplinary themes.

This is the first time any of these books have been published in English for international readers. The series aims to put forward a Chinese perspective, give insights into cutting-edge academic thinking in China, and inspire researchers globally.

To submit proposals, please contact the Taylor & Francis Publisher for China Publishing Programme, Lian Sun (Lian.Sun@informa.com)

Titles in education currently include:

Understanding the Professional Agency of Female Language Teachers in a Chinese University
Rhetoric and Reality
Xiaolei Ruan

Research on Investment Scale and Allocation Structure of Chinese Higher Education Finance
Yongmei Hu and Yipeng Tang

Children's Museums as a New Informal Learning Environment in China
Practice, Impact and Implications
Xin Gong

Deeper Learning
A Voice from Laboratory to Classroom
Hang Hu

Embracing the New Two-Child Policy Era
Challenge and Countermeasures of Early Care and Education in China
Xiumin Hong, Wenting Zhu, Qun Ma

For more information, please visit https://www.routledge.com/China-Perspectives/book-series/CPH

Deeper Learning

A Voice from Laboratory to Classroom

Hang Hu

Routledge
Taylor & Francis Group

LONDON AND NEW YORK

First published 2022
by Routledge
4 Park Square, Milton Park, Abingdon, Oxon OX14 4RN

and by Routledge
605 Third Avenue, New York, NY 10158

Routledge is an imprint of the Taylor & Francis Group, an informa business

British Library Cataloguing in Publication Data
A catalogue record for this book is available from the British Library

Library of Congress Cataloging in Publication Data
A catalog record for this book has been requested

ISBN: 978-1-032-24397-9 (hbk)
ISBN: 978-1-032-24467-9 (pbk)
ISBN: 978-1-003-27870-2 (ebk)

DOI: 10.4324/9781003278702

Typeset in Times New Roman
by Deanta Global Publishing Services, Chennai, India

Contents

Figures

Tables

Acknowledgements

The last period is drawn, the volume is closed but there is no long-awaited excitement. Looking up at the starry sky, a bright moon through the window and a small table with a thick pile of books. Looking back, I only hear the sound of children sleeping. And the heart has left a few hints of apprehension and inexplicable contemplation so I open the volume again.

I am grateful to my PhD supervisor, Professor Dong Yuqi. A "common ideal" has brought "reckless people" into the fold. I am grateful to my master's supervisor, Professor Ren Youqun. Twelve years ago, despite my stupidity, he introduced me to the field of "learning science" and opened a window for me. I am grateful to Professor Xie Yueguang of Northeast Normal University. I am grateful to Professor Liu Dianzhi of Soochow University, Professor Yu Ping of Nanjing Normal University, Professor Wu Zhengji, Vice President of Taiwan Normal University, Professor Zhang Ling of Ningxia University and Professor Zhao Lizhu of Shanghai Normal University for providing research materials and ideas. I am grateful to Professor Tu Tao of Southwest University, Professor Liu Ge Ping and Associate Professor Yang Hailu of Xihua Normal University for their support and concern during the dissertation; and Professor Jo Bolar of Stanford University, Professor Liu Ge Ping and Associate Professor Yang Hailu of Xihua Normal University for their support and concern during the dissertation. I am grateful to Professor Jo Bolar of Stanford University and Professor Charles M. Reigeluth of Indiana University for their valuable information and inspiration!

Thank you to the primary and secondary school teachers who supported and helped in the implementation of the study: Liu Dong, Yuan Manli, Li Zhen, Ding Dan, Liu Ying, Wang Bo, Zhang Hongyan, Chen Yunmei, Zhou Hong and other leaders and teachers. The above teachers are my friends, classmates and students, thank you again for your support, help and encouragement!

I would like to thank Professor Li He, Associate Professor Liu Xiangyong, Associate Professor Xu Jihong, Associate Professor Yang Ning, Associate Professor Zhang Yan, Associate Professor Wang Jing, Associate Professor Qian Songling, Associate Professor Wang Qiushuang and Dr. Bao Zhengwei for their discussions of academic and guidance; I would like to thank Dr. Yi Liangliang, Dr. Pang Jingwen, Xie Jian, Bao Naiyuan, Bian Jiasheng, Qian Weixu, Zheng Yi, Wang Jue, Bi Jinggang, Han Ying, Yu Ying, Lu Dan and others who worked together during their studies. Zhang Xiyan, Jiang Xunxun, Sun Kai, Liu Guihong, Xu Chengcheng, Ni Dan, Ma Fang, Yin Xiangjie, Liu Hanlong, Yang Qin and other students provided research advice and life concerns. We are lucky to have you all with us on our journey!

I am grateful to my parents, my beloved and my children. It is a shame that my parents are still sewing for me at an advanced age; my beloved, apart from sharing family matters, actively provides me with information and research ideas from a professional perspective and revises my theses together with me, and my children's laughter inspires my research. Thank you for letting me experience the sweetness and sourness of life!

I am grateful to my master students majoring in English Education, they helped me with the terminology and language correction:

He Shiyu, terminology translator and language corrector of Chapter 3, is a master student at Southwest University.

Jiang Linhui, terminology translator and language corrector of Chapter 4, is a master student at Southwest University.

Li Xiaoqian, terminology translator and language corrector of Chapters 1, 5 and 6, is a master student at Southwest University.

Lu Jiayi, terminology translator and language corrector of Chapter 8, is a master student at Southwest University.

Ma Hui, terminology translator and language corrector of Chapter 3, is a master student at Southwest University.

Yang Wendi, terminology translator and language corrector of Chapter 3, is a master student at Southwest University.

Preface

The long history – from the spring and autumn periods to post-industrial society which is entering from East to West and back again. For centuries, the world's educational centres have rotated, yet educators have tirelessly pursued the "teaching of the individual", the maximization of human potential and an educational paradigm that satisfies the harmonious development of the individual and society. Learner-Centred Design (LCD) has consciously become the syllabus of education. Under its guidance, many contemporary educational paradigms with the characteristics of "the times" have come to light, such as personalized learning, deeper learning, adaptive learning and active learning. These paradigms describe the learning process from different perspectives: personalized learning in terms of learning styles, deeper learning in terms of the extent of learning, adaptive learning in terms of learning monitoring, active learning in terms of learning attitudes, etc. However, they are all designed and delivered with a strong focus on "Learner-Centred Design".

First, from "industrial society" to "post-industrial society": how is the "learner-centred" education paradigm transforming?

In 1973, the term "post-industrial society" was coined by the American sociologist Daniel Bell in his book *The Coming of Post-Industrial Society*. He divided the development of human society into pre-industrial, industrial and post-industrial societies (Bell, 1976). Each stage is characterized by a different central axis that establishes a form of different social ways of being. Pre-industrial societies, i.e. agricultural societies, were characterized by agriculture, forestry, livestock and fishing, challenged by natural resources such as land and minerals, and centred on traditional farming. Industrial society was characterized by the production and exchange of commodities, with resources such as naturally processed machines as its challenge and economic growth as its axis. In contrast, the most important resource in post-industrial societies is information and the competition for knowledge. Social ethics present an egocentric consciousness and a plurality of values. People are no longer bound to the pursuit of traditional moral and social ideals such as family and national sentiments and the meaning of life. People's minds have been greatly liberated and they are beginning to understand their "self" and strive for the release of their values and potential. Economies of scale based on personalized services replaced the standard economies of scale of industrial societies, which are "tailored" for consumers and large-scale services with low enough value. In this social form, technology, services and education become its leading industries. This is certainly not a rejection of industries such as electronics, aerospace and new energy, but rather highlights the fact that the main body of industrial society will also inevitably be led by educational development, technological innovation and information sharing.

As can be seen, the idea that "science and technology is the first productive force" is even more prominent in post-industrial societies. This productivity requires an educational system (not a traditional school) to create and transform theoretical knowledge. The new education system therefore needs to "mutate" and adapt to the progress of the society as it develops. Education itself is a product of social development, and at the same time it reacts to the society, showing a "two-way" interaction between the two. Today, China is moving from an industrial society to a post-industrial society. History is taking great strides forward. The shape of education has not changed significantly from 100 years ago. Education is still lost in the flood of technology (block-chain, big data, artificial intelligence (AI), etc.). Every period of social change is a period of shifting educational, economic, political and cultural centres of the world. In the character of the post-industrial era, whoever becomes the centre of world education also becomes the centre of world politics, economy and culture.

The world centre of education is not a simple drift of objects, but a system of development and a process of construction. The Tang Dynasty of the 7th–10th centuries made China the centre of world education. Hundreds of thousands of international students gathered in the city of Chang'an, which then became the economic centre of the world; in the 12th and 13th centuries, modern universities such as Bologna in Italy were born, leading to a rapid growth in productivity. In the 18th and 19th centuries, Germany and England grew to become the world's educational centres; the first industrial revolution was born in England. In the 20th century, the United States became the world's centre of education. The second industrial revolution broke out here. With the advent of post-industrial society, the ability of the educational paradigm to adapt to the new needs of society will be one of the major influencing factors in the process of building the world's educational centres, and a central factor in determining whether new opportunities for change can be seized.

Charles M. Reigeth, a leading American expert in instructional design, has proposed a post-industrial educational paradigm that focuses on learning rather than selection. He believes that education in this paradigm should focus on the development of each learner, their genetic characteristics, family background, personal experiences, learning styles, learning needs and other elements, and be learner-centred, reflecting the characteristics of post-industrial instructional design, which is a blend of "personalization and scaling". For learning itself, attention should be paid to the cognitive, brain and social mechanisms of learning, and to the systems of teaching and learning practices that improve the learner's performance, motivation and quality of learning (Charles M, 2017). Regulus highlights six characteristics of the educational paradigm in a post-industrial society: firstly, students should learn by doing; secondly, content and stages of learning should be adjusted based on individual learner outcomes rather than learning time; thirdly, teaching should be personalized rather than standardized; fourthly, criterion-referenced assessment should be based on different learner characteristics rather than the current norm-referenced assessment; fifthly, we should value collaborative learning in learning communities rather than independent learning; and sixthly, we should value the pleasure of the learner in the learning process. As can be seen, these six aspects are personalized to the pursuit of people in post-industrial society. They can meet the positive response to technological innovation and the growth of the knowledge economy in post-industrial society; they are also the landing point for the practice of education to go into positive action.

Second, from "ought" to "real": How far is "learner-centered design" from being applied to school education?

"Learner-centred design" is an educational paradigm that has been recognized by academics for many years and has been pursued and explored in practice over the last decade. However, current schooling, such as the classroom teaching system and the current system of admission, training and completion of schooling, has been developed in industrial societies to meet the need for "standardization and scale". The education system is process-oriented and linear, with different learners learning pre-determined content at a fixed time. The less efficient learners "pass" their learning stages by reading without understanding the whole thing, while the more efficient learners "wait" and waste time, losing opportunities to learn and create. There are different levels and degrees of contradiction between school education and the needs of society. The authority of schooling is slipping. Scholars, teachers, parents, businesses and employers of all kinds have entered a strange circle of deeper anxiety and uncertainty. Everyone seems to know how to reform, but there is very little that can be done in school education – neither empirical research nor school implementation has a strong operational paradigm.

Why is this? What are the reasons? Deeply reflecting and observing the research, the author and team members spent five months visiting more than 30 primary and secondary schools in four cities – S, C, W and K. More than 4,000 primary and secondary school students, more than 100 primary and secondary school teachers and more than 10 headmasters were interviewed face-to-face. The reasons for the current educational paradigm were explored from the perspectives of educators and learners respectively. From the educator's point of view, there are three obvious reasons: firstly, there are too many new ideas, methods and models, and the theories are too advanced and difficult to get off the ground. The teachers are well-informed about the theory, but still use their past "experience" as a model in class. Secondly, the new technologies and products under the guise of "learner-centred design" are changing day by day, such as the interactive use of electronic whiteboards, big data analysis, block-chain platforms and smart learning PDAs. Technology is trendy but does not really reflect the laws of learning, nor has it ever been deeply integrated with education and effectively designed for teaching and learning. After more than a decade of building information technology hardware and equipment, standardized management has largely been achieved. Instead of individual development for learners and teachers, it has become more "standard" and "dull". While other industries, such as finance and drop-shipping, are moving towards post-industrial "personalized, large-scale" services, the education sector is becoming more and more "standardized" in industrial society. The education administration has forgotten the need for the "learner-centred" nature of education for the sake of so-called "scientific, regulatory and standardized" assessment. The human nature of learners and teachers have been diluted, and under the guise of "personalization" they have actually been labelled as "machines" operating in a standardized manner.

From the learner's perspective, this is reflected in eight main areas: firstly, learners' reverence for iPads and smartphones, simply because they are lonely; the "playmates" of over 30 years ago – the learning community – have disappeared in the steel and concrete of the city. Secondly, their pride in their academic performance is a weapon for parents and education authorities to show off, while the people they care most about have long been cut off by "regulatory norms". 46.19% of children say they are the most proud of having good friends and being able to help people around them solve problems. Only 9.81% of the students wanted to be "academically successful". Thirdly, their disinterest in the classroom is due to the fact that our methods and content is boring and no longer fits into their "society". This may be the need of tomorrow's post-industrial society. Fourthly, learners want teachers who are emotional. Nearly half of the children said they most liked teachers who were funny and happy, kind and calm, understanding, who always had a smile on their faces, who cared about each student and who could talk to them like a friend. When asked what kind of teacher you would be, 48.21% of children said they would treat their students like a friend. Fifthly, students are eager for inspiring and interactive classes. 81.22% of children say they like to break into small groups for discussion and practice, with opportunities to share and ask questions. Learners want to be the real owners of the classroom, not the "masters" of the education system. Sixthly, they want their parents to trust, respect and help them appropriately. 57.31% of children said they want their parents to "calmly work with me" when they are in trouble, rather than always seeing the good in "other people's kids" and not their own. This is not the case. Seventhly, students want to travel and read more than school and remedial classes, but are not resistant to spending time outside of school to learn additional knowledge and skills. Eighthly, students want to realize their dreams through learning, with 61.11% of children saying they want to "do what they like and realize their dreams" in the future.[1]

In summary, there is still a long way to go if we are to achieve ultimate success in the paradigm of schooling from "what should be" to "what is". This distance is often an artificial obstacle set by our management of educational and evaluation, often a "conjecture" of the adult world about children, and often a human inertia that makes us unwilling to change ourselves and unable to accept our "new selves".

Last, from "theory" to "classroom": what should we do?

The above-mentioned post-industrial society demands a "personalized and large-scale" educational paradigm that has been agreed upon by the academic community. However, the distance from "what should be" to "what is" has led every researcher of educational researcher, reformer and practitioner to sigh that "it is difficult to start a business with a hundred battles". The above-mentioned phenomena have led to the fact that learner-centred design is still mostly at the level of theoretical research. It mainly explores the connotations, models and strategies of various learning styles supported by information technology, such as adaptive learning and deeper learning, but it is difficult to explore them in the classroom. For various reasons and difficulties, researchers seldom go into schools to conduct empirical evidence, and therefore lack a practical paradigm to work with. What to do? This is the cry of every researcher of responsible educational and every conscientious educational practitioner. The current educational paradigm does not truly reflect learner-centred design. It is more concerned with the "marks" of academic achievement. This means that the learner is stuck at the superficial level of learning. Deeper learning and development of individual quality is not really happening-at least not on a large scale. We need to move from the "laboratory" to the "classroom". We need to move from the translation of foreign literature, theoretical design and model building to the teacher, to the learner, to the problem solving of real situations, and to build our own "community of deeper learning and development".

Note

1 The education your child most desires is very different from what you think! http://mp.weixin.qq., 2017-04-26.

References

Bell, D. (1976). *The coming of post-industrial society*. New York: Basic Books: 11–18.
Reigeth, C.M. (2017). *Instructional-design theories and models: The learner-centered paradigm of education* (Volume 4). New York and London: Routledge: 58–87.
The education your child most desires is very different from what you think! http://mp.weixin.qq., 2017-04-26.

Contributor

Fei Yunqian, writer of Chapter 6, 7, and 8 (a total of over 20, 000 words), is a teacher of Southwest University

1 Theoretical foundations of deeper learning

The connotation of CTCL

CTCL, a new paradigm of educational technology research, was formally proposed by Professor Dong Yuqi's team in 2012, with the initial intention of focusing deeply on learners. This research paradigm embodies not only the intrinsic methodological attributes of educational technology but also the ability to promote the development of learners from angles of technology and learning content within a cultural perspective.

What is CTCL?

CTCL paradigm advocates the integration of technology, content and learners within a cultural (C) perspective. Technology (T) consists of two aspects: the first is physical technology such as computers and networks; the second is intellectual technology with performance technology as the core and the pursuit of system optimization as the objective. On this basis, special attention is paid to and emphasis is placed on the optimizing function of technology in the process of learning, which is oriented towards the development of "problem solving". This optimizing function visualizes that through the use of technology learners improve their psychological states like learning cognition and their differences from the targets. The content of learning (C) is not confined to a particular subject but rather focuses on the intersection and integration of content between subjects. For the learner (L), this includes the individual student and the learning community of students, teachers, parents and other members of society (Dong, 2012).

    The four elements of the CTCL paradigm are interrelated and interdependent, with the learner (L) using technology (T) to facilitate his or her own learning of the content (C), and technology (T) being designed and developed primarily on the basis of the learning content (C) and the condition (e.g. psychological) of the learner (L). Culture, if taken in its upper connotation, affects every element of the whole system, and if taken in its lower connotation, functions mainly in the circle of the learner element. Therefore, in the CTCL paradigm, the technology (T) element not only corresponds to the learning content (C) and the learner (L)

DOI: 10.4324/9781003278702-1

respectively, but also to the unity of the learning content (C) and the learner (L), with due regard to the culture (C) element.

From "media application" to "learning technology": the formation of the CTCL paradigm

The formation of the CTCL research paradigm reflects the development and transformation of the educational technology research paradigm, which consists of the following three stages (Dong, 2013).

The first is the media application phase. This stage mainly focuses on the huge impact of the development of media technology on education and teaching. It emphasizes the advantages and effects of media technology applied to education and teaching, and stresses a research paradigm that optimizes the process and effects of education and teaching through the universal application of media technology, which includes three stages of characteristics concern, application design and effect evaluation. However, due to the rapid pace of new media updates, most of the research has stagnated in the feature concern stage, while the lack of the latter two stages is bound to end up in the introduction of new media over and over again, without really improving the quality of teaching and learning, causing confusion and resentment in education practice.

The second is the stage of curriculum integration. At the height of the curriculum, this research paradigm has broken through the previous limitations of simply emphasizing technology or the application of media education, looking at the role of technology in a comprehensive and systematic way, emphasizing the impact of technology on all aspects of the curriculum. It is not simply the application of technology to teaching but high-level integration and active adaptation, which emphasizes the interaction between technology and the curriculum, in-depth exploration into subjects and research at the strategic level. After more than a decade of practice, it was found that improving teaching methods and strategies without considering learners did not yield the desired results. Good teaching methods and strategies must occur based on the learner, so people gradually explored ways to change learning in a technology-rich environment from the learners themselves – the psychology of learning.

The third stage is the formation of learning technology. In 2008, based on the author's understanding of learning science, he argued:

> learning technology is the technology based on learning science, which refers to the hardware and smart technologies (software and methods) used for learning based on the theoretical research and practical results of learning science, and on a deep understanding of "how people learn" and the nature of learning. It is the systematic design of hardware and intelligent technologies for learning, based on a deep understanding of how people learn and the nature of learning, to build learner-centred learning environments that better support learners' knowledge construction, social negotiation and practical participation through the mediation of technology.
>
> (Hu & Ren, 2008, pp. 1)

The physical and intelligent technologies in the CTCL research paradigm are consistent with the understanding in this definition. The definition clarifies the foundations and underlying mechanisms of learning technologies and emphasizes "learner-centredness". However, due to the level of development and application of technology, the understanding did not reach the point where "Technology is a way of life for learners" (Yan, 2015). Therefore, based on its mechanism – that "how people learn" must be based on the findings of cognitive and brain sciences, subject learning psychology and other research findings – the author in 2017 developed a new understanding of learning technology, explaining that

> "learning technology" refers to the description of models, methods and strategies that are nurtured by "technology enablement" in the whole learning process, including the learning behaviours of learners in selecting and reconstructing learning contents, constructing suitable learning environments, implementing learning activities according to scientific learning strategies, and achieving specific learning goals. It includes the elements of learning design, learning contents, learning strategies, and learning activities, which belong to "smart learning technology", the fusion of "physical technology" and "intelligent technology".
>
> (Hu & Dong, 2017, pp.89)

The definition is clearer in the following aspects: firstly, it clarifies the function of technology being nurtured in the whole learning process; secondly, it clarifies the object of its operation, including learning content, learning strategies, etc.; thirdly, it emphasizes the structured fitness and clarifies the relationship between the elements. These three clarifications provide an operational definition and understanding for the research and practice of learning science and technology, strengthen the definition of the attributes of "learning technology" in the CTCL paradigm and provide a theoretical basis and framework for the development of this study.

Learner-centredness: the focus of the CTCL paradigm

The CTCL paradigm focuses on "learner-centredness", and the learner is always the starting and ending point of CTCL research. Based on a series of empirical research results, the study by Dong (2004) summarizes eight major propositions of the CTCL paradigm, including elements and their relationships, learning resources, learning processes and learning styles, as follows (Dong, 2014). Firstly, the core of educational technology research is to effectively promote the development of learners. Secondly, the use of technology should be adapted to the learner's situation and learning content in order to effectively improve learning. Thirdly, research in educational technology is directed towards the optimization of the learning system consisting of technology, learning content and learners under the umbrella of learning culture. Fourthly, when developing and applying digital learning platforms and resources, full consideration should be given to the learners' condition and the fitness of the learning content for the learners. Fifthly, when designing the learning process, full consideration should be given to the seamless integration with the learning environment created by technology, so that it can maximize the learners' active participation, active experience and creative passion. Sixth, the choice of learning methods should be fit for the learning culture, technology, content and learners. Seventh, the application of technology should facilitate the development of learners' problem-solving skills. Eighth, the highest goal of educational technology research is to improve the quality of learning. The logical diagram of the eight propositions is shown in Figure 1.1. The eight propositions are seamlessly aligned and mutually relevant, and focus on learners' learning at a deeper level, providing actionable research ideas and directions for the study and practice of learning technologies in learner-centred design.

Subject teaching: the orientation of CTCL

The emphasis on "learning content" in the basic theory of CTCL paradigm predestines the research paradigm to aim at "subject teaching" rather than "physical technology" per se, let alone the generalization of "technology", but a "precision instruction" (Zhu & Peng, 2016, 2017). Thus, the CTCL paradigm embodies the attribute of "subject teaching" from its embryonic conception. Of course, this "subject teaching" is not narrowly defined according to its understanding of "learning content", but it comprises two forms of curriculum: "subject curriculum" and the "integrated curriculum". "Subject curriculum" refers mainly to the classical courses in school education such as mathematics, English, science and physics, and also includes integrated subject-based or project-based courses; it can also be used in early childhood education, vocational education and higher education, especially in subject-based teaching and learning for young children and

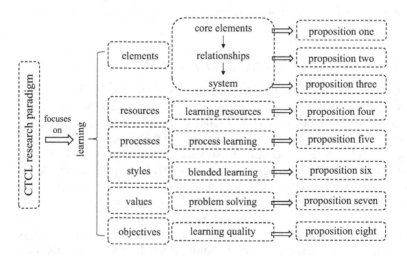

Figure 1.1 Logical diagram of CTCL propositions

work process-based experimental training. The subject orientation of the CTCL research paradigm not only calls for innovation in school education but also fits in with the current school education system and status quo, and has strong practical applicability and application value. With this guidance, this study will focus on the reform and practice of classroom teaching in primary school mathematics.

New developments in CTCL paradigm research

Senior high school IT: development of cognitive diagnostic tools

Dr. Wang Jing developed a cognitive diagnostic tool for senior high school IT in the aspect of empirical research on the CTCL research paradigm, including the following content. First, he investigated the cognitive status of junior high school graduates before learning IT in senior high school and came up with four cognitive types, namely, fuzzy replacement of terminology, inappropriate cognitive structure, unstructured cognition and cognitive black box (Wang & Dong, 2012). Second, based on the findings, a second-order diagnostic tool for senior high IT learning was developed with good reliability and validity (Wang & Dong, 2013). Third, the developed tool was applied to 12 schools in six provinces (municipalities directly under the Central Government and autonomous regions) across China to investigate the conceptual changes of high school students before and after learning IT, and to obtain the types and structures of conceptual changes of senior high school students in IT subjects (Wang & Dong, 2014, 2015). Fourthly, based on the above study, an instructional design was conducted, and an empirical study and application was carried out in Shandong Province. Finally, conceptual change strategies were summarized, mainly including three categories of methods to trigger cognitive conflict, reflection on original cognition and contexts in which cognitive changes occur (Wang & Dong, 2016). The study applied the empirical approach to develop a cognitive diagnostic tool for senior high school students in China in the IT subject, assessed their conceptual change types and structures, and provided operational strategies for instructional design. In a follow-up study, Ding Yibing and Qiao Wen applied this method to two units of "Computer Virus" (Ding, 2016) and "Binary" (Qiao, 2016) in the IT subject at city senior high schools in Shanghai and achieved good results, again proving the validity and operability of this cognitive diagnostic tool.

Junior high physics: designing effective digital resources

Dr. Yi Liangliang conducted an in-depth empirical study on the development of digital resources based on the CTCL research paradigm for the junior high school physics unit "Light Phenomena", which mainly included the following contents. Firstly, based on the results of the pre-concept test of the unit, a learner-friendly micro-video learning resource was developed and applied in teaching, and the micro-video learning resource development path was summarized (Yi & Dong, 2015). Secondly, the CVL micro-video resource design model was designed based on the "Compensation for Visual Limitations" mechanism, and its six functions were analyzed (Yi & Dong, 2017). This study provides a reference model for the design of digital resources under the CTCL paradigm, especially for the development of resources for the physics subject.

College foreign languages: research on motivation and conceptual change

Dr. Li Zairong conducted a diagnostic study of undergraduates' motivation to learn English based on the CTCL research paradigm, identified four types of learners and designed instructional and "precision" interventions to improve undergraduates' motivation and academic performance (Li & Dong, 2015). Dr. Bian Jiasheng analyzes the characteristics of the research on conceptual change strategies in Japan and the United States from the perspective of foreign language learning and constructs a research genealogy (Bian & Dong, 2015). At the same time, he analyzes the research track of conceptual change strategies in Japan, reflecting the transformation between two tracks – from cognitivism to constructivism (Bian & Dong, 2016). Finally, he reflects on the development trend of educational technology research in China.

To sum up, the current research on CTCL shows the following characteristics. Firstly, it is mainly manifested as empirical research, practising the idea of theoretical summary and induction from empirical evidence. Secondly, it focuses on school subject education, which currently mainly includes the subjects of junior high school physics, senior high school IT and college foreign languages. Thirdly, it fully reflects the concern for learners, starting from their cognitive state to the development of their learning qualities, including their academic performance, learning motivation and learning strategies. This study intends to continue the ideas of the CTCL research paradigm from the perspective of primary school mathematics, to provide an actionable paradigm for primary school mathematics education and to enrich and develop the CTCL research theory from the perspective of deeper learning.

Research orientation of deeper learning

In response to these challenges, since the 1990s, learning science has advocated and researchers have adopted a new paradigm of learning research – "design research" – which places the study of learning rules, methods and paradigms (theories) in natural and authentic contexts (practice). Through the bidirectional interaction between theory and practice, a learning community of educational researchers, administrators, teachers, learners and volunteers is built to promote the development and continuous innovation of education in a subtle way. Based on the fulcrum of "deeper learning", studies explore its learning content, learning methods, learning processes and evaluation methods from the perspective of learning science and technological design. Through revealing the mechanism of deeper learning through systematic exploration, a framework for its research and practice is built, providing an operable paradigm and organizational implementation strategy for the development and promotion of deeper learning in class. In order to enhance the effectiveness of the research and practice framework, the study focuses on the following three aspects.

Empirical induction and theoretical construction, rooted in real-life contexts

The research is rooted in the real class context of school teaching. Based on theories related to learning science, cognitive psychology, instructional design and digital resource development, the research variables and observations related to deeper learning are selected, and real classes with different characteristics of the variables are designed. In the experiment, the teaching strategies are continuously adjusted through observations and feedback to the learners. After one month of experimentation, the changes in academic performance are analyzed through pre-tests and post-tests, and the data are analyzed through eye-movement and ERP Electroencephalograph (EEG) observations to test the pre-determined variables and discover non-predetermined phenomena, so as to objectively reveal the occurrence mechanism of deeper learning and the effect of the strategies. On this basis, the theory is then constructed through original data analysis. This research method, rooted in the real class, focuses on the selection of variables and the discovery of new phenomena, and is infinitely closer to the real environment and the state of everyday learning; it avoids the "simple and brutal" approach of traditional educational research in which the application model is designed and then consciously verified.

Focus on school education and paradigm innovation in class teaching

Learning research in the learning science encompasses a variety of learning paradigms, including formal and informal learning, offline and online learning, classroom and field learning, school learning and lifelong learning. Each of these learning paradigms is useful for human development and progress, and all are worthy of further study. However, at the current stage of social development, school class teaching is still the foundation and main part of learning; in other words school education is the basis for all other learning paradigms currently advocated and is still the main battleground of the nation's educational lifeline. Therefore, the study grasps the roots of school education, focuses on the innovation of the class-teaching paradigm, promotes deeper learning into the everyday class and makes deeper learning normal and natural in class.

Exploration of subject content and developing effective subject teaching technologies

Class teaching is divided on the basis of subjects – regardless of the scientific and rational nature of this classification – which are currently at the heart of

Table 1.1 Deeper learning competence framework

21st century competence domains (NRC)	Competence dimensions of deeper learning (AIR)
Cognitive domain	Dimension 1 Mastery of core academic content
	Dimension 2 Critical thinking and problem solving
Interpersonal domain	Dimension 3 Effective communication
	Dimension 4 Working collaboratively
Individual domain	Dimension 5 Learning to learn
	Dimension 6 Will to learn

basic education in the country and even around the world. Traditional educational technology research has focused on the generic nature of a particular learning study, always trying to find a golden key that can solve all the problems of education and teaching, but always ending up with "looking good but not feeling good". Different subjects have their commonalities, but they also have their individual subject attributes. By grasping the intersection of subject attributes and new technologies and methods, deeper learning can "take root", "sprout" and "blossom" in the subject. Therefore, the study takes the "operations and problem solving" component of Primary Mathematics in Grade 4 and 5 as a carrier, and focuses on the core issues of "number and shape combination and problem solving" in mathematics, with the aim of developing mathematical thinking on the ground and then moving on to other subjects in the next round of experiments. The project aims to develop highly effective teaching technologies for the subject.

The National Research Council (NRC) of the USA, based on a comprehensive analysis of theory and practice in various fields of learning, has outlined the essence of deeper learning as "the process in which individuals are able to apply what they have learned in one context to a new context, i.e. transfer". The NRC identifies this process with the specific requirements of "21st century competence" and divides deeper learning into three domains of competence: cognitive, interpersonal and individual. These three domains contain sub-domains that coincide with the six dimensions of competence that the American Institutes for Research (AIR) has initiated and implemented with the "deeper learning" project, which has led to a framework for research and practice on deeper learning, as shown in Table 1.1.

Table 1.1 shows: (1) deeper learning emphasizes the collaborative development of learners in the cognitive, interpersonal and personal domains; (2) deeper learning lays emphasis on the development of critical thinking and problem-solving skills in addition to core content mastery (dimensions 1 and 2); (3) deeper learning advocates interpersonal and social interaction (dimensions 3 and 4); and (4) deeper learning stresses the development of the individual learner's capacity to learn (dimensions 5 and 6).

References

Bian, J.S., & Dong, Y.Q. (2015). The research and inspiration of Japanese and American conceptual change strategy from CTCL perspective. *China Educational Technology, 36*(11), 18–26.

Bian, J.S., & Dong, Y.Q. (2016). The explanation and analysis of concept change in subject learning science: A literature review based on the research of concept change in Japan. *Studies in Foreign Education, 43*(3), 94–107.

Ding, Y.B. (2016). *An empirical study on improving teaching effect based on CTCL: Taking computer virus of high school information technology as an example*. Unpublished doctoral dissertation, Shanghai Normal University, China.

Dong, Y.Q. (2012). CTCL: A new paradigm of education technology research (1): The basic conception and preliminary study. *Journal of Distance Education, 30*(2), 3–14.

Dong, Y.Q. (2013). CTCL: A new paradigm of Educational technology research (2): From media application, curriculum integration to CTCL. *Journal of Distance Education, 31*(2), 3–12.

Dong, Y.Q. (2014). CTCL: A new paradigm of educational technology research (3): Bases, philosophy and practice. *Journal of Distance Education, 32*(3), 23–32.

Hu, H., & Dong, Y.Q. (2017). How technology promotes learning performance: An empirical study based on three types of classes. *Modern Distance Education Research, 30*(2), 88–94.

Hu, H., & Ren, Y.Q. (2008). The new development of learning technology and its significance to educational research. *China Educational Technology, 29*(4), 1–6.

Li, Z.R., & Dong, Y.Q. (2015). Study on promoting college English learners' learning motivation in CTCL. *Modern Distance Education Research, 28*(5), 73–79.

Qiao, W. (2016). *A study on improving the effectiveness of teaching binary units of information technology in high schools in the conceptual shift perspective*. Unpublished doctoral dissertation, Shanghai Normal University, China.

Wang, J., & Dong Y.Q. (2013). The development of cognitive assessment tool for high school students' naive needs about information technology: Research on psychology in learning information technology based on CTCL (2). *Journal of Distance Education, 31*(1), 67–72.

Wang, J., & Dong, Y.Q. (2012). On high school students' cognitive status before learning information technology: Research on psychology in learning information technology based on CTCL(1). *Journal of Distance Education, 30*(5), 56–62.

Wang, J., & Dong, Y.Q. (2014). Investigation of high school students' conceptual change in information technology: Research on psychology in learning information technology based on CTCL (3). *Journal of Distance Education, 32*(4), 14–29.

Wang, J., & Dong, Y.Q. (2015). Students' conceptual types and structures in the perspective of conceptual change: Research on psychology in learning information technology based on CTCL (4). *Journal of Distance Education, 33*(1), 93–99.

Wang, J., & Dong, Y.Q. (2016). Research on construction and application of teaching strategies to convert students' cognitive deviation. *e-Education Research , 37*(12), 74–81.

Yan, S.G. (2015). *Philosophy of education technology*. Beijing: China Social Sciences Press.

Yi, L.L., & Dong, Y.Q. (2015). The canonical form of CTCL micro video learning resources the development and application. *e-Education Research, 36*(8), 40–66.

Yi, L.L., & Dong, Y.Q. (2017). Micro-video resources design model based on "compensation for visual limitations". *China Educational Technology, 38* (3), 121–126.

Zhu, Z.T., & Peng, H.C. (2016). Technology enable efficient teaching of knowledge: Activating the power of precision instruction. *China Educational Technology, 37*(1), 18–25.

Zhu, Z.T., & Peng, H.C. (2017). Measurement-assisted learning: A core mechanism of precision instruction in smart education. *e-Education Research , 38*(3), 94–103.

2 The connotation and mechanism of deeper learning

Multiple understandings of deeper learning

Deeper learning from the perspective of learning science

Since the birth of learning science in 1991, a series of research results have explained and understood learning and deeper learning from multiple dimensions. Andre Giordan, a Swiss scholar, believes that there are three major types of learning (Giordan, 2015): One is to portray the ability to learn as a simple, mechanical record; the acquisition of knowledge is a direct result of transmission. This teaching model is called "direct transmission" teaching, which assumes that there is only a linear and direct relationship between the sender of information, namely the "owner" of knowledge (such as teachers, elders, museum narrators, etc.) and the receiver (such as students or the public), and the receiver will memorize the information in turn. The second is based on the behaviourism and cognitivism learning theory, with "training" as its core and rising to a set of strategies. People set up situations in which learning is facilitated by either "reward" (positive reinforcement) or "punishment" (negative reinforcement) with questions that immediately elicit a variety of answers. By forming such a reflex, the individual will eventually choose the appropriate behaviour, that is, the behaviour that will save him from punishment. At present, the teaching form that widely exists in school teaching is actually such, also known as "behaviour intervention" teaching. The third is based on the constructivist learning theory. Starting from the spontaneous needs of individuals, it advocates the freedom of expression, creation and awareness of individuals. Individuals are no longer content to receive raw information, but to select and assimilate it. Learners in a certain situation, through conversation and collaboration, finally achieve meaning construction, known as "meaning construction" teaching. This model endows "learning subject" with an extremely important position in cognitive development and intelligence development. Individual transcendental knowledge – the starting point of cognition – constitutes the determinants of learning, and learning is no longer the result of sensory stimuli leaving imprints on students' minds; nor is learning the result of operant conditioning caused by the environment. Learning is a process of meaning construction in which learners and the environment constantly adapt to each other and finally reach a circle, which has the characteristics of iteration. Obviously the first

DOI: 10.4324/9781003278702-2

two are shallow learning, and the third is beginning to take on the characteristics of deeper learning.

In *How People Learn*, American scholar John D. Bransford put forward the characteristics of understanding, initiative, interaction, situational and constructiveness of learning, focusing on learners' ability to solve problems (Brandsford, 2002). The concept of "deeper learning" is not explicitly proposed in the classics of learning science, such as *The Cambridge Handbook of Learning Science* (Sawyer, 2010), *The Handbook of Educational Communication and Technology Research* (Spector & Merrill, 2012, 2015) and *Key Words in Learning Science* (Gao, 2009). But they all cover the following from different aspects: first, they cover constructivism, cognitive apprenticeship, situational cognition, distributed cognition, metacognition and other learning theories from a theoretical basis; secondly, they advocate the research paradigm of learner-centred design and design-based research from the perspective of methodology; thirdly, they emphasize the characteristics of concept change, case-based reasoning and model-based reasoning from the perspective of the essence of knowledge; fourth, from the perspective of learning styles, we should encourage personalized learning, active learning and the construction of learning community based on collaborative conversation; fifthly, it is required from a learning environment perspective, created by learners who are good at constructing their own meaning from their own experience. Emphasis is placed on the authentic contextual pulse of the learning environment supported by technology. It is conducive to the development of the above learning activities for learners and the practice of interactive intention-action-reflection activities for learners (Gao, 2009).

To sum up, the following conclusions can be drawn: first, the current research results of learning science design a research and practice framework from the connotation of learning, models, strategies, environment and other aspects of descriptive representation. Second, the above descriptive representation is not a tinkering with the learning guided by traditional classical learning theories such as communication, behaviourism and cognitivism, but an innovation of the understanding of the essence of learning. Third, the new descriptions of learning are all aimed at promoting the development of individual learners, advocating learners' understanding of knowledge and construction after social connection through dialogue and collaboration based on individual characteristics, so as to integrate all kinds of information, solve practical problems and enhance creativity. In fact, all these point to the degree of learning in the end, which requires the depth of the learning process, and finally help realize the deeper learning of learners.

In domestic research on deeper learning, Li Jiahou's team introduced the concept of deeper learning first (He & Li, 2005). This point of view has been widely recognized, but this kind of interpretation belongs to descriptive definition, which is easy for researchers to accept but difficult for practitioners to operate.

On this basis, Zhang Hao's team conducted an empirical study on deeper learning based on reflection, which explored in greater depth the connotations, characteristics, theoretical basis and evaluation systems of deeper learning and other frameworks (Wu, Zhang & Ni, 2014) (Wu & Zhang, 2015). It mainly includes the following contents (Zhang & Wu, 2012) (Zhang, Wu, & Wang, 2014): first, according to Bloom's classification of educational objectives, the six levels directly correspond to learning progression. In Bloom's classification, "memory" and "understanding" correspond to shallow learning, while "application, analysis, evaluation and creation" correspond to deeper learning; second, the theoretical basis of deeper learning is analyzed, including constructivism theory, situational cognition theory, distributed cognition theory and metacognition theory; third, a multi-dimensional theoretical system of deeper learning evaluation is constructed, including four dimensions of cognitive goals, thinking structure, motor skills and emotions; fourthly, the deeper learning strategy based on reflection is proposed, including the knowledge construction process of "conflict-reflection-generation" and the knowledge transformation process of "change-reflection-transfer", and the deeper learning process model based on reflection is constructed. This study provides a certain theoretical basis and practical framework for the localization of deeper learning practices. However, it is based on Bloom's taxonomy of educational goals, which simply corresponds to shallow and deeper learning. It seems arbitrary to interpret the mechanism of occurrence of deeper learning in this way. The study believes there has a big gap between shallow learning and deeper learning, nor is it a natural progression in learning. However, these two learning qualities and learning processes have essential differences, which will be explained in detail through theoretical and empirical studies in the future. If the understanding of the essence of deeper learning changes, then its corresponding strategies, models and evaluation system should also be modified accordingly.

Duan Jinju made some attempts to analyze deeper learning in the E-learning environment from the perspectives of theory, model and strategy (Duan, 2012) (Duan & Yu, 2013). It mainly includes the following contents: first, this study extended Bloom's educational goal taxonomy. The difference with Zhang Hao's study is that the first three levels are set as shallow learning, while the last three levels are set as deeper learning, which directly corresponds to higher-order thinking, that is, that learning can be "instantly" transferred from shallow learning to higher-level learning. Second, he believes that constructivism, situational cognition, connectivism and metacognition theories are the theoretical basis of deeper learning, which is basically consistent with Zhang Hao's research. Third, in the analytical framework of e-learning, deeper learning is constructed from the deeper learning environment, learning process, learning results and emotional experience. Other scholars have conducted scattered studies on the status and significance of deeper learning. Fourth, the structural form of mind mapping is also used to represent the state of shallow learning and deeper learning. This study examines the connotation of deeper learning in the e-learning environment and provides user inspiration for online learning. However, it lacks effective empirical research and specific research groups and contents, so it needs to be further deepened in practice.

Other scholars have done some piecemeal research on deeper learning. Zhang Jing accepted Bloom's idea of taxonomy of educational objectives to define deeper learning and designed teaching strategies in an informationalized environment (Zhang & Chen, 2013). Du Juan et al. also use Bloom's six levels of goals to understand what deeper learning is all about. She equates deeper learning with higher-order thinking skills. And from this perspective, she summarizes the five characteristics of deeper learning: critical understanding, information integration, constructive reflection, transfer application and problem solving. At the same time, the study proposes to reorganize the learning content and construct the teaching strategy of learner-centred design (Du, Li & Guo, 2013). Liu Zheyu and others denied the above scholars' understanding of deeper learning according to Bloom's educational goal taxonomy. They believed that deeper learning is not an advanced stage of shallow learning, but two learning processes with essential differences. The research divides deeper learning into two stages: one is the understanding of new knowledge. The other is the transfer of internal association and external expansion. They believe that deeper learning should be a spontaneous, active and active processing process from the beginning, and "problem solving" is the importance of deeper learning (Liu & Wang, 2017).

Deeper learning in the vision of artificial intelligence

Another area of deeper learning research is in the field of computers and artificial intelligence, which aims to build neural networks that mimic the human brain and enable machines to form deeper learning structures similar to the human brain to facilitate the formation of expert systems that can interpret data such as images, sound and text. The concept of deeper learning was proposed by Hinton et al. in 2006. Based on the Deep Belief Networks (DBN), they proposed the unsupervised greedy layer, which by using a layer training algorithm would bring hope to solve optimization problems related to the deep structure, and then proposed the deep structure of the multi-layer autoencoder. In order to solve the optimization problems related to the deep structure, the deep structure of multi-layer autoencoder is proposed. In addition, the convolutional neural network proposed by LeCun et al. is the first real multi-layer structure learning algorithm, which uses spatial relative relation to reduce the number of parameters to improve training performance.

Deeper learning in the field of artificial intelligence has been widely used in computer vision, language recognition, natural language processing and other fields. IBM, Google, Baidu, Alibaba, automation of the Chinese Academy of Sciences and iFlytek Co. Ltd quickly launched deeper learning or research units in the field of applied research, such as automatic correction function of Google translate, Baidu translation of speech recognition and simultaneous interpretation, IBM's cognitive marketing system, Alibaba's intelligent supply system, handwritten Chinese character recognition system, face recognition system and so on. Deeper learning by machines is already playing a role in the military, industry, finance, health care and education. Deeper learning in the field of artificial intelligence and deeper learning from the perspective of learning science are not two parallel ideas. The development of machine deeper learning provides technical support for the realization of deeper learning in the field of learning science. According to the SOAR cognitive model, the intelligent learning research team of the Open University in the Netherland has developed a brain-like intelligent learning and guidance system LID (Learning and Instruction based on the Data) with deeper learning ability by applying big data technology and the principle of artificial neural network. The system focuses on specific topics in science courses such as chemistry and biology. And through deeper learning algorithms such as search and reasoning, the machine is equipped with visual modality, hearing modality, touch modality, sensory modality, cognitive modality, long-term and short-term memory and decision-making, and motion vision, so that the machine can carry out deeper learning and have the ability of "problem solving". After deeper learning, learners can communicate with the machine through natural language, facial expressions, movements, etc., so as to realize the guidance of the machine for learners (Hu & Dong, 2016). At the same time, deeper learning of machines can learn and analyze the big data of learners' individual attributes such as learning style, cognitive starting point, family background, etc., which can select, organize and recommend learning contents for learners in the process of deeper learning, and provide an operational path for monitoring and adjustment in the learning process; it provides the possibility for personalized learning and distributed collaborative dialogue in the network environment.

The connotation of deeper learning

The connotation of deeper learning involves two fields of research: one is learner deeper learning based on cognition, brain science, pedagogy and sociology, and the other is machine deeper learning based on computer and artificial intelligence. Although the learning subjects of the two are different, their learning mechanisms tend to be the same: to explore the learning rules of human beings, maximize or simulate the neural network operation mechanism of the human brain, and finally achieve "problem solving"; at the same time, the application of machine learning in the field of education aims to promote the realization of deeper learning for learners.

Deeper learning in this book mainly refers to deeper learning from the perspective of learning science, pointing to learner-centred design. At present, research in this field has reached consensus in the following four aspects: first, learners in deeper learning are characterized by initiative, enthusiasm, criticality and constructiveness. Second, deeper learning focuses on situation transfer, problem solving and innovation. Thirdly, learners have a good emotional experience in the process of deeper learning. Fourth, based on learner-centred design, meeting learners' personalized needs is the guiding ideology of their teaching activities. However, there are differences in the following aspects and the need for further research and practice: first, the essence of deeper learning, whether it is a high-level or high-level thinking of Bloom's taxonomy of educational objectives or another learning process with essential differences, needs to be deeply considered based on the new teaching design theory, cognitive psychology research results and empirical research. This is also the focus of this book. Second, deeper learning research remains at the theoretical level of connotation discussion and model construction, with few empirical studies and a lack of operational paradigms. This problem is particularly obvious in formal learning, such as the operational paradigm of classroom learning, which is difficult to be promoted and applied in practice. This book will focus on classroom research in elementary school mathematics for empirical observation. Third, deeper learning has begun to focus on learning methods, learning contents and learning strategies, but it still remains at the revision level of classical learning design, lacking concrete embodiment and qualitative innovation of deeper learning characteristics. This study will be deeply designed and implemented in the empirical study, and investigated through academic performance analysis, eye movement and event-related potentials, interpersonal interdependence relationships, etc.

Deeper learning refers to

> learning in which learners are able to critically learn new ideas and facts on the basis of understanding, integrate them into the original cognitive structure, make connections among many ideas, and transfer existing knowledge to new situations to make decisions and solve problems.
>
> (He & Li, 2005, 29)

Some learners also use higher-order thinking to describe the qualities of deeper learning, such as critical ability, creativity and problem solving. These views are widely accepted, but this kind of interpretation is a descriptive definition, which is easy for readers to accept but difficult for practitioners to operate. Therefore, we strive to explore measures of school education that are easy to operate and have good explanatory significance for the quality of deeper learning.

The system of deeper learning

The cognitive process of deeper learning

The research on classroom deeper learning technology can analyze the cognitive process of deeper learning and construct the S-ACIG deeper learning process model, as shown in Figure 2.1. First, the cognitive process of deeper learning is the whole process of schema construction, including four stages of awareness, compromise, including and generalization. Second, any stage of compromise, induction and generalization can be returned and recycled according to the individual

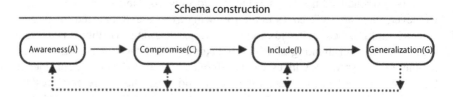

Figure 2.1 S-ACIG cognitive process of deeper learning

situation of learners. Thirdly, the awareness stage is the entrance of learning, that is, the process in which learners participate, perceive, experience and understand the learning content through PCL activities. Fourthly, the compromise stage is mainly carried out on the basis of awareness. Learners will have various understandings, doubts and even misunderstandings in this stage, and need to select, reorganize and reflect on various cognitions, and then start to construct their own cognitive structure. Fifth, the include phase mainly reflects on the compromise phase's gradually unified cognition and finishing, this stage has two functions: one is to form a reasonable cognitive structure, the second is on the basis of scientific cognitive structure, integration and choice of different strategies to solve the same problem, the optimal path to form, to achieve "automation". Sixth, the stable schema is gradually formed in the migration stage, and can be transferred to different situations and problem solving. Meanwhile, the existing schema will be constantly revised and improved in this process.

To sum up, the construction of digital resources of learning and teaching should be carried out closely around the cognitive process of learning. The construction process of learners' schema and cognitive structure is the process of cognitive development and the occurrence and progression of learning activities. Cognitive load theory clarifies the key points of digital resource design by "modular" through schema representation. The concept of educational information-based resources emphasizes the characteristics of digital resources. The cognitive process of deeper learning provides guiding and operational core clues for the dynamic design and phased application of digital resources. Based on the above views of schema, cognition and digital resources, this paper presents the representation and development of deeper learning resources.

The mechanism of deeper learning

Mechanism refers to the inner workings of the elements of a system structure in order to achieve a particular function. It also realizes the rules and principles of operation of the elements in relation to each other and their interaction under certain environmental conditions. This study mainly refers to the interaction, function and operation principle of learners, teachers, learning content, learning environment, learning technology and other elements in the process of deeper learning in primary school mathematics classroom.

The research process of deeper learning

Based on the analysis of the multivariable experimental exploration of deeper learning (Chapter 3), the composition of deeper learning content and its resource representation, the univariate experimental verification of "personalized cooperative" learning mode (Chapter 4) and the deeper learning process, the full text research can be analyzed and explained from four aspects.

From the perspective of the learning environment, in the early stages of the empirical study, we had more in-depth communication with the vice principal of teaching, teaching director, head teacher, teachers and parents on the connotation, value and practice mode of deeper learning, which was fully supported and recognized by them. The communication process is not only to obtain the "license" of in-depth empirical research in the experimental school, but also to let them enter the "deeper learning research community" (Hu, 2008), hoping that they will gradually enter the "center" from the "legitimate marginal participation" (Hu & Ren, 2008). In this process, the vice president and the director of teaching went deep into the classroom many times to encourage teachers and students; the head teacher participated in the whole process of empirical research, and the teachers and researchers communicated, discussed and reflected on the contents and teaching methods of each class with the researchers before and after class; some parents also communicated with researchers, teachers and head teachers and participated in some activities of empirical research. It can be seen that the recognition of deeper learning thinking and the support of all parties are the primary guarantees for the smooth implementation of the practice. According to the CTCL research paradigm,[1] the above process of communication, exchange, participation and collaboration is classified as "culture", that is, school administrators, teachers and parents and other personnel related to learning should form a common learning culture, which not only supports the effective development of classroom deeper learning, but also constitutes the humanistic culture of the learning environment. This part is not the focus of this study, and will be further studied in the follow-up study.

From the perspective of the learning process, Chapter 4 also explains the design principle, development mode and application strategy of deeper learning resources. In Chapter 5, the structure of desks and chairs in the classroom and the structure of learners' groups are explained in detail. The "deeper learning spatial structure" should be further studied in the intelligent learning environment; at the same time, in Chapter 5 and Appendix 10 (operation manual of deeper learning), combined with the description of "4S" learning content and its digital resources and the application in learning activities, it explains the development process of deeper learning activities – "personalized cooperative" learning. The design, development, organization and implementation of the above fields, resources and activities all need the support of technical design, including materialized technology and intellectualized technology. Therefore, this part is collectively referred to as "technology" in CTCL, which is also the core of this study.

From the perspective of learning content, this study constructs and verifies the "4S" learning content composition based on the integration of subject knowledge (SK), knowledge strategy (KS), social skills (SS) and cognitive structure (CS) through the practice in Chapter 4: first, learning content is not isolated, it is selected and reconstructed based on the cognitive starting point of learners, and its content is integrated with learners. Second, the representation of learning content itself and the learning process are not single, which fully embodies the idea of "the transformation of number and shape" in mathematics learning, ① The transformation of number and shape in "content" representation, such as the "shape" of different arrangement and the "number" of corresponding calculation formula in a tree planting problem; ② The "number" of mathematical content, the "shape" of learning strategies and learning activities; ③ The "number" of content in cognitive structure and the "shape" of schema structure; ④ The "number" of mathematical problems and the "shape" of mathematical problem solving. The above four aspects fully embody the mathematician Hua Luogeng's idea of the unity of opposites about "the transformation of number and shape", that is, to transform shape into number and solve shape by number.

From the perspective of learners, there are two aspects: the first is learner and learning content, which selects and reconstructs the appropriate learning content based on learners' cognitive starting point; the second is about learners and learning activities, which is based on the cognitive starting point of learners. It has a personalized learning process suitable for individuals, which is classified as individual cognition. There are also researches on the interaction between members inside and outside the group through resources, activities, media and other aspects, which classify it as distributed cognition, and the individual cognition and distributed cognition are not parallel, but a process of mutual integration; the learning object in this process is the process of "the transformation of number and shape". In the process of deeper learning, learners constantly perceive, understand, analyze, induce, synthesize and transfer, that is, the psychological process of assimilation and adaptation, based on the contradiction between learning starting point and learning goal. Finally, they reach a new balance, form a new cognitive starting point and start a new round of learning.

The construction of a mechanism model

To sum up, the operation mechanism of deeper learning in the classroom (mathematics) is described in Figure 2.2. The operation mechanism of deeper learning (mathematics) is a three-dimensional model, which can be analyzed from horizontal and vertical dimensions in order to visually represent the data. A detailed explanation is as follows.

In terms of cross section, there are three concentric circles including learners, technology and culture: (1) the outermost circle is culture, representing habits, beliefs, mechanisms, atmosphere (school spirit, study style), etc., which transcend specific learning and working situations, but affect the operation of the whole learning community. (2) The circle in the middle is technology, including learning fields, resources, activities, etc. The concept of "Field Theory" was put forward by Kurt Lewin in 1935. He introduced the concept of "field" into sociology by analogy with the concept of "field" in physics. The public statement $B = F(P,E)$, B stands for behaviour, P stands for people and E stands for environment, emphasizing that human behaviour is the result of the interaction between individuals and environment. Individual behaviour changes with a change of themselves and their environment, emphasize the role of learners and field, that is, that learners can carry out various activities with the support of technology, environment and services provided by the specific field. Classroom structure, resources and activities are the services that support the operation of the learning field under the technology design and development, in which teachers and students are formed. The

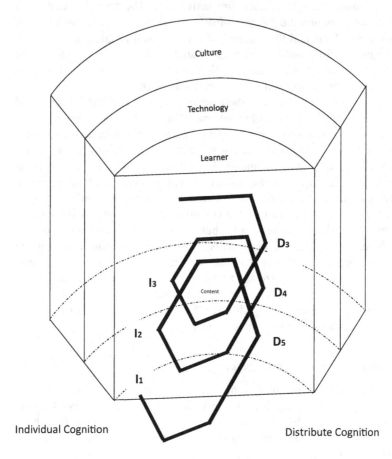

Figure 2.2 The mechanism of technology promoting deeper learning of primary school
        mathematics

field relationship between students: (3) the most core circle is learners. On the one
hand, it refers to the cognition and experience brought by individuals in the local
learning field, and on the other hand, it means that the development of learners
is the core of research. They respectively reflect learning power, technical power
and cultural power. In the learning community, they are interdependent and interact with each other. Learners' cognition is formed in the interaction with peers,
teachers and the cultural circles of the community, supported by the resources and
activities provided by the community, and influenced by the cultural value of the
community. The interest and experience that learners bring into the community
will make them arrange or adjust the learning tasks of the community and provide
corresponding resources, and the cultural values and expectations of learners will
be constantly generated and developed by the members of the community and the
interaction among them.

Viewed from the longitudinal section, it is mainly a spiralling process of learners with the support of culture and technology. The specific analysis is as follows: (1) the spiral process includes three aspects: the individual, the community and the learning content. The individual shows the individual cognition based on individuation, the community shows the distributed cognition based on cooperation and interaction, and the learning content in this study shows the transformation of number and shape. (2) Distributed cognition is a system including cognitive subject and environment. It is a new analysis unit including all the things involved in cognition. It is a cognitive activity and an information processing process of internal and external representation. It exists in individuals and between individuals and media, environment, culture, society and time.

To sum up, the operation mechanism model of deeper learning (in mathematics) emphasizes the following three aspects: first, from the perspective of learners, it emphasizes the appropriateness between learners and various elements, which fully reflects the learner-centred design; second, from the perspective of learning style, it emphasizes the distributed interaction among individuals, communities, resources, activities and environment in the learning process; third, from the perspective of learning content, it emphasizes the transformation of number and shape. Therefore, the deeper learning mechanism of mathematics classroom is summarized as "the transformation of number and shape in distributed interaction".

Theoretical explanation of mechanism

The mechanism of deeper learning (in mathematics) is "the transformation of number and shape in distributed interaction". Distributed cognition emphasizes that cognitive phenomenon exists in the interaction between cognitive subject and external environment, including all units involved in cognition. The specific explanation is as follows.

Representation: the transformation of cognition in media. Cognition is to realize the transformation of number and shape through the transmission representation between media. This transformation is characterized by the relationship between life (trees, distance, commodities, etc.) and tree planting, distance, sales and other issues, and is represented by the use of data calculation (charts, arithmetic, equations) to solve the judgment of distance and price.

Interaction: cognition transforms in activities. Cognition is to promote perception, understanding, analysis and synthesis through activity interaction to realize the transformation of number and shape. Learners are active in thinking and have different styles, so they have different classification and thinking characteristics, such as image and abstraction, radiation and aggregation, field independence and field dependence, rich language and introverted thinking. This means that we need to learn from each other and promote each other. Those with strong mathematical abstract thinking can help image thinking to transform through arithmetic representation, or help them to describe real problems. Rich language can help introverts to clarify the mathematical process or help them to understand deeply.

Debug: cognition transforms in time. Cognition constantly debugs the perception of logarithmic transformation between individual and community through the flow of time. Time is horizontally distributed in the individual's unique time dimension, and vertically distributed in the individual's past, present and future. On the time line, individuals and communities constantly achieve vertical and horizontal collision, interaction and change through media, activities and other life experiences, and finally achieve deep understanding and problem solving of the transformation of the number form.

Construction: the transformation of cognition within individuals. Cognition is to realize the transformation of number and form in an individual through construction. Data, information, knowledge and wisdom are the processes of individual thinking development, which are unevenly distributed in the mind. Modularity is an important theory in cognitive science and cognitive neuroscience which supports this view. Through the above-mentioned resources, activities and time, each individual constructs his own knowledge structure by combining his own growth and learning experience.

Generation: the cultural transformation of cognition. The above process involves a number of individuals forming a community that generates a new mathematical culture and learning culture in the process of numerical transformation. It contains norms, patterned beliefs, values, symbols, tools and other things that people share, for example, the number-shape transformation that resolves real problems into mathematical models in a culture. In this process, learners' thinking is rigorous and logically clear in the learning culture. The process includes normative and patterned beliefs, values, symbols, tools and other things shared by people, such as the number-shape transformation culture of transforming realistic problems into mathematical models, and the learning culture of rigorous thinking and clear logic. Culture affects learners' mathematics learning and cognitive processes indirectly. The new learning culture formed by the learning community will continue to affect the further development of learners in the future.

To sum up, it is summarized from the following four aspects: first, the design subject of representation and interaction is the teacher. The teacher should fully understand the mechanism of deeper learning, play a guiding role in learning, and make use of deeper learning activities to promote learners to enter the process of deeper learning, reflecting the teacher's "leading role"; secondly, the subject of interaction, adjustment and construction is the learner, and the learner is the implementation of deeper learning behaviour, which fully reflects their "subjectivity" status; the third is the generation of learning culture, involving the above teachers and learners as well as education administrators and parents related to education and teaching activities; the fourth is about the existing form of technology. The above five aspects do not specifically mention "technology", but it seems that every aspect is inseparable from "technology". Technology has been contained in the operation of every link, which fully reflects the view that "technology is the way of learners' existence".

The system of deeper learning

Deeper learning is a deep connection and transformation process of complex problems. It is the three-dimensional construction of learners' cognition, the growth and change of thinking. From the research process of learning systems, at the end of the 20th century, learning science began to develop and reached a consensus on "how people learn", that is, emphasizing the solution of problems. At the beginning of the 21st century, Dr. Marie Sontag, an American scholar, put forward the concept of cognitive connectivity and social-cognitive connectivity schemata (SCCS). Under its paradigm, great changes have taken place in the teaching field through the use of information technology. In the age of wisdom, classical learning theories and learning ideas such as cognitivism and constructivism do not meet the real needs of learners for learning, and hinder the occurrence of learning and the formation of a lifelong learning society to a certain extent[2] (Zhu, 2012). The cognitive connectivity model reflects learners' ability and appeal to construct the connection between existing knowledge and social situations, and urges learners to regard knowledge as a complete and related structure rather than fragmented information. At present, the pursuit of learning usually means that learners actively promote problem solving and enhance their creativity, that is, deeper learning. From the perspective of constructivism, situational cognitivism and metacognition, they all have a certain degree of "subjective imagination", but the real occurrence of learning needs to be confirmed by brief experiments. Therefore, deeper learning intuitively observes the changes of implicit behaviours such as brain, mind, cognition, thinking and behaviour through brain imaging technology, artificial intelligence technology, deep exploration technology and multimodal behaviour analysis technology. In this sense, by realizing "real understanding" and integrating knowledge into their own cognitive structure, we can cause the growth of neurons and the enhancement of the brain's connections. On the one hand, the cognitive form changes because the human life field is more intelligent, on the other hand, the human cognitive representation is more fragmented.

Based on the above understanding, the deeper learning research team carried out a series of theoretical and empirical studies on deeper learning in recent years: first, in the multivariable exploratory experiment of "how technology promotes learning", it answered the question "can technology promote learning", that is, that the existing multimedia applications will increase cognitive load but based on "learner centered design" deeper learning technology can promote learning (Hu & Dong, 2017a). Second, in the univariate confirmatory experiment of "personalized cooperative learning", we answered the question of "how technology promotes deeper learning", and solved the problem of "how to do" deeper learning, that is, PCL learning (Hu & Dong, 2017). Third, in the univariate verification of the learning content of "deeper learning content and its resource representation", it answered the question of "what to learn to achieve deeper learning", solved the problem of "what to learn" in deeper learning, and put forward the composition of "4S" learning content and the reconstruction framework and strategy of the "awareness, discussion, practice" curriculum (Hu & Dong, 2017a). The representation state of S-DIP deeper learning resources is found, and the representation method of deeper learning resources, the CRF deeper learning resource development model and its application strategy are formed. Fourth, in the "occurrence process of deeper learning and its design model and mechanism", it puts forward the cognitive process of deeper learning S-ACIG and forms a deeper learning mechanism, solves the problem of "how to learn" and forms the mechanism of the deeper learning process (Hu, Li, Lang, Yang, Zhao, & Cao, 2020). Fifth, the problem of "how to evaluate deeper learning" is solved by building a "deeper learning prediction model" to form a "deeper learning evaluation path and strategy" (Hu, Yang & Fei, 2021).

Based on the above empirical research process, conclusions and cases, the study intends to reveal the occurrence mechanism and process of deeper learning, provide a theoretical basis for the theory and practice of deeper learning, and thus enrich the theoretical system of deeper learning. Based on the cognitive connectivity theory, the occurrence process of deeper learning is discussed from four levels of point, structure, connectivity and transformation, as shown in Figure 2.3.

Perception forms "dots" in the medium. The transformation of number and shape is realized through the transfer representation between media. What it represents is the "point to point" relationship between "point" (tree, road, commodity, etc.) and tree planting, distance, sales, etc. Its performance is to use value and calculation to solve the judgment of the number of trees, distance, profit and so on.

Compromise forms a "bond" between activity and time. "Bond" refers to the formation of perception, understanding, analysis and generalization in the interaction and transformation of activities, as shown in Figure 2.4. Due to the differences in social activities, problem solving and individual cognition, a continuous connection is formed. Cognitive structure forms a structured knowledge system through the connection of knowledge points. The cognitive mode through the retelling of the learned content is the formation of personalized explanation. Cognitive interaction forms conceptual interaction between objects through the information interconnection and complementarity of learner and teacher, learner and learner, and learner and teaching resources – characteristics of thinking through the specific description of the problem, the formation of abstract problem solutions.

Conclude forms the "bond" within an individual. "Structure" refers to the continuous debugging of the relationship between individuals and the world through the accumulation of experience, as shown in Figure 2.5. Through the accumulation of time, the perception of individual and community to tree transformation is constantly adjusted. In space, time horizontally points to the individual's unique time dimension, and vertically points to the individual's past, present and future. On the time line, individuals and communities constantly realize the vertical and horizontal interaction and change in time and space through media, activities and different life experiences, and finally form the "structure" of several lines of transformation – deep understanding and problem solving.

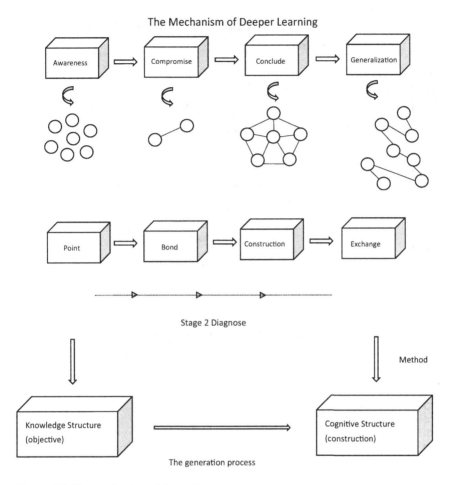

Figure 2.3 The mechanism of deeper learning

Transfer forms the "exchange" in problem solving. Through the construction of an individual interior, the transformation of number and shape is realized. The development process of individual thinking includes data, knowledge, information and wisdom, which is a non-linear distribution in the human brain. In cognitive science and cognitive neuroscience, the important theory of "modularity" supports this view. Through the role of resources, activities and time in the activities of "point", "bond" and "structure", individuals construct their own cognitive structure by combining their own unique growth process and learning experience.

Virtual reality, big data, brain science and other emerging technologies have broken through the traditional ways of transmission and learning of education. Through the integration of information technology and education, based on

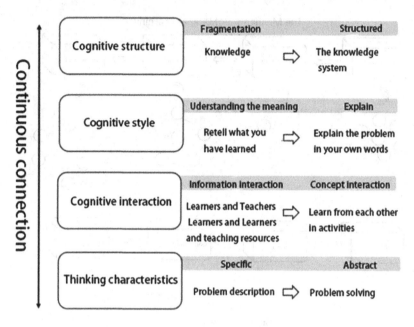

Figure 2.4 Connection hierarchy development diagram

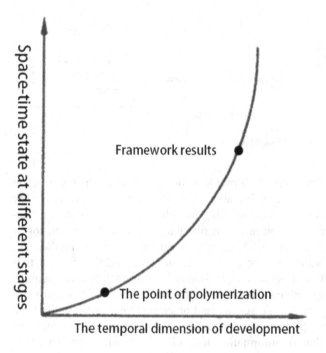

Figure 2.5 Sequence diagram of individual space-time development

deeper learning, they describe the representation form and process from "point" to "transformation", showing the possibility of operation in the scope of practice. The analysis based on the mechanism and occurrence system of deeper learning can provide an empirical basis for the creation of educational theories, reveal the occurrence mechanism of deeper learning from "point" to "transformation", and focus on the research content of deeper learning.

Notes

1 CTCL was founded by Professor Dong Yuqi and refers to the integration of Technology, Content and Learner within the vision of Culture.
2 Sontag, M. A Learning Theory for 21st Century Students [DB/OL]. www.innovateonline.info/index.php? view =article&id =524.

References

Brandsford, D.J. (2002). *How people learn-brain, mind, experience, and school: Expanded edition.* Shanghai: East China Normal University Press.

Du, J., Li Z.J., & Guo, W.L. (2013). Research on strategies of informationized instructional design to promote deeper learning. *China Educational Technology, 34*(4), 20–24.

Duan, J.J., & Yu, S.Q. (2013). Overview of study on deeper learning with e-learning based on learning science. *Journal of Distance Education, 31*(4), 43–51.

Duan, J.J. (2012). E-learning research on strategies to promote deeper learning in e-learning environment. *China Educational Technology, 33*(5), 38–43.

Gao, W. (2009). *Key words learning in science.* Shanghai: East China Normal University Press.

Giordan, A. (2015). *The nature of learning.* Shanghai: East China Normal University Press: 3–8.

He, L., & Li, J.H. (2005). Promoting students' deeper learning. *Computer Teaching and Learning, 13*(5), 29–30.

Hu, H., & Dong, Y.Q. (2016). The future trend of educational media research: to promote the learner- centered design. *Research on Modern Distance Education, 34*(6), 11–17, 38.

Hu, H., & Dong, Y.Q. (2017). How technology promotes deeper learning: An empirical study and theories construction about "personalized-cooperative" learning. *Research on Modern Distance Education, 35*(3), 48–61.

Hu, H., & Dong, Y.Q. (2017a). How technology promotes learning performance: An empirical study based on three types of classes. *Research on Modern Distance Education, V*(2), 88–94.

Hu, H., & Dong, Y.Q. (2017b). The composition of deeper learning content and its reshaping strategies. *Distance Education in China, 35*(10), 72–78, 80.

Hu, H., & Dong, Y.Q. (2017c). Towards a representation mode and development model of digital deeper learning resources. *Distance Education in China, 35*(12), 5–11, 20, 79.

Hu, H., Li, Y.X., Lang, Q.E., Yang, H.R., Zhao, Q.H., & Cao, Y.F. (2020). Deeper learning: occurrence, design model and mechanism interpretation. *Distance Education in China, 38*(01), 54–6, 77.

Hu, H., & Ren, Y.Q. (2008). The new development of learning technology and its significance to educational research. *China Educational Technology, 29*(4), 1–6.

Hu, H., Yang, Y., & Fei, Y.Q. (2021). Educational informatization promotes educational modernization: mission, pathways and strategies. *Teaching Research, 44*(01), 24–31.

Hu, H. (2008). *The study of community of practice in school context.* Shanghai: East China Normal University: 56–58.

Liu, Z.Y., & Wang, Z.J. (2017). The empirical study of behaviour engagement influence on deeper learning: Exemplified with video learning in virtual reality(VR) environment. *Journal of Distance Education, 35(*1), 72–81.

Sawyer, R.K. (2010). *The Cambridge handbook of the learning sciences.* Beijing: Education Science Press.

Spector, J.M., & Merrill, M.D. (2012). *Handbook of research on educational communications and technology.* Third edition. Shanghai: East China Normal University Press.

Spector. J.M., & Merrill, M.D. (2015). *Handbook of research on educational communications and technology.* Fourth edition. Shanghai: East China Normal University Press.

Wu, X.J., Zhang, H., & Ni, C.Q. (2014). Based on the depth of the reflection learning: the connotation and process. *China Audio-visual Education, 35*(12), 23–28, 33.

Wu, X.J., & Zhang, H. (2015). An experimental research on reflection-based deeper learning. *Journal of Distance Education, 33*(4), 67–74.

Zhang, H., Wu, X.j., & Wang, J. (2014). Study on the evaluation theoretical structure building of deeper learning. *China Audio-visual Education, 35*(7), 51–55.

Zhang, H., & Wu, X.J. (2012). The connotation of the deeper learning and cognitive theory analysis. *China Educational Technology, 33*(10), 7–10, 21.

Zhang, J., & Chen, Y.Q. (2013). Learning scientific horizon in deeper learning oriented information teaching mode change. *China Educational Technology, 34*(4), 20–24.

Zhu, Z.T. (2012). Educational technology foresight research report. *Audio-visual Education Research, 33*(4), 5–14.

3 Exploring the major influencing factors of technology-enhanced deeper learning of mathematics in primary schools

Experimental design and implementation

Based on the view that "technology is the life style of learners", this study no longer narrowly defines technology, but focuses on learners. This study introduces the author's new understanding of learning technology in the literature review at home and abroad: it refers to the description of the mode, method and strategy of technology in the whole learning process, including learning behaviour such as the selection and reconstruction of learning content, creating a suitable learning environment, carrying out scientific learning activities and achieving specific learning goals. It includes learning design, learning content, learning strategies, learning activities and other structural elements (Hu & Dong, 2017).

The CTCL paradigm accepts the above "technology view" and the new understanding of "learning technology", emphasizing the combination of culture, technology, content and learners. Technology includes the following four aspects: first, technology builds a bridge between learners and content through the starting point of cognition; second, technology opens the channel between learners and content through resource representation. Thirdly, technology helps learners to enter appropriate learning activities through the construction of a learning environment. Fourth, technology combines the above three to build a new learning culture or a new relationship between education and people.

At the same time, the research of cognitive and brain science and subject learning psychology shows that learning is more influenced by content and teaching strategies than by media, and that the integration of mathematical knowledge and strategies is positively related to academic achievement (Liu & Huang, 2005). There is a positive correlation between mathematics cognitive structure and academic achievement (Liu, 2013). These two points are consistent with the conclusion of diagnostic research on children's mathematical thinking visualization, which shows that the digital learning resources based on pattern representation are more consistent with the cognitive law of the learner's brain (Hegarty, 1999). As Clark puts it, "The medium is not information, but only the carrier of instruction, which has no effect on instruction, just as the truck used to transport goods to the store has no effect on the groceries it carries" (Clark, 1983). So let's go back to our "view of technology". The diversity and novelty of the media itself cannot

DOI: 10.4324/9781003278702-3

promote the development of learners, but technology intervenes the relationship between learners, learning content and learning activities appropriately, that is, that the deep intervention and influence of the learning process may promote the development of learners.

The experimental design

Research question

Based on the above discussion, through the empirical study of classroom teaching, this paper discusses the above problems from the perspectives of academic performance, ERP error analysis, learning strategies and visual diagnosis of cognitive structure. The first question is whether technology can promote deeper learning. The second question is how technology can promote deeper learning. The hypotheses based on the foregoing questions are shown as follows. First, learning styles can significantly affect learning outcomes. Second, learning content representation can significantly affect learning outcomes. Third, technical design can effectively improve learning styles and content. In this study, "operation and problem solving" in the fourth-grade mathematics of a primary school is selected as the experimental object.

Overall design

The study was based on two variables, "technology" and "brain and cognition", as shown in Figure 3.1.

At the level of "technology" clues, according to the existing classroom technology application level and methods, it is divided into group basic courses (Class G), multimedia teaching (Class M) and learner-centred teaching (deeper learning class, referred to as Class D). Table 3.1 shows the basic properties of these three categories.

In Table 3.1, personalized cooperative learning (PCL) is a new teaching strategy based on cognitive and brain science, subjective learning psychology, constructivism and other theories, that is, through the diagnosis of learners' cognitive starting point, to form a typical learner cluster. We provide targeted learning content and learning resources according to the different structures of clusters, and group them into homogeneous or heterogeneous groups according to the actual situation in the learning process. As a whole, each learner can obtain personalized

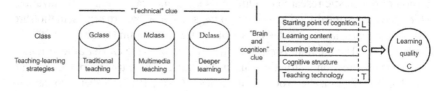

Figure 3.1 Research design clue

Table 3.1 G-M-D class properties

Class	Learning contents	Teaching-learning strategies	Properties
G Class	Teachers determine their own teaching contents in a natural state according to teaching materials, teaching experience and habits	Lecture style	Control group 1
M Class	Teachers apply supporting digital resources in a natural state to determine their own teaching content according to teaching materials, teaching experience and habits	Multimedia teaching in the teacher's experience, which has the form of situational, cooperative, flip classroom and so on	Control group 1
D Class	Based on the psychological theory of brain science, cognition and subject learning, the researchers reconstructed the learning content, designed and developed the corresponding digital learning resources, embodying the idea of "learner-centred design"	Personalized cooperative learning	Violation group

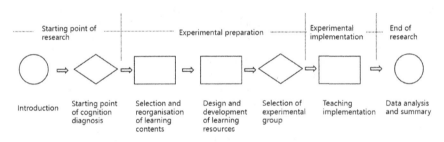

Figure 3.2 The research route

learning content and learning resources according to his own actual situation. At the same time, learners can carry out cooperation, dialogue and experience sharing in the learning process, which ultimately promote the meaning construction of learners.

The operation route of the study is shown in Figure 3.2. Before "the starting point of cognitive diagnosis", we should first let students understand the basic knowledge of learning content: otherwise, the starting point of cognitive diagnosis will lose its significance. According to the diagnosis results, researchers select and organize the learning content, design and develop supporting digital learning resources, and determine the control group and experimental group according to the situation of the experimental class. When everything is ready, the real experiment can be conducted, and data can be summarized in the classroom.

Detailed design

In the detailed design stage of the experiment, due to the complexity of terms involving cognitive and brain science, discipline learning psychology, educational technology and other fields, unified interpretation and coding of terms in the research are carried out, as shown in Table 3.2.

At the level of "brain and cognition" in Figure 3.1, the cognitive starting point is the basic attribute of learners. Learning content, learning strategy and cognitive structure are learning content, teaching technology is technology, and learning quality is culture. According to the CTCL paradigm and the visual diagnosis conclusion of children's mathematical thinking, cognitive structure deviation, visual spatial representation, learning strategies and other related factors are significantly related to academic performance, and the intervention methods of educational technology are determined, as shown in Table 3.3.

In order to facilitate the analysis of educational research, the above seven intervention strategies are integrated into four research variables, as shown in Table 3.4.

Table 3.2 Research terminology coding and interpretation table

Serial number	Term encoding	Interpretation	Source
1	SK	Refers to "subject knowledge", that is, the representation of subject knowledge points	English word "subject knowledge", educational academic term
2	KS	Refers to the learning strategy corresponding to the subject knowledge, such as the "consolidation method" in the "four mixed operations"	English word "strategy to knowledge", a psychological term
3	CS	Refers to the "cognitive structure", that is, the knowledge structure in the learner's mind, all the conceptual content and organization they already have	English word "cognitive structure", psychological terms, such as "mathematical cognitive structure" as "MCS"
4	SPC	Refers to the "starting point of cognition", the initial state of the cognitive structure before the learner begins the next stage of learning	English word "starting point of cognition", a psychological term
5	VSP	"Visual-spatial representations" refers to the strategies in the brain when an individual solves a problem, including graphs and images	"Visual–spatial representations", psychological term
6	ERP	Event-related brain potential, which reflect changes in the brain's EGG in the process of solving problems based on time clues	English word "event-related brain potential", psychological and medical measurement tools for brain activation

Table 3.3 Theoretical rationale, teaching design and CTCL mapping table

Theoretical rationale		Intervention strategy	Coding	Technical methods	Teaching design	CTCL
Cognitive and Brain Sciences	There are different brain mechanisms in visual-spatial representation	Digital resources representations (schema, image)	A	Presentation, interactive resource design, development and application	Learning resources	Co- Cu-Te-
	There are different brain mechanisms in the learning order	Adjust the order of teaching	B	Staggered	Teaching strategy	Te-
	There are different brain mechanisms between mechanical learning and meaningful learning	Adjust multimedia resources, design and representation strategy	C	"SK, KS, CS" are integrated into "SC", and the visual learning strategy of thinking is applied (concept schema)	Learning resources, learn contents, learn strategies	Co- Te-
Learning psychology	Cognitive structure	Build a good subject cognitive structure	D			
	Learning strategies	Combining subject knowledge with corresponding strategies	E			
	Starting point of cognition	Starting point of cognition diagnosis	F	Second-order diagnostics, Interview method	Learner analysis	Co- Le-
Constructivism	Learning is the process of constructing meaning through dialogue and collaboration	Adjust the learning way	G	Personalized cooperative learning	The learning way	Te-

(Note in column between Theoretical rationale and Intervention strategy, first row: There was a significant correlation between six items and academic performance)

(*Note: Term encoding in technical methods corresponds to Table 3.2 interpretation; the first two abbreviations in CTCL indicate the corresponding dimension*)

Table 3.4 Research variable-intervention strategy mapping tables

Serial number	Research variables	Intervention strategy	The level of the variable	Description
1	Learning contents	E	0	Based on the SK content of the teaching material and the teaching reference books
			1	SK personalized learning content developed based on starting point of cognition
			2	Develop SK and KS content based on SPC
2	Learning resources	A, C, D	0	No multimedia teaching resources
			1	Multimedia teaching resources for textbook
			2	DLR resources developed by experimental
3	Learning order	B	0	Classic "central"
			1	experiment "alternative"
4	Learning way	G	0	Classic collective lecture or free cooperation, discussion
			1	Personalized cooperative learning

Table 3.5 Experimental class properties

Properties Class	Learning contents	Learning resources	Learning way	Learning order	Number of students	Class property
C_1	0	0	0	0	30	G class
C_2	0	1	0	0	30	M class
C_3	1	2	1	0	30	D_1 D
C_4	2	2	1	0	30	D_2 class
C_5	2	2	1	1	30	D_3

Based on the theoretical basis and research design, five classes in grade 4 of a better primary school (C school) in T city are selected as the research objects, and classes G, M and D are constructed respectively. Table 3.5 shows the operating characteristics of each class.

Research methods

1. Visual diagnosis of thinking. The research uses the visual diagnostic tool of children's mathematical thinking to evaluate the SPC of learners to provide the basis for the resources, grouping and teaching guidance.
2. Quasi-experimental research methods. The research is carried out in the real classroom situation, in which variables such as learning resources, learning activities and teaching strategies are partially controlled in order to explore the effectiveness of the learning operation mode closest.

3. SPSS data analysis. The study used SPSS23.0 to analyze the data in the experiment, including t-test, correlation analysis, etc., for explanation of the validity of the results.

The experimental implementation

The subject of the experiment

This study takes five normal classes in grade four of C school in T City as the object. The education level of T city is at the forefront of the country, and school C also represents the higher education level of T city. There are 150 students in five normal classes, 30 students in each class. There was no significant difference in the pre-test results of each class. The research objects are real students and can be regarded as "independent samples".

The contents of the experiment

This research takes "operation and problem solving" as the basic content, including three parts: operation rules, calculation strategies and problem solving. The teaching time is four weeks, one hour a day, a total of 20 hours.

The implementation process

This study is divided into four stages in the implementation process. The first stage is the confirmation and training of experimental teachers. The five classes of grade 4 in C school are taught by three teachers, one of whom is an expert (director of teaching and research section), responsible for one class, and two mature (10 years and 12 years of experience) teachers, each of whom is responsible for two classes. The expert teachers were selected as C_1 control group without any intervention or experimental training. Two mature teachers correspond to C_2, C_3 and C_4, C_5 respectively, and receive experimental training in order to minimize the difference of variables in the class that the same teacher is responsible for. The second stage is four-week teaching work, in which researchers observe and record the teaching process. In the third stage, the three teachers jointly release the post test, unit test and learning strategies, and diagnose the students' cognitive structure. At the same time, the teacher randomly selected two students with three levels of excellent, medium and poor in each class, a total of 30 students, for ERP observation. In the fourth stage, SPSS data analysis and ERP waveform analysis were carried out.

Data analysis and discussion

Based on the four variables of learning content, learning resources, learning order and learning style of G, M and D classes and different variable levels, this paper makes an exploratory experiment to answer two questions: whether the current technology application can promote learning and what the main influencing factors of promoting deeper learning are. In order to draw a conclusion, the data are analyzed and discussed.

Academic achievement data

The average score and standard deviation are shown in Table 3.6. It can be seen from the table that, from the perspective of average post-test academic performance, in the G-M-D classes, class D is the highest and class G is the lowest; in the experimental group D_1-D_2-D_3 class, class D_3 is the highest and class D_1 is the lowest. From the dimension of standard deviation, in G-M-D classes, G class is the highest and D class is the lowest; in D_1-D_2-D_3 class, D_1 class is the highest and D_3 class is the lowest.

Table 3.7 shows the results of pairwise comparison of the average academic achievement differences of the three classes (five classes). It can be seen from the table that: D-M > M-G, D_2-D_1 > D_3-D_2, that is, the difference between Class D and class M is far greater than that between class M and class G, and the difference between class D_2 and class D_1 is greater than that between class D_3 and class D_2. Among them, D_3 class with the highest average academic performance is 18.14 points higher than G class with the lowest average academic performance, while D class is 15.36 points higher than G class.

There is no one-to-one correspondence between the average academic achievement of three types of classes (five classes) because at least one sample size between two classes is 30, and the individuals in any two samples are randomly selected. Therefore, a t-test of the average difference of independent samples is adopted. The t-test of G-M-D class average academic achievement difference is shown in Table 3.8, and the t-test of D_1-D_2-D_3 class average academic achievement difference is shown in Table 3.9.

Table 3.6 Average academic achievement in the G-M-D class (five classes)

Class	G Class	M Class	D Class	D_1 Class	D_2 Class	D_3 Class
Academic achievement (Average)	78.03	81.37	93.39	89.67	94.33	96.17
Standard deviation	16.308	7.351	6.294	8.719	3.845	2.743

Table 3.7 G-M-D class (five classes) average difference in academic achievement

G Class	G Class					
M Class	3.34	M Class				
D Class	15.36	12.02	D Class			
D1 Class	11.64	8.3	-3.72	D_1 Class		
D2 Class	16.3	12.96	0.94	4.46	D_2 Class	
D3 Class	18.14	14.8	2.78	6.5	1.84	D_3 Class

Table 3.8 G-M-D class average academic performance achievement t-test

property Variance	G-M		M-D		G-D	
	t	Sig. (two way)	t	Sig. (two way)	t	Sig. (two way)
Suppose the variance is equal	-6.006	.000	-8.681	.000	-7.464	.000
Suppose the variance is not equal	-6.006	.000	-8.030	.000	-5.034	.000

Table 3.9 Average academic achievement test for class D_1-D_2-D_3

properties variance	D_1-D_2		D_2-D_3		D_1-D_3	
	t	Sig. (two way)	t	Sig. (two way)	t	Sig. (two way)
Suppose the variance is equal	-2.682	.010	-2.126	.038	-3.895	.000
Suppose the variance is unequal	-2.682	.011	-2.126	.038	-3.895	.000

It can be seen from Table 3.8 that in the statistical decision, every Sig. is bilateral, DF = 58, t (58) 0.01 = 2.660, t (58) 0.05 = 2.000, and |t|=6.006, then t(58)0.01< |t|, P<0.01, indicating that there are extremely significant differences between G-M classes. If DF = 118, t (118) 0.01 = 2.626, t (118) 0.05 = 1.984, and |t|=8.681 or |t|=8.030, t（118）0.01< |t|, P<0.01, no matter whether the variance is equal or not, shows that there is an extremely significant difference between M-D classes; similarly, there is also an extremely significant difference between G-D classes.

As can be seen from Table 3.9, in statistical determination, every Sig. is bilateral and the degree of freedom (i.e., df) between E_1 and E_2 is 58. Checking the value table (P2), t $_{(58)\ 0.01}$=2.660, t $_{(58)\ 0.05}$=2.000, |t|=2.682, so t$_{(58)0.01}$< |t|, P<0.01, indicating that there are significant differences between E_1-E_2 classrooms. Similarly, the difference between D_1-D_3 classes is significant. Between D_2-D_3 |t|=2.126, so t$_{(58)0.05}$< |t|< t$_{(58)0.05}$, 0.01<P<0.05, it indicates that there are significant differences between D_2-D_3 classrooms.

ERP EGG

Among the students in the three types of classes (five classes), teachers in each class selected two students from each class to participate in the ERP EEG evaluation according to the experience and the academic performance before and after the test, according to the standard of excellent, medium and poor. There were six students in each class, a total of 30 students. The pre- and post-ERP EEG of each

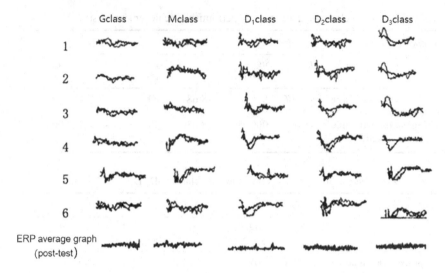

Figure 3.3 G-M-D class student ERP EGG. (Note: thick = first test, thin = second test)

student and the average post-ERP EEG of each class are shown in Figure 3.3. The following characteristics can be directly reflected from the figure: (1) the difference of amplitude before and after D_3 class is the largest, and that in M class is the smallest; the order of amplitude difference from big to small is $D_3 > D_1 > D_2 > G > M$. This shows that D_3 classroom intervention changes the most, and M classroom changes the least. (2) In D_3 class, the average ERP chart is the smoothest, while in M class, the fluctuation is the most obvious; the order of the smoothness degree of the five classes from smooth to obvious fluctuation is $D_3 > D_2 > D_1 > G > M$. This shows that M class is the most active and D_3 class is the least.

Learning strategy and cognitive structure data

Diagnostic data of learning strategy

In this study, the primary school students' mathematics learning strategy diagnosis system is applied to diagnose the strategies of three types of classes, as shown in Figure 3.4. According to the figure: (1) compared with Figure 8.24, the three types of classrooms are generally higher than the average level of the four cities, but not very significant. This is because C school is a high level school in T city. (2) Regarding the distribution score of learning strategies, D class has the highest level and M class the lowest, a phenomenon consistent with the ERP EEG findings, indicating that multimedia in G class was conducive to learners' learning strategy development, while multimedia in M class had no advantage in learning strategies and was even inferior to G class. It was suggested that the rich multimedia context interfered with learners' reflection and summarisation of learning strategies. (3) The learning strategies for Classes D_1- D_2- D_3 in the D

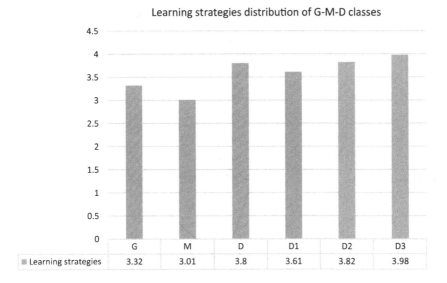

Figure 3.4 Learning strategies distribution of G-M-D classes

Table 3.10 Distribution of cognitive structures in G-M-D classes (percentage)

Class type	G	M	D	D_1	D_2	D_3
Single-point schema	10.0	6.7	3.3	6.7	3.3	0
Merge schema	56.7	50	42.2	43.3	43.3	40
Graphical schema	26.7	33.3	40.0	40	40	40
Multi-linked schema	6.7	10.0	14.4	10	13.3	20

classroom are ranked as $D_1 < D_2 < D_3$, which is consistent with the ranking of academic achievement and ERP EEG. (4) In conclusion, the results of D class, especially D_3, reflect the most effective methods in the experiment.

Diagnostic data of cognitive structure

In this study, the visual diagnostic tool of children's cognitive structure, csv-pda, was used to evaluate the cognitive structure of three types of classes, as shown in Table 3.10. The trend of G-M-D class is shown in Figure 3.5, and the trend of D_1-D_2-D_3 class is shown in Figure 3.6.

From Table 3.9, Figure 3.5 and Figure 3.6, we can see that (1) in Figure 3.5, the students' percentages of the four types of schemata from small to large at single-point schemata and merge schemata are D < M < G, and graphical schemata and multi-linked schemata are G < M < D. According to solo classification theory, the proportion of low-level cognitive structure in Class D is the lowest, while the

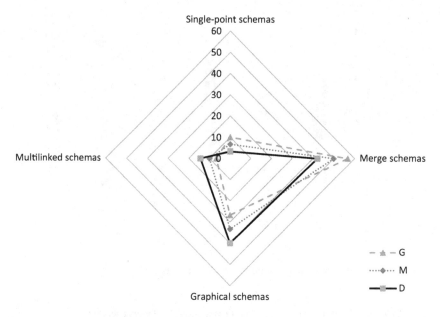

Figure 3.5 Distribution of the cognitive structure of the G-M-D classes

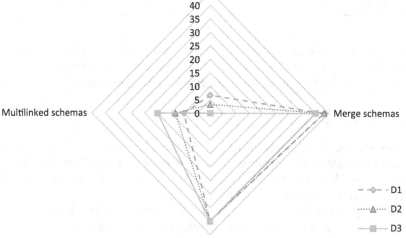

Figure 3.6 Distribution of the cognitive structure of classes D_1- D_2- D_3

proportion of high-level cognitive structure is the highest; the proportion of four schemata in class M is at the middle level. (2) Compared with Figure 3.4, the level of Class M is higher than that of Class G, which is inconsistent with the ranking of learning strategies, indicating that multimedia teaching is conducive to the formation of learners' structural schemata. (3) In Figure 3.6, the order of D_1-D_2-D_3 class is consistent with academic achievement, ERP EEG and learning strategy, which fully shows the influence of the technical design of learning content and learning style on learning quality. (4) Compared with Figure 3.5 and Figure 3.6, it can be seen that the merge schema is dominant, which is consistent with the distribution of cognitive structure in four cities; the graphical schema and multi-linked schema in Class D, especially the multi-linked schema in Class D_3, are obviously more than that in Class G and M, which shows the advantages of class D, especially class D_3.

Data on the correlation between academic achievement and four study variables

In the study, the dependent variable is "academic achievement", and the independent variable is "learning content", "learning resources", "learning sequence" and "learning style". Due to the large number of independent variables, it is difficult to design and operate the independent influence of each variable on academic achievement in real experiments. However, according to the design and change relationship between dependent variable and independent variable, the correlation analysis is carried out, and the qualitative comparison of size is carried out. The correlation coefficient is shown in Table 3.11.

Table 3.11 illustrates that (1) the correlation coefficient between academic achievement and the four independent variables is as follows: learning style > learning content > learning resources > learning sequence. The gap between learning style and learning content is very small, greater than that between learning style and other factors. (2) The correlation between learning content and learning resources is the largest, followed by learning style, which is far greater than that with learning sequence. (3) The correlation between learning resources and learning style is second only to learning content, which is far greater than that with learning sequence. (4) The correlation between learning sequence and other variables is not as significant as that between other factors.

Experimental conclusions and next work

Through the comparison of the academic performance and ERP EEG of G, M and D classes (five classes), this paper analyzes which kind of classroom technology design and application is more effective. Through the correlation analysis of academic performance and four research variables, this paper explores the main influencing factors of academic performance and ERP EEG of learners, so as to lay the foundation for follow-up research. Research conclusions and thinking, the next step of work arrangement analysis, are as follows.

Table 3.11 Table of factors related to academic achievement and study variables

			Learning achieve-ment	Learning content	Learning resources	Learning sequence	Learning style
Kendall's taub	Learning achieve-ment	Correlation coefficient	1	.561**	.498**	.384**	.562**
		Sig. (two-tailed test)		0	0	0	0
		N	150	150	150	150	150
	Learning content	Correlation coefficient	.561**	1	.875**	.530**	.868**
		Sig. (two-tailed test)	0		0	0	0
		N	150	150	150	150	150
	Learning resources	Correlation coefficient	.498**	.875**	1	.530**	.722**
		Sig. (two-tailed test)	0	0		0	0
		N	150	150	150	150	150
	Learning sequence	Correlation coefficient	.384**	.530**	.530**	1	.408**
		Sig. (two-tailed test)	0	0	0		0
		N	150	150	150	150	150
	Learning style	Correlation coefficient	.562**	.866**	.722**	.408**	1
		Sig. (two-tailed test)	0	0	0	0	
		N	150	150	150	150	150

**When confidence interval is 0.01 (two-tailed test), the correlation is significant.

Experimental conclusions

Based on the above average academic achievement comparison and ERP EEG changes, the study can make pairwise comparison and comprehensive analysis from the perspective of academic achievement and ERP EEG development between different classes.

G-M-D three types of classroom analysis: the effectiveness of current multimedia technology applications

According to the above research data, the following conclusions can be drawn. (1) The average academic performance of G-M-D classes is L > M > D from high to low, and the range of L and M is greater than that of M and G, which indicates that the current multimedia teaching method is conducive to improving academic performance, but its improvement is not as good as the learner-centred design based on CTCL research paradigm. (2) Due to the G-M-D class the order of the standard deviation of the average academic achievement from low to high is D < M < G, and the range of L and M is less than that of M and G, which indicates that the current multimedia teaching method can greatly narrow the gap between learners, but learner-centred design can further narrow the gap between learners. (3) In G-M-D classes, the difference of D is the largest, the difference of M is the smallest, and D is the smoothest, the fluctuation of M is the largest, which indicates that learner-centred design has the least activation degree and consumes the least brain power. Although the current multimedia teaching method has the above advantages, it has no obvious influence on brain development, and increases cognitive load and plays a negative role. In other words, it is not as effective as the traditional classical teaching. (4) To sum up, because the difference between M-D and G-M in all aspects is greater than that between G-M, combined with the variable correlation coefficient, the correlation between "learning content", "learning style" and "academic performance" is more obvious, and between the two groups of classrooms is the most obvious embodiment of these two variables, so it shows that "learning style" and "learning content" have a significant impact on "academic performance". The key is how to design the most effective technology.

Three types of classroom (D_1-D_2-D_3) analysis: analysis
of the main influencing factors of deeper learning

According to the above data, the following conclusions can be drawn: (1) For D_1-D_2 and D_2-D_3, the difference of academic achievement of the former is greater than that of the latter, and the standard deviation of the former is less than that of the latter, and the learning style is the same. The difference lies in the composition of "learning content" and the representation of "learning resources", while the correlation between "learning content" and "learning resources" is relatively large, which indicates that in the improved "learning style", the composition of "learning content" and the representation of "learning resources" have the greatest impact on learning outcomes, while 'learning sequence' has less impact. (2) For D_1-D_2 and D_2-D_3, the order of smoothness of ERP EEG from small to large is $D_3 < D_2 < D_1$. At the same time, the correlation coefficient between "learning sequence" and other factors shows that "learning sequence" has a certain effect on learners' brain development, although it is not as significant as other factors. (3) To sum up, in order to improve the effectiveness of technology promoting learning in teaching practice, we should focus on the composition of "learning style", "learning content" and the integration of "learning resources".

CTCL research paradigm: focus on learners
and exert technical effectiveness

Based on the analysis of the above two parts, we can further draw the following conclusions. (1) Attention should be paid to the improvement of "learning style" and highlight "personalized cooperative" learning, that is, pay attention to the diagnosis of learners' cognitive starting point. (2) Attention should be paid to the composition of "learning content" and its integration with the representation of "learning resources", and highlight the selection and reconstruction of "learning content" and personalized learning design and development of digital learning resources. To sum up, the experimental data on the one hand answer the question whether technology can promote learning, and on the other hand can verify the effectiveness of the CTCL research paradigm in the "calculation and simple problem solving" part of primary school mathematics, that is, how to promote learning based on learner-centred technology design.

Further thinking about the experiment conclusion

Looking back at the research conclusion and returning to the origin and problems of the research, the author reflects as follows: Based on the data analysis of the above empirical research, the questioning of whether technology is effective and the confusion of how technology can be effective, we still dare not draw a conclusion rashly – after all, the data sample size is still small – but we can get a glimpse of it, which can also serve as a reference for the further development of empirical research.

Explanation of technical effectiveness: contest of positive and negative

This summary was intended to be summarized by "technical effectiveness conclusion", but it was found to be too hasty. The object of education research is "people", which is an extremely complex ontology. Therefore, the research can only be responsible for the samples and data of this empirical study, and can only summarize the problems explained, rather than "having reached a conclusion". It is not easy to draw a conclusion on the problems of modern technology, modern education, and the new problems arising from the integration of the two. The realistic research of educational practice is only a possible way to a utopia.

First, technology has changed the way of learning and narrowed the learner gap.

Through the comparative study of G-M classes, we can see that the current application of information technology provides support and possibility for the change of learning style, constructs a rich learning environment, and some content can provide students with an immersive learning situation. At the same time, the gap between learners is narrowed. Through interviews, it is found that this phenomenon is mainly due to the narrowing of the differences brought about by the family environment. Different families provide learners with relatively different information growth environments and knowledge source channels. The application in the classroom narrows the gap between learners' self-efficacy and provides almost equal numbers for each learner. It's a learning environment.

The above phenomenon confirms a conclusion of a PISA international survey. The conclusion shows that if we only look at the correlation between PISA and computer application at home or in school, the correlation coefficient is positive, but if we take school attributes and family factors into the research variables, the correlation coefficient of school is not significant, and family is even negative

(Fuch & Wvbwmann, 2004). This research shows that it is actually other factors in the school and family that affect the academic performance of learners. In fact, other factors are more concerned with the development of the learners themselves. Similarly, John Hattie conducted a meta-analysis of education in 2008 (Petko, 2014). This study shows that other factors in the school and family actually affect the academic performance of learners. In fact, other factors are more concerned about the development of learners themselves. Similarly, Hattie's meta-analysis of education in 2008, which is the largest in the history of pedagogy, is based on the secondary meta-analysis of 800 meta-analyses, of which 81 are based on new media and new technology learning. Research shows that the effect of new media learning on academic performance is not significant. It can be seen that studies at home and abroad show that although technology has made some achievements in the current classroom environment, it still stays at the level of learning style transformation.

Second, the current application of multimedia technology has increased cognitive load without a significant improvement in academic performance.

The data show that there is no significant improvement in the academic performance of learners in M class, and the cognitive load of learners increases compared with G class. This shows that the current application of educational technology – or which can be called the application of a "technology centre" – teachers and learners are subject to the generalization of the functional level of "technology", and their main role is to construct the situation or replace the blackboard, which all stay in the sense of "tool theory" of technology. It can be seen that technology is not moving towards "education or learner's way of existence" or "learner-centred design". The key words in M class are "cooperative learning", "flipped classroom", "digital learning situation" and so on, and the learner's ontology attribute has not been involved. Similarly, studies have shown that the application of new media in kindergartens leads to attention deficit disorders and dyslexia in children; online activities and virtual social interaction lead to loneliness and depression. These studies are similar to the ERP research results of M class. In the two-week experimental study, learners' cognitive load is higher than that of G class. If the comparative application is continued, the negative effect may be more obvious, which also verifies the scientific nature of this exploratory experiment.

Third, the CTCL research paradigm improves learning.

"Learning ability" is one of the core concepts in "learning organization" (Diff, 2003). Dr. Chen Weiwei understands learning ability from the following three aspects: first, from the perspective of existence, learning ability objectively exists in learners, which is the essential attribute of learners; second, from the perspective of essential attribute, learning ability is the essential power of people who are in a learning relationship to transform themselves for survival and development; third, from the perspective of development process, learning ability of learners is a historical and developing concept (Chen, 2010). The comparative study of G-M-D classrooms shows that the D classroom based on the CTCL research paradigm has a significant improvement in academic performance, less brain activation and smoother learning process. This shows that CTCL learning technology not only has a bigger effect in improving academic performance but is also conducive to the healthy development of learners' physical and mental health and improves their learning abilities. In contrast, the focus of the CTCL research paradigm may be more able to find the reason. CTCL advocates "learner-centred design" in the true sense, and pays attention to the technological enabling in the following relationships: (1) the relationship between learners' cognitive starting point and learning content; (2) the relationship between learning content and representation of digital learning resources; (3) the relationship between learners and learning styles; (4) the enabling and effect in the new learning culture space formed by the above contents. It can be seen that CTCL is striving to pursue and embody the philosophy of educational technology that "technology is the way of learners' existence", abandoning the instrumental value of technology, striving to realize "learner-centred".

Technology effectiveness strategy: learner-centred design

Based on the above analysis, the CTCL research paradigm based on learner-centred design is effective in both academic achievement and learning ability improvement. However, how can it be effective and how to operate learner-centred design? This paper considers these questions and gives a specific explanation in the way of empirical research.

First, cognitive starting point diagnosis is the basis of learning.

Vygotsky's "zone of proximal development theory" holds that there are two levels of students' development: one is the current level of students, that is, the level of problem solving that can be achieved in independent activities; the other is the level of students' possible development, that is, the potential development obtained through teaching; the difference between the two is the zone of proximal development. Teaching should focus on students' zone of proximal development and provide students with content with appropriate difficulty so as to mobilize students' enthusiasm, develop their potential, surpass their zone of proximal development and reach the level of the next stage, and then carry on the development of the next zone on this basis. So how to determine the nearest development area of a specific subject system is actually a very difficult thing. Cognitive starting point diagnosis is the process of mining learners' current level and zone of proximal development based on learning content. In this study, the visual diagnostic tools and methods of children's mathematical thinking provide a useful attempt for the evaluation of cognitive starting point, and the second-order diagnostic method provides an operable method and strategy for this abstract theory (Wang & Dong, 2012; Wang, 2013). This study mainly adopts the thinking visualization method, combined with the second-order diagnosis, to diagnose and classify the cognitive starting point of learners, which is also the operation starting point of the follow-up experiment implementation of this study, and also the basis of "learner-personalized learning design".

Second, integration of knowledge and strategy constitutes learning content.

Learning based on the diagnosis of cognitive starting point means that learners should choose the content that meets their own needs among individuals or clusters. Traditional personalized learning pays more attention to the "personalized" selection and push of knowledge itself. The data from the empirical study of D_1-D_2 verified Wilbur Schramm's theory that the integration of knowledge and strategy has a significant impact on academic performance. The subject knowledge "SK" and the corresponding learning strategy "KS" constitute the learning content, which is a complete knowledge system. This just confirms Gagne's classification of learning results as "declarative knowledge", "procedural knowledge" and "strategic knowledge", which are interconnected and constitute the content ontology. However, the integration of knowledge and strategy is different for individual learners and clusters. Therefore, instructional designers are required to select and reorganize learning content, rather than direct teaching based on textbook content in traditional classroom teaching, or mainly "replication" of "declarative" and "procedural knowledge" – even some teachers stay at "procedural knowledge" in the representation stage of "declarative knowledge".

Third, schematic representation guides the design of learning resources.

According to the research data, there is a high correlation between learning content and learning resources, and learning resources themselves are a representation of learning content. A traditional digital learning resource is a kind of graphic expression based on experience design, which focuses on "situation creation" and "abstract content visualization" or "electronic version replacing paper or handwritten version". Are these two phenomena really effective for learning? The theory of visual spatial representation (VSP) holds that the representation ability of learners' brains includes visual image and spatial relationship (Hegarty, 1999), which corresponds to two forms of digital language: visual images are image representations, which are negatively correlated with academic performance; spatial relationships are schema representations, which are positively correlated with academic performance (Xu & Shi, 1992; Yu & Zeng, 2003). However, "situation creation" and "abstract content concretization" are just image representation. Although constructivism requires "situation and life" to facilitate learners' understanding, it also forgets that the ultimate goal of learning is to understand the law and essence of knowledge, and to return to the "schema" stage to realize "meaning construction". At present, the promotion of "happy learning" and "life-oriented education" by businesses has greatly strengthened this trend of thought in the market; at the same time, there is no doubt that the expression of digital "replacement" is just from "one form" to "another form", which does not really touch the mechanism of learning. The data in this study also verifies this fact. In the comparison of the G-M classrooms, the academic performance of M classroom has no significant improvement, and the cognitive load has increased. The reason is that most of the supporting digital teaching resources in the market are developed based on the idea of "contextualization", which leads to the opposite road of "image" representation; while the D classroom just reflects the internal characteristics of learning "integration" and "schema representation" of content and learning resources.

Fourth, personalization-cooperative learning generates learning activities and interactive relationships.

Activity is the basic way of human existence, and learning activity is the basic way of learners' existence. It is in learning activities that learners combine learning objects (learning content) through technology to form a learning whole, and the three interact and influence each other. In learning activities, learners form a learning relationship with others, including instructors, peers and learning resource providers. The formation of a well-structured learning relationship is conducive to the better use of technology, the improvement of learners' self-efficacy and the final improvement of academic performance. Based on the above understanding, personalized cooperative learning deepens the connotation of "learner-centred design", which includes not only individual learners, but also clusters or learning groups, and it also conforms to the constructivism theory that individuals in a certain situation, through group cooperation and conversation, finally achieve the process of meaning construction. The data of the relationship between academic performance and learning in the three G-M-D classes verify this theory.

Fifth, technology enablement integrates multiple elements of the learning process.

In the above diagnosis of cognitive starting point, integration of learning content, representation of digital resources and construction of good relationships between learning activities and learning all reflect the energy of technology. This kind of energy includes not only the direct materialization technology of resource representation, but also the indirect materialization technology of personalized cooperative learning resource diversity, and the intelligent technology of knowledge and strategy integration and learning relationship construction in the process of learning design. Technology, such as the link and lubricant in the learning process, integrates the above elements to realize the unity of learning practice. In the representation of learning content and resources, it is the carrier; in learning activities, it is the intermediary; in learning relationship, it is the communication; in a learning environment, it is the space; in learning wisdom, it is the value.

Sixth, learning culture generates and iterates learning wisdom.

Learning wisdom is the learning quality of pursuing life wisdom in learning activities. In learning activities, learners may acquire knowledge, but not necessarily wisdom. Knowledge is only the knowledge and experience of sub-disciplines in nature, society and human beings' own fields, which is the result of previous practice. Most of the acquisition of knowledge only inherits and aims at the acquisition of problem conclusions. Learning wisdom depends on learners' deeper understanding of the essence of learning, and "Understanding is the whole relationship between people and the object of understanding at a certain time" (Yin, 1998). Therefore, learners need to understand themselves, understand learning content, understand learning technology, understand learning partners, and understand the role and relationship between them. Learning wisdom is generated from the interaction and relationship among learners, learning content, learning resources, teachers and peers, and is expressed in the way learners treat themselves, their learning content, their learning resources and their teachers and peers. In the process of learning and self-development, this kind of wisdom will continue to iterate and evolve, and then gradually form a learning culture. The enrichment and development of learning culture with intelligence attributes will promote the generation of learners' wisdom. This is the cultural essence of the CTCL research paradigm on the basis of emphasizing the integration of learners, content and technology.

Technical effectiveness levels: from "physical level" to "emotional level"

For modern people, this means learning to survive in technology. The effectiveness of technology is ultimately reflected in the level of learners' development, which can be represented by "learning ability" and can be divided into three levels according to its influencing factors: physical ability, cognitive ability and emotional ability. Based on this, the study divides the learning ability level in the perspective of technology into three levels: physical level, cognitive level and emotional level, which represents the triple realm of technology effectiveness, as shown in Figure 3.7.

First, at a physical level the way of learning is changed.

Physical level refers to technology involved in learners' physiological organs (except the brain), including information acquisition, perception and the expression of their own information. It is relatively stable, limited and explicit, such as watching multimedia animation, experiencing virtual reality technology, WeChat expression communication, remote interactive communication and so on. It is in the outermost layer of effectiveness. From the essence of learning practice, it only changes the way of learning. The M class in the research belongs to this level and

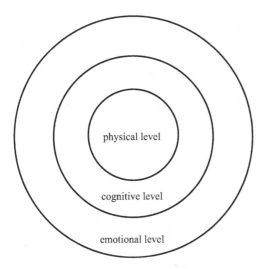

Figure 3.7 Three levels of learning ability

category, and the typical application of current technology is more concerned about whether the situation is created, whether the learners use mobile media devices, whether the classroom is installed with an interactive learning platform and so on.

Second, at a cognitive level academic performance is improved.

Cognitive level refers to the application of technology that affects the development of human thinking organs, including knowledge acquisition and understanding, lasting changes in cognitive structure and the formation of new schema. Its external representation is the improvement of academic performance, and it is the backbone of learning ability. It is in the middle layer of effectiveness structure, such as D classroom in research. Learners' academic performance has been significantly improved, ERP EEG gradually smoothed, and learners' cognitive level has been effectively developed.

Third, at an emotional level learner development is promoted.

Emotional level is the most implicit, the core of learning ability, and also the highest level of the effectiveness of technology application. It mainly affects learners' motivation (learning goal, interest, motivation, etc.), perseverance (learners' spirit, psychological quality, will and values, etc.) and innovation (seeking difference, criticism, creation, etc.), which determines the character of learners' learning behaviour, and has great significance on relative stability, such as the focus on learners' self-efficacy. At present, the research team's empirical research on intervention strategies is only on the cognitive level; emotional level factors are only involved in the research process. The research team will design the intervention strategy of emotional level in the follow-up research, and carry out empirical research and verification, which is the value pursuit of "learning culture" in the CTCL research paradigm.

To sum up, the "deeper learning" classroom is designed according to the CTCL research paradigm, and compared with "traditional teaching" and "multimedia teaching" classroom, to explore the effectiveness of technology in promoting learning and the factors influencing learning, and to seek the reasons. CTCL advocates "learner-centred design" in the true sense and pays attention to the technological enabling in the following relationships: (1) the relationship between learners' cognitive starting point and learning content, that is, the composition mechanism and integration method between cognitive structure and subject knowledge and corresponding strategies; (2) the relationship between learning content and digital resource representation, that is, the design mechanism of digital learning resources and its impact on content appropriate representation strategies; (3) the relationship between learners and learning styles, that is, the form and structure of learning activities and the relationship between learners in this activity; (4) the integration of the above content forms of CTCL learning technology, giving birth to a new learning culture in which technology plays its role. It can be seen that CTCL is striving to pursue and embody the philosophy of educational technology that "technology is the way of learners' existence", abandoning the instrumental value of technology, striving to realize "learner-centred" and returning to the essential significance of education.

From the philosophical point of view of "technology existentialism", this paper examines the current situation and problems of technology application in education and teaching. Based on the CTCL research paradigm, this book designs three types of G-M-D classrooms and five models to conduct empirical research on classroom teaching in order to answer two questions in educational technology to a certain extent: first, is technology really effective? And second, how is technology effective? Based on the data analysis and discussion of empirical research, the author summarizes and explains the effectiveness of technology, the strategy of effective design of technology and the three levels of effectiveness from three aspects: the positive and negative contest of technology effectiveness, the methods of learner-centred design, and from "physical level" to "emotional level". As Marx said, "the positive and negative value of technology to human beings is not determined by technology, but by the application of technology in different social situations" (1962).

The next step of research

Based on the conclusion of the exploratory experiment, further research questions are determined: first, the classroom teaching of deeper learning is effective and can be further studied. Second, in-depth research focuses on two research variables: (1) personalized cooperative learning about learning style; (2) composition and reconstruction of learning content and representation and development of digital resources. Learning content and learning resources are originally two research variables, because resources are the carrier of content, and the correlation between them is the largest. It shows that they can be combined into one variable; (3) the above two variables are experimented separately, in order to change the multivariable exploration into single variable verification.

Summary

This chapter is about the exploratory experimental research of "classroom deeper learning technology".

Based on the research review, brain science, cognitive psychology, constructivism and other theories on mathematics learning, this chapter takes "operation and problem solving" as the carrier, and carries out a four-week, one hour classroom experiment every day in the fourth grade of C primary school in T city. Through the visual diagnosis of academic performance, ERP EEG, learning strategy and cognitive structure, this paper compares and analyzes the three classes of G, M and D in the experiment from physical level, cognitive level and emotional level, and draws the following conclusions: first, technology is effective in promoting learning; second, the effectiveness of technology mainly lies in how to design technology.

Through the above classroom experiments and data analysis, the author clarifies the main influencing variables of deeper learning in the mathematics classroom: first, the composition of learning content and the representation of digital resources should conform to the cognitive law of learners; second, the learning style should meet the needs of individual and social interaction of learners. In the follow-up, the research will focus on these two variables to explore the specific operation paradigm.

References

Chen, W.W. (2010). *Learning ability in the field of technology survival.* Beijing: Education Science Press.

Clark, R.E. (1983). Reconsidering research on learning from media. *Review of Educational Research, 53*(4), 445–459.

Diff, S. (2003). *Learning ability.* Yanji: Yanbian People's Publishing House.

Fuch, T., & Wvbwmann, I. (2004). Computers and student learning: Bivariate and multivariate evidence on the availability and use of computer at home and at school. *Social Science Electronic Publishing, 47*(11), 339 –347.

Hegarty, M., & Kozhevnikov, M. (1999). Types of visual-spatial representations and mathematical problem solving. *Journal of Educational Psychology, 91*(4), 684 –689.

Hu, H., & Dong, Y.Q. (2017). How technology promotes learning performance: an empirical study based on three types of classes. *Modern Distance Education Research, 30*(2), 88 –94.

Liu, D.Z., & Huang, X.T. (2005). The application and development characteristics of primary school pupils' math learning strategies. *Psychological Science, 28*(2), 272 –276.

Liu, D.Z. (2013). *The research on the development and processing mechanism of primary school students' Mathematic learning strategies.* Unpublished doctoral dissertation. Southwest Normal University, Chong Qing.

Marx, E. (1962). *The complete works of Marx and Engels: volume 12.* Beijing: People's Publishing House.

Petko, D.E. (2014). *Lehren und lemen mit digitalen medien.* Weinheim: Beitz.

Wang, J., & Dong, Y.Q. (2012). A survey of cognitive status before high school information technology learning. *Journal of Distance Education, 30*(5), 56 –62.

Wang, J. (2013). *Research on the concept change of information technology for high school students.* Unpublished doctoral dissertation. Northeast Normal University, Changchun.

Xu, F., & Shi, J.N. (1992). A preliminary study of the correlation of spatial ability and geometrical ability of 4 - and 5 - grade students. *Acta Psychologica Sinica, 24*(1), 20 –27.

Yin, D. (1998). *The destiny of understanding.* Beijing: Sanlian Bookstore of Life Reading New Knowledge.

Yu, G.L., & Zeng, P.P. (2003). Visual-spatial representation and Mathematical problem solving for children with Mathematics learning disabilities. *Acta Psychology, 35*(5), 643–648.

4 Classroom verification of deeper learning

Verification 1: the experimental design and implementation of "4S" learning content and its resource representation

At present, deeper learning under the guidance of learner-centred design is not only the core idea of instructional design, but also has become a hot topic in the field of learning science research and educational technology practice. It is also the guiding ideology of front-line classroom teaching. So, what is learner-centred design? How to implement deeper learning? So far, there are few practical examples, and little cognitive and psychological evidence. "Learner centre" is definited that

> teaching should combine the attention to each learner with the attention to learning itself, in which the attention to each learner is to pay attention to their genetic characteristics, personal experience, talent and other personal needs and individual attributes(McCombs & Whisler, 1997) . The focus on learning itself is on what to learn, how it happens, motivation and performance. Learning science takes human's deeper learning as an important research content. It holds that learning is not only a cognitive process of individual perception, memory and thinking, but also a social construction process rooted in social culture, historical background and real life
>
> (Feng & Ren, 2009).

It can be seen that deeper learning must be personalized learning based on the individual attributes of learners, and at the same time, it is a socialized process of collaboration between individuals. Therefore, how to design and implement deeper learning, how to understand technology and whether technology can promote deeper learning have become important topics in the field of educational practice.

Based on the understanding of "learner-centred design" and the viewpoint of "technology is the learner's way of living (Yan, 2015)", the research makes a new understanding on the basis of the original understanding of learning technology:

> It refers to the description of the models, methods and strategies that are incubated by technology embodiment in the whole learning process, including

DOI: 10.4324/9781003278702-4

learning behaviours such as learners' selection and reconstruction of learning content, construction of appropriate learning environment, implementation of learning activities in accordance with scientific learning strategies to achieve specific learning goals; it includes structural elements such as Learning Design, Learning Contents, Learning Strategies and Learning Activities.

(Hu & Dong, 2017, p88)

Based on the above understanding of learning technology, in the multivariate exploratory experiment of "How technology facilitates learning" (Hu & Dong, 2017), the question "Can technology facilitate learning" was answered. First, existing multimedia application methods would increase cognitive load. Second, deeper learning technology based on "learner-centred design" can promote learning.

So, what should the object or content of deeper learning be? That is, what should deeper learning "learn"? In his sixth book *Instruction-Design Theories and Models: The Learner-Centered Paradigm of Education*, Charles M. Reigeluth (2016) expounds "the value, strategies and methods of learner-centred instructional design, especially the connotation and principle of learner-centred instructional design, which is based on the starting point of learning", and reconstructs the curriculum form, and emphasizes that the composition of subject content and its resource representation should conform to the cognitive law of learners (Hu & Dong, 2016).

Experimental design

Basis one: learning content and resource representation

Learning content includes content composition and resource representation. There are various forms of content presentation, but how to make learners accept and understand such abstract things requires the help of tools such as symbols, graphics and words. This kind of form which can be presented on the surface is called resource representation (Xiang, 2008). It can be seen that resource representation is the external presentation form of content. This presentation form expresses the content in a visual way, so that the content can be spread and understood by learners. In short, content composition and resource representation complement each other, so as to convey to learners the knowledge, emotions, attitudes and values that the learning content wants to express. Resource representation can materialize and visualize the learning content, and reflects the related attribute of learning content.

Digital resource representation is a more advanced form of information representation. The development of information technology provides a powerful visual help for digital resources. The development of information technology has provided a powerful aid to the visualization of digital resources, drawing attention to the openness of resource representation, the contextual nature of virtual reality technology representation and the interactivity and intelligence of artificial intelligence representation. Representation and cognition of information in a digital learning environment enhances the thinking and subjective initiative of learners.

Basis two: overview of exploratory experiments

In the exploratory experiment stage, the study includes four variables: learning style, learning content, learning resources and learning sequence, with learning content and learning resources (.561 and .498) being second only to learning style (.562) in terms of their correlation with academic achievement, and with very small differences (Hu & Dong, 2017). At the same time, learning content and resource representation themselves are twin brothers, but the former emphasizes the composition of content, while the latter emphasizes the representation of content. Therefore, in the confirmatory experiment stage, the research unified the two as a univariate "learning content" to further verify its effectiveness.

Experimental problems

Based on the basis and conclusion of the exploratory experiment, this study plans to implement two kinds of classes (four classes and four variables). The empirical study of teaching is conducted from three dimensions of academic achievement, eye movement changes and ERP EEG changes to answer three questions: first, to test the effectiveness of the reconstruction of learning content and the corresponding development of digital resources. The second is to analyze the elements and structure of learning content and summarize its organizational strategies through empirical research. The third is to summarize the representation methods and development modes of digital learning resources.

Experimental method

1. **Quasi-experimental research method.** The study was carried out in real classroom situations, with learning content and its resources as the only variables, and variables such as learning style and teaching strategy were controlled to explore effective learning operation modes.
2. **Experimental study.** Through eye tracker and ERP EEG observation, the data of eye movement behaviour and brain wave of learners were collected to analyze the relationship between learning content, attention and academic achievement.

Detailed design

According to the relevant research and exploratory experimental conclusions, the composition of learning content and its resource representation have a great correlation with academic performance, and they are two sides of "content", so they are merged into the same variable "learning content" in the confirmatory experiment stage. The relevant design, research terms, data analysis and research conclusions of the exploratory experiment are detailed in Chapter 3. For continuity and clarity of expression, the design descriptions of the two types of experiments are shown in Table 4.1.

The research is explained from the five design dimensions in Table 4.1 as follows. (1) From the perspective of research purpose, the exploratory experiment is to seek the main influencing factors of the "learner-centred" classroom and explore comprehensive practice methods; the confirmatory experiment is mainly to further confirm the validity of the "learning content" in the exploratory experiment and its specific operation mode. (2) From the point of view of

Table 4.1 Description table of two types of experimental design

The research type	Exploratory experiment	Confirmatory experiment
Research purpose	The first is to explore whether technology can enhance learning; the second is to explore how technology can promote learning, mainly including learning style (PCL), learning content (SK+KS+CS+SS), resource representation (SR), learning sequence and other contents	The first is to verify the validity of "learning content (SK+KS+CS+SS, 4S)" and its resource representation based on cognitive processes. The second is to analyze the elements and structure of learning content and conclude its organizational strategies. The third is to summarize the representation methods and development modes of digital learning resources
The research object	Five parallel classes in grade 4 of C primary school in T city participate in this experiment. The education level of T city is among the top in China. School C can also represent the higher education level of T city. Each class has 30 students, a total of 150 students	Four parallel classes in grade 5 of Y Primary School in T City participate in this experiment. Y Primary School is at the middle level in T City, second to C Primary School, with 40 students per class, 160 students in total
Experimental environment and tools	Real classroom, ERP EEG	Real classroom, eye tracker, ERP EEG
The experiment content	"Operation and Simple Problem Solving" is the basic content of the fourth grade in primary school, including three parts: operation rules, operation strategies and simple problem solving	"Operation and solving more complex problems" is the basic content of the fifth grade in primary school, which includes three parts: operation rules, operation strategies and solving more complex problems
The experimental time	Four weeks, one class hour per day, a total of 20 class hours	

the research object, the exploratory experiment selects a primary school with a good level, which is conducive to the experiment to achieve a better effect. In the confirmatory experiment, a middle level primary school was selected and the experimental grade was adjusted, mainly to verify the applicability and generalization of the "learning content" variable. (3) From the perspective of experimental environment and tools, real classrooms were selected to explore the operability of the research. At the same time, an eye tracker was added in the confirmatory experiment stage to obtain the mutual verification of academic performance, external eye movement behaviour and internal brain wave changes, so as to enhance the persuasive power of research evidence. (4) From the point of view of the contents of the experiments, they are all "operation and problem solving" in primary school mathematics, but the fourth grade is simpler and the fifth grade is more complex, with the same purpose as the second dimension. (5) From the perspective of experimental time, four weeks and a total of 20 class hours were used, which was the minimum amount in empirical research on real classroom situations, otherwise it would be difficult to illustrate the effectiveness. In the follow-up practice, the experimental time of the research will be increased.

In the verification experiment, the teaching methods of the four classes were designed by the teachers themselves according to the learning content and learning resources. The learning method was the only variable, and the class code was represented by the school name "Y". The four classes were divided into the following four categories according to the properties of the classroom content. (1) Based on the classic content without digital resource representation (Classic Content Class, C_1 for short). (2) Based on the classical content and a classic digital resource representation (Classic Content and Representation Class, C_2 for short). (3) Based on 4S content and without digital resource representation (SK+KS+CS+SS, referred to as S_1 for short). (4) Based on 4S content and with digital resource representation representing cognitive processes (SK+KS+CS+ SAND representation, referred to as S_2 for short), operation attributes are shown in Table 4.2.

It can be seen from Table 4.2 that the teaching activities of Classroom C and S are designed by teachers themselves according to their experience, instead of adopting the "Personalized Cooperative Learning" (Hu & Dong, 2017) method in the exploratory experiment and the variable verification experiment of "learning style" (Hu & Dong, 2017). The exploratory experiment showed that PCL mode had the greatest influence on academic performance. In order to eliminate the influence of this variable, this study only interfered with one variable, "learning content", and the learning mode was controlled by teachers according to their experience.

The experiment

Selection and reorganization of learning content

This stage is in the experimental preparation stage of the exploratory experimental operation route, and 4S learning content has been researched and developed, which mainly includes the following four aspects. The first is subject knowledge (SK),

Table 4.2 C-S experimental class operation attribute table

Class level	Variable attributes	Operational definition	Number of students	The name of the class		Class attribute
Y_1	The classic content	Teachers organize teaching in natural state according to teaching experience, and multimedia teaching is not applicable, which corresponds to G class in exploratory experiment	40	Class C_1	Class C	Controlled group 1
Y_2	Classic content + classic digital resources	At present, there is a typical multimedia classroom in the school. Teachers organize teaching behaviours and teaching content by themselves, and apply supporting digital resources in the natural state, which corresponds to the M classroom in the exploratory experiment	40	Class C_2		Controlled group 2
Y_3	4S content	Teachers apply the 4S teaching content selected and reconstructed by the study and design their own teaching activities without applying the accompanying digital learning resources	40	Class S_1	Class S	Experimental group 1
Y_4	4S content + cognitive digital resources	Teachers apply the 4S teaching content selected and reconstructed by the study and design their own teaching activities without applying the accompanying digital learning resources	40	Class S_2		Experimental group 2

which refers to the representation of subject knowledge points as a unit, that is, classic learning content in Classroom C. The second comes to the learning strategy (KS) corresponding to the subject knowledge, such as the "Rounding Method" in "elementary arithmetic". The third is organizational cognitive structure (CS), which refers to guiding learners to consciously construct their own schemas and cognitive structures in the learning process. The fourth is social skills (SS), which refers to "the behaviour of communicating with others, such as accepting authority, conversational skills, cooperative behaviour. Self-related behaviours, such as emotional expression, moral behaviour, and positive attitudes towards the self; task-related behaviours: participation behaviour, task completion, following instructions, etc." (Xin & Zou, 2000), in order to promote the metacognitive ability of learners in the learning process and ensure the efficient development of learning activities.

Design and development of digital resources

Based on the selection and reorganization of the learning content mentioned above, the research has designed the S-DIP deeper learning resource representation state according to schema theory, adaptive control of thought (ACT theory) and action-process-object-schema theory (APOS theory), as well as the digital resource development mode in the exploratory experiment.

The process

The implementation process of the research includes four stages. The first stage is to confirm and train the experimental teachers. There are four classes of grade 5 in Y School, which are taught by two teachers, including a mature teacher (18 years, backbone teacher of district level, bachelor's degree) and a novice teacher (2 years, master's degree of primary education). Each teacher is responsible for two classes. Therefore, it is confirmed that matured teachers are given charge of Class Y_1 and Y_2, namely the controlled group, without any intervention or participation in experimental training. Novice teachers in charge of Class Y_3 and Y_4 should receive experimental training, i.e. the experimental group, to minimize the variable difference between the classes in the charge of the same teacher.

The second is a four-week teaching period, in which researchers observe and record the teaching process. Third, two teachers jointly issue post-test questions and conduct unit tests and interviews. At the same time, teachers randomly selected six students of each class from the three grades of excellent students, intermediate students and poor students, and two students from each grade. A total of 24 students were observed by eye tracker and ERP EEG during the learning process. The fourth is SPSS data analysis and ERP waveform analysis.

Data analysis

Two types of classroom academic performance data

The mean scores and standard deviations for the two types of classrooms with different levels of control and intervention for the "learning content" variable are shown in Table 4.3. The table shows that, from the dimension of the average academic achievement in four types of classroom, S_2 class is the highest and C_1 class is the lowest; the order from high to low was $S_2 > S_1 > C_2 > C_1$. In terms of the standard deviation dimension, classroom S_2 is the lowest and Classroom C_1 is

Table 4.3 The average grades of C-S class

Class	Class C_1	Class C_2	Class C	Class S_1	Class S_2	Class S
Grades (average value)	80.07	82.13	81.10	87.49	91.56	89.53
Standard deviation	14.308	7.359	8.827	8.719	3.165	4.642

the highest, ranked from lowest to highest as $S_2 < S_1 < C_2 < C_1$, i.e. S<C. The results of the two-by-two comparison of the mean academic performance difference between the two types of classrooms are shown in Figure 4.1. As can be seen from Table 4.4: $S-C > S_2 - S_1 > C_2 - C_1$ i.e. the mean academic performance of S and C classrooms is much greater than the difference between the levels of the different variables within the two classrooms, and the difference within S classrooms is greater than the difference within C classrooms. The highest average academic performance in classroom S_2 was as high as 11.49 points higher than the lowest Classroom C_1, while the average academic performance in classroom S was also 8.43 points higher than that in Classroom C.

The data of eye movement in two types of class

Researchers use the SMI company Iview X RED eye tracking system, and in the eyes tracking sampling, the sampling rate can reach 500 hz. The tracking resolution is 0.03 deg, and the gaze of positional accuracy is <0.4 deg. The equipment is non-contact measurement; a remote control infrared camera automatically records the subject's eye movement information. It includes eye gaze position, pupil diameter, location and tracking the location of the pupil, eye image and so on. After image acquisition and analysis, real-time data such as horizontal and vertical eye movement time, gaze position, displacement distance, velocity and pupil diameter are calculated. In the process of reading, "Longer eye gaze, larger average pupil diameter, lower blink frequency, longer scan path, larger eye flutter

C_1 Class	C_1 Class					
C_2 Class	2.06	C_2 Class				
C Class	1.03	-1.03	C Class			
S_1 Class	7.42	5.36	6.39	S_1 Class		
S_2 Class	11.49	9.43	10.46	4.07	S_2 Class	
S Class	9.46	7.40	8.43	2.04	-2.03	S Class

Figure 4.1 The average deviation of academic achievements of C-S classes

Table 4.4 Description of learner eye movements (mean) in the C-S classroom

Class type	Fixation Duration (ms)	Pupil Size (mm)	Blink Count (s)	The length of scanning path [activity]	Total eye flutter range (°)	Number of eye flutters
C_1 Class	186.30	12.24	0.25	11100.5	226.42	46
C_2 Class	209.40	12.65	0.13	11689.3	245.97	45.25
C Class	197.85	12.46	0.19	11394.9	236.20	45.63
S_1 Class	198.65	12.51	0.18	11645.5	263.80	45.36
S_2 Class	253.80	12.93	0.05	12871.8	318.22	44.25
S Class	226.23	12.72	0.12	12258.6	291.01	44.81

and fewer eye flutters are some indications that the reading content is more attractive to the subject" (Cheng, Yang & Wang, 2007). Due to equipment limitations, two students from each of the two types of classrooms (four classes) are selected by the teachers of each class to participate in the eye movement experiment, based on experience and pre-test and post-test academic performance, according to the criteria of academic excellence, intermediate and low academic achievement. Six students per class, a total of 24 students, are divided into four groups, i.e. one group per class for one round. In each round, the subjects are observed through three consecutive sessions of ten minutes each, with a five-minute break in between. Learner eye movement data for the four variable levels in the two types of classrooms are shown in the data in Table 4.4.

According to Table 4.4, the data can be obtained from the six dimensions of observation: (1) from the fixation duration, pupil size, scanning path length, the high to low order is $S_2 > C_2 > S_1 > C_1$, $S > C$; (2) from the point of total twitch amplitude, the high to low order is $S_2 > S_1 > C_2 > C_1$, $S > C$; (3) from the point of blink frequency count and number of DE, the low to high order is $S_2 < C_2 < S_1 < C_1$, $S < C$.

ERP EEG data in C-S classroom

In this study, the Mindwave Mobile electroencephalograph made by the Neurosky company is used, and its sampling rate is 512 hz, which can measure ERP EEG signals with high accuracy. After the operation of the ERP EEG data through complex mathematics, it can be interpreted as a number of parameters that reflect people's mental states.

At the same time, the study used the Baiyitong ERP EEG biofeedback training system to monitor the learner's EEG data in a timely manner. The eSenseTM algorithm quantifies the learner's mental state as an attention value, which is used as a basis for analyzing the learner's concentration, with parameter values ranging from 0 to 100.

During the experiment, due to equipment limitations (a total of 30 sets of equipment in the laboratory) and in order to minimize the variability of the subjects, participation in the ERP EEG experiment was restricted to the 24 students who participated in the eye movements and ran simultaneously.

1. The effect of learning content on learners' attention

To understand the relationship between the four levels of the learning content variables and learner attention, the attention data from four groups of learners in four classes are tested for homogeneity of variance, with significance much greater than 0.05, satisfying the requirement of homogeneity of variance. On this basis, the attention of four groups of learners is analyzed by one-way analysis of variance (ANOVA), and the results are shown in Table 4.5. As can be seen from the table, there are significant differences between the different learning contents and their resource representations on learners' attention (F(3, 119) = 8.326, p<0.001), and their influence (M-value) is ranked from highest to lowest as

Table 4.5 One-way ANOVA of learning content on attention

Group	Participants	M	SD	F	P
C_1	30	61.53	8.724	8.326	.000***
C_2	30	64.81	8.134		
S_1	30	63.26	7.981		
S_2	30	72.08	8.207		

(***P<0.001)

Table 4.6 Post hoc multiple comparisons of learning content on attention

Group	Mean difference	P
C_1-C_2	-3.28	.089
C_1-S_1	-1.73	.099
C_1-S_2	-10.55	.000**
C_2-S_1	1.55	.106
C_2-S_2	-7.27	.001**
S_1-S_2	-8.82	.002**

(**P<0.01)

$S_2>C_2>S_1>C_1$. To further investigate the differences in attention between the four groups of learning content and their resource representations, post hoc multiple comparisons are conducted and the results are shown in Tables 4.5–4.6. The table shows that the attention of group S_2 is significantly higher than group C_1, C_2 and S_1, and there is no significant difference between group C_1, C_2 and S_1.

2. The influence of learning content and attention to academic performance

To understand the effect of learning content paired with three different levels (high, medium and low) of attention on academic achievement, the study examines the effect of different learning content paired with different levels of attention on academic achievement using a factorial ANOVA, and the results are shown in Table 4.7. As can be seen from the table, there is an interaction between learning content and attention on academic achievement ($F(6, 120) = 2.164$, $p<0.05$), i.e. the effect of learning content and its resource representation on academic achievement differ across different levels of attention, as shown in Figure 4.2. According to the table: at low concentration levels, the high to low order is $S_2>C_2>S_1>C_1$; at the medium concentration level, the high to low order is $S_2>S_1>C_2>C_1$; at the high level of attention, the high to low order is $S_2>S_1>C_1>C_2$.

Table 4.7 also shows that learning content composition and resource representation have a major effect on academic performance ($F(3,160) = 21.071$, $P < 0.001$). In order to further understand whether there is a significant difference in academic performance among different levels of learning content variables,

Table 4.7 Analysis of the interaction between learning content and attention on academic performance

	SS	df	MS	F	P
Learning content	3528.827	3	1246.176	21.071	.000***
Attention	10056.283	2	5021.481	96.853	.000***
Learning content* attention	798.969	6	128.867	2.164	.032*
Error	5984.019	108	52.953		
Total	570388.000	120			

(*P<0.05, ***P<0.001)

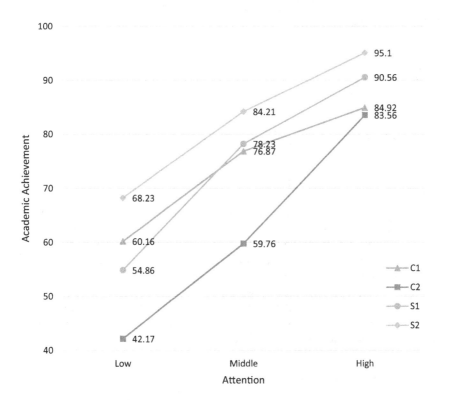

Figure 4.2 The interaction between learning content and attention on academic performance

the homogeneity of variance is tested on the academic performance of the four groups of learners, which meets the requirement of homogeneity of variance. Then, one-way ANOVA is performed on the academic performance, and the results are shown in Table 4.10. As can be seen from the table, there is a significant difference in academic achievement between levels of the learning content

Table 4.8 One-way ANOVA of learning content on academic achievement

Group	Participants	M	SD	F	P
C_1	30	80.07	12.324	8.419	.000***
C_2	30	82.13	10.547		
S_1	30	87.49	11.989		
S_2	30	91.56	8.231		

(***P<0.001)

Table 4.9 Post hoc multiple comparisons of learning
content on academic performance

Class	Mean difference	P
C_1-C_2	-2.06	.051
C_1-S_1	-7.42	.004**
C_1-S_2	-11.49	.000**
C_2-S_1	-5.36	.007**
C_2-S_2	-9.43	.001**
S_1-S_2	-4.07	.009**
C-S	-8.43	.002**

(**P<0.01)

variable (F(3, 119) = 8.419, p<0.001). The high to low order of the four groups is S_2>S_1>C_2>C_1.

In order to further study the academic performance differences between the four groups of variables, the post hoc multiple comparison is carried out, as shown in Table 4.9. It can be seen from the table that except for no significant difference between C_1 and C_2, the difference between other classrooms is purely significant, and the order of difference from high to low is C_1-S_2>C_2-S_2>C-S>C_1-S_1>C_2-S_1>S_1-S_2. Table 4.7 also shows the main effect of attention on academic achievement (F(2, 120)=96.853, p<0.001). However, as the observed variable in this study is "learning content", the effect of attention on academic performance is not part of the main study and is therefore not analyzed in detail.

Diagnostic data on mathematical thinking visualization

1. **Diagnostic data on mathematical learning strategies.** The study applies the Mathematics Learning Strategy Diagnostic System for Primary School Students to diagnose strategies in two types of classrooms (four variable levels), C and S, as shown in Figure 4.3. According to the figure, (1) S is significantly higher than C, with S_2 being the highest and C_2 the lowest. This phenomenon is consistent with the findings of the ERP EEG and learning strategy distribution in Classroom M in the exploratory experiment, indicating that Classroom C_1 is conducive to learners' learning strategy development, while Classroom C_2 does not have any advantage in terms of learning

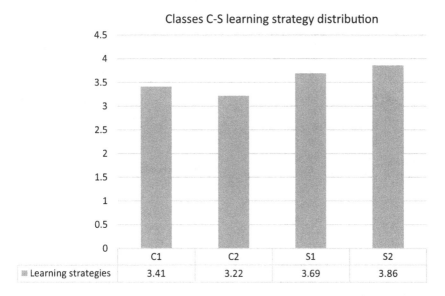

Figure 4.3 Classes C-S learning strategy distribution

strategies. The validation experiment again indicates that the rich multimedia context interferes with learners' reflections and summaries of learning strategies. (2) In the S classrooms, the results show that $S_1 < S_2$, which is consistent with the ranking of academic performance, the exploratory experiment and the ERP EEG in this validation experiment, as well as with the ranking of eye movements. (3) In summary, it suggests that the S classroom, and S_2 in particular, is the most effective classroom approach for the validation experiment. This phenomenon suggests that the "4S" content structure combined with the cognitively designed digital resource representations are conducive to the development of learners' learning strategies.

2. **Diagnostic data on mathematical cognitive structure.** The study applies the CSV-PDA, a visual diagnostic tool for children's cognitive structure, to two types of classrooms (four variable levels), as shown in Table 4.12, and the trends across the four classrooms are shown in Figure 4.4.

  Table 4.10 and Figure 4.4 show: (1) the percentages of learners for the four types of schemas, in descending order, are: $S_2 < S_1 < C_2 < C_1$ for both single-point and merge schemas, $C_1 < C_2 < S_1 < S_2$ for graphical schemas and $C_1 < C_2 = S_2 < S_1$ for multi-linked schemas. According to SOLO classification theory, classroom S_2 has the lowest proportion of low-level cognitive structures and the highest proportion of high-level cognitive structures; the C_1, C_2 and S_1 classrooms have exactly the same number of intermediate level schemas, with the middle two coming to 85%. (2) Comparing Figure 4.4 with Table 4.4, the C_1 and C_2 sequencing is inconsistent, indicating that multimedia instruction facilitates the formation of structured schemas for learners; however, the C_2 and S_1

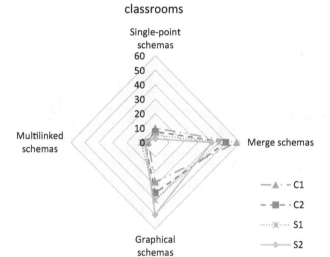

The map of cognitive structure in C-S classrooms

Single-point schemas

Multilinked schemas

Merge schemas

Graphical schemas

— ▲ - C1
- ■- C2
⋯ ✕ ⋯ S1
— ◆ — S2

Figure 4.4 The map of cognitive structure in C-S classrooms

Table 4.10 C-S classroom cognitive structure distribution table (percentage)

Class	C_1	C_2	S_1	S_2
Single point of schema	10.0	7.5	5	2.5
Merge schema	57.5	50.0	45.0	40.0
Graphical schema	27.5	35.0	40.0	50.0
Multi-way schema	5.0	7.5	10.0	7.5

sequencing is consistent, indicating that designed content composition is more effective than the generic use of multimedia. (3) By comparing C_1 with C_2; C_2 with S_1; and S_1 with S_2, it can be seen that the combined application of content composition and digital resource representation design is the most effective. This is consistent with academic performance, exploratory experiments and ERP EEG, eye movements and learning strategies in this validation, and fully demonstrates the impact of learning content selection, reconfiguration and resource design and development on learning quality.

Conclusion

By combining the above mean academic performance comparisons, eye movement observations and ERP EEG changes, the study analyzes and generalizes the findings from both physical (eye movement and EEG) and cognitive (academic performance) levels through "triangulation".

High effectiveness of cognitive process-based
reconstruction of learning content and its resources

According to academic research data, the following conclusions are drawn. (1) First, the average academic performance of the two types of classrooms is ranked from highest to lowest as $S_2 > S_1 > C_2 > C_1$. Second, the magnitude of S vs. C is greater than that of S_2 vs. S_1 and C_2 vs. C_1. Third, there is a significant difference between C and S. The three facts indicate that a qualitative change has taken place between S and C classrooms. (2) As the standard deviation of the mean academic performance of the two types of classrooms is ranked from lowest to highest as $S_2 < S_1 < C_2 < C_1$, and S<C, it indicates that in this order, the gap between learners is gradually decreasing from C_1 to S_2 classrooms. (3) As the academic performance in the S classroom is ranked $S_2 > S_1$ and the standard deviation is ranked $S_2 < S_1$, this indicates that the combined application of 4S learning content and S-APT digital resources is more effective than the individual applications. (4) Based on the analysis of the above, 4S learning content and S-APT digital resources are highly effective in improving academic performance.

The interaction relationship between learning quality and technology

According to the ERP EEG data, the effects of learning content and attention on academic performance are as follows. At low concentration levels, from high to low the order is $S_2 > C_2 > S_1 > C_1$. At the medium concentration levels, from high to low the order is $S_2 > S_1 > C_2 > C_1$. At the high level of attention, from high to low the order is $S_2 > S_1 > C_1 > C_2$. This phenomenon means the following. (1) In low, medium and high levels of concentration, S_2 has the best utility. (2) At low concentration levels, multimedia technologies are more likely to engage learners' attention than cognitive processes, resulting in slightly better academic performance ($C_2 > S_1$). (3) In the medium level of attention, the synergy of cognition and technology is more effective ($S_2 > S_1 > C_2 > C_1$). (4) In the high level of attention, the effectiveness of cognition outweighs the multimedia technology ($S_1 > C_1 > C_2$). All in all, there is an interactive relationship between learning quality and technology, with most learners more at low attention levels, ranked from highest to lowest as $S_2 > C_2 > S_1 > C_1$, mostly at moderate attention levels for longer periods of time, and learning design should reconcile cognition and technology to optimize utility.

Technical design to promote deeper learning

According to academic performance, eye movement and ERP EEG data, in terms of two types of class levels of four variables, academic performance from high to low order is $S_2 > S_1 > C_2 > C_1$. And fixation duration, pupil size, scanning path length and eye movement amplitude is $S_2 > C_2 > S_1 > C_1$. And consistent with the order of the attention the influence of learning content, the attention of S_2 group is significantly higher than C_1, C_2 and S_1 group. But there was no significant difference between C_1 and C_2 and S_1. This interesting phenomenon indicates that: (1)

multimedia technology can improve the learner's attention $(C_2>S_1>C_1)$. (2) The design of learning technologies that reflect cognitive processes is better for learner development than the current way of using multimedia technology $(S_2>S_1>C_2)$. (3) If technical design can reflect the cognitive process it can achieve the optimal utility, otherwise it will increase the cognitive load.

The conclusions of the validation experiment are generally consistent with the exploratory experiment

Based on the above findings, it shows that the findings of the validation experiment and the exploratory experiment (Hu & Dong, 2017) are basically consistent. (1) Learning content and resource representation have a high correlation (.875**,P>0.01), and the two can be combined as "learning content" variables for research. (2) Learning content composition and resource representation methods are highly correlated with academic performance (.561** & .498**, p>0.01), with a main effect (F(3, 160)=21.071, p<0.001). (3) The traditional multimedia M classroom is able to improve academic performance over the lecture-based G classroom because the technology enhances learners' attention $(M>G\&C_2>C_1,$ $C_2>S_1>C_1)$; and the reason for the lack of significant improvement is the lack of representation of cognitive processes $(S_2>S_1>C_2)$. (4) The difference in academic achievement in the S_2-C_1 classroom (11.49) does not reach the difference in the L_3-G classroom (18.14) because the activities are designed by the teacher and do not use the individualized-collaborative learning approach. Conversely, this again demonstrates the strong correlation between learning style and academic achievement (.562**,p>0.01) and the effectiveness of the content and learning style together (.866**,p>0.01).

Academic performance, eye movement and ERP EEG may constitute a "triangulation" research method

According to the above comprehensive analysis, we can draw the following conclusions. (1) For S-C classrooms, academic performance is ranked from highest to lowest as S>C. This order is consistent with eye movement in terms of gaze duration, pupil size, scan path length, and eye movement amplitude, and also consistent with the ranking of the effect of learning content on attention, all of which indicate that S classrooms are more effective than C classrooms, suggesting that the three correlate with each other and can form triangular reciprocal evidence. (2) In terms of level of four variables, the data relationships between academic performance and eye movements and ERP EEG, although with some differences (academic performance $S_2>S_1>C_2>C_1$, physiological indicators $S_2>S_1>C_2>C_1$, etc.), in turn reveal an inherent interaction between cognition and technology: first, it provides evidence against the "technology-only" theory. The second is to strengthen the position of the "cognitive" learning design. The third is to reveal that the technology design should be based on cognitive learning and teaching activity design. Based on this, academic performance, eye movement and ERP

EEG may constitute a "triangle" formation for each research method, reciprocal evidence and contradictions, thereby enabling better study of the laws of learning.

In summary, the study selects and reconstructs classroom learning content based on the view that "technology is the learner's way of being", designs and develops digital resources based on cognitive processes and practices them in the primary school mathematics curriculum. Finally, the study verifies the effectiveness of the reconstructed and developed learning content and its resources at three levels: body (eye movement behaviour), cognition (academic achievement) and learning quality (attention). It also reflects the advanced process of deeper learning from body to learning quality, and then explains the operation paradigm of deeper learning under the guidance of learner-centred design from the dimension of "what to learn".

Verification 2: "personalized-cooperation" experimental design and implementation of learning style

Cooperation, competition and individualization are the three main ways of working in human society and the three main ways of learning that are common in the schooling process (Wu & Guan, 2010). In terms of social production, individuation is the most basic mode of production, cooperation is the core mode of production in contemporary society and competition is an important way to drive the continuous progress of society. However, competition in contemporary society is all about team competition based on cooperation. In terms of school education and classroom learning, the only way to effectively promote the development of individual students and the school community is to use the idea of individualized effort as the basis, cooperative learning as the core, and moderate competition for development to guide the actual teaching. However, in our traditional classrooms there is a strong emphasis on competition and individualized learning, with the "independent completion of homework" being a typical example of this idea. These two types of learning are characterized by the interdependence between learners: individualized learning, where learners are not interdependent and work individually on content and assessment; their knowledge comes from two channels: the teacher-student communication channel and the student-learning resource communication channel. Competitive learning, where there is a negative interdependence between learners and where the success of anyone means the failure of others, has been debated; thus, researchers have attempted to construct positive interdependence between learners – "cooperative learning". At the same time, with the enrichment of digital learning, the development of intelligent learning and the development of big data and learning analytics, researchers have begun to focus on "personalized learning", which means creating intelligent learning environments and designing learning activities based on individual factors such as the cognitive starting point, learning interests and learning styles of individual learners or clusters of learners, in order to facilitate their development. The individual is the basic unit of personalization, and personalization is the expression of the individual. The difference between personalized learning and individualized learning is a world of difference: firstly, personalized learning emphasizes individual learner differentiation, which includes many factors such as learning style, learning attitude and motivation; individualized learning only emphasizes individual forms of existence. Secondly, personalized learning can also include clusters of individuals with similar characteristics, rather than just a single individual. Thirdly, personalized learning does not completely deny the element of cooperation, and also expects to build positive learner interdependence (Chen & Yang, 2015). However, in the current classroom teaching, teachers tend to ignore the cooperation among learners when focusing on individualization, and often neglect the individual differences among learners when focusing on cooperative learning, resulting in the situation of losing sight of the other.

Therefore, the CTCL research paradigm proposed by Dong Yuqi's team advocates the generation of a new learning culture based on the convergence of learners, content and technology to facilitate the transformation of learning and ultimately the development of learners. Based on this paradigm, this study here integrates the advantages of personalized learning and collaborative learning in an attempt to construct a new classroom learning organization, exploring how to focus on learners' individual characteristics while collaborating, and building a learner-centred personalized-cooperative learning approach (Personalized-Cooperative Learning, PCL approach).

Experimental design

Experimental problems

Based on the above discussion, this study intends to answer two questions through an empirical study of four types of classroom teaching from the analysis of academic achievement, and the dimension of the relationship between learner interdependence and academic achievement, interpersonal structure and psychological well-being: firstly, to test the effectiveness of personalized-collaborative learning; and secondly, to summarize the elements, connotations, structure and implementation strategies of personalized-collaborative learning. This paper focuses on a detailed explanation of the effectiveness of PCL through data. The study will be followed by a theoretical construction in the next section, which summarizes the elements and connotations of PCL through empirical research.

Experimental method

1. **Second-order diagnostic approach.** The study uses a second-order diagnostic approach to assess learners' cognitive starting points in order to inform the provision of learner resources, personalized-collaborative learning groupings and instructional guidance.
2. **Quasi-experimental research method.** The research is conducted in an authentic classroom context, with learning styles as the only variable, and variables such as learning resources and teaching strategies are controlled in order to explore models of effective learning operations.

3. **Questionnaire and interview method.** Student questionnaires and individualized interviews with students, teachers and parents were used to understand the social interdependence between students and the state of social support.

Detailed design

In summary, both the physiological and social dimensions provide the theoretical basis and implementation rationale for personalized-collaborative learning. The study is based on a prototype classroom participation structure design, a synthesis of the above-mentioned literature, an empirical study design and a summary of the elements, structures, design models and implementation strategies of personalized-collaborative learning. The study consists of two phases: an exploratory experiment and a validation experiment, with the validation experiment being conducted on the basis of the exploratory experiment. The relevant design, research terminology, data analysis and findings from the exploratory experiment are explained in detail in Chapter 3 and are not repeated in this paper and are used directly. For the sake of continuity and clarity of presentation, the designs of the two types of experiments are described in Table 4.11.

In the validation experiment, all four classes used the learning content and resources from the L_3 classroom, with the learning mode as the only variable and the class code denoted by the name of the school "X", and the four classes were named according to the classroom attributes as Multimedia Class (M class), Competition Class (C class), Individual Class (I class) and Learner-Centred Class (L class) with personalized and collaborative learning. Table 4.12.

The four fourth grade classes at School X are taught by three teachers, one expert (28 years of teaching experience, municipal subject leader) and one novice teacher (two years of teaching experience), and each is in charge of one class; one mature (14 years, district key teacher) teacher is in charge of two classes. Therefore, the expert teacher is identified as the control group X_1 and is not given any intervention, and they did not participate in the experimental training. Mature teachers, corresponding to groups X_2 and X_3, and the novice teacher, corresponding to group X_4, are given experimental training to minimize differences in variables for classes under the responsibility of the same teacher. The X_2 and X_3 groups, which appear to be the two extremes, are in fact basically the same in terms of teaching strategies, except for the assessment strategies, which are at the two extremes and are therefore under the responsibility of the same teacher.

Implementation

In the implementation process of the study, Class M, Class C and Class I are mainly different in classroom organization and evaluation strategies, which can be implemented according to the operational definition in Table 4.12. For Class L, the operability is more complex, and the implementation process is explained in detail.

Table 4.11 Two types of experimental designs description table

Research type	Exploratory experiment	Confirmatory experiment
Research purpose	The first is to explore whether technology can facilitate learning; and the other is to explore how technology can facilitate learning, which mainly including learning styles (PCL), learning content (SK+KS+CS+SS) and resource representation (SR)	The first is to verify the effectiveness of personalized-collaborative learning; the second is to verify the elements, structures and behaviours of personalized-collaborative learning
Research object	Five parallel classes in grade 4 at Primary School C in T. The standard of education in T is one of the highest in the country and School C is representative of the higher standard of education in T. Each class has 30 students, making a total of 150 students	Four parallel classes in grade 4 at Primary X in T. Primary X is at the same level as Primary C, with 30 students in each class, making a total of 120 students
Experimental period	Four weeks, one hour a day, a total of 20 hours	
Research method	See the "research methods"	
Experimental content	The basic content for Primary 4 is "Calculation and Simple Problem Solving", which contains three parts: rules of arithmetic, arithmetic strategies and simple problem solving	

Cognitive diagnosis

Pre-tests are administered to four classes on the basis of learners "initial knowledge" of the subject matter, with each class showing no significant difference between their usual performance and the pre-test. The cognitive starting point has also been diagnosed in Class L, as shown in Table 4.13. As can be seen from Table 4.13, the learners are categorized into four main categories according to clusters, with the rest being "basic scientific type". Within each category, there are a number of categories based on specific question types. Accordingly, the study has developed corresponding learning resources for teachers to use the PCL adaptive learning system to target learners and give them personalized guidance. The distribution of individual cognitive starting points for learners in Class L is shown in Table 4.14. The table shows: (1) the "Symbol priority" problem has the highest proportion, followed by the "addition and subtraction column" problem. (2) One learner can have one or more cognitive biases, for example, Learner 1 has three types, A, B and C.

Implementation process

1. Operating routes

Based on the implementation process in the exploratory experiments, the research further clarifies the control process of "learning style" variables and operating

Table 4.12 The experimental class action attribute table of M-C-I-L

Class	Operational definition	Number of students	The name of the class	Class attribute
X_1	Teachers organize teaching according to teaching experience in the natural condition, containing features such as moderate competition, individual and traditional cooperative learning, consistent with exploratory experiment M class	30	Class M	Control group
X_2	In individual learning, publish the results to the whole class according to the order of academic performance, and give rewards and penalties	30	Class C	Experimental 1
X_3	In individual learning, academic performance is not sorted, not released, nor reward and punishment	30	Class I	Experimental 2
X_4	According to the starting point of the learner's cognitive diagnosis, forming typical learners' cluster. According to the different structure of learner characteristics and cluster providing targeted learning content and learning resources, and consistent with exploratory experiment class L	30	Class L	Experimental 3

line. Based on Bloom's taxonomy of educational objectives and the cognitive diagnosis of learners with multiple biases, the study designed a personalized-collaborative learning operational road map with "circular" features, as shown in Figure 4.5.

Figure 4.5 shows that: (1) for learners with only one deviation, round 1 focuses on cognitive awareness and comprehension, round 2 on application and analysis, and round 3 on synthesis and evaluation. (2) For learners with multiple deviations, multiple rounds are used to address recognition and comprehension and to gradually improve application, analysis, synthesis and evaluation skills in a spiral with other learners. The specific learning numbers for each round in the PC classroom are indicated in the four quadrants of the diagram. (3) Teachers can conduct multiple rounds of the cycle depending on the actual class situation.

2. Team group

Round 1: Based on the natural grouping of social relations

The study begins with a questionnaire (Appendix 2) in which students are asked to select their preferred partners in order to find out who and what type of classmates (e.g. good grades or good interpersonal skills, etc.) they prefer to study in the

Table 4.13 Subject content deviation distribution table

Typical problems (coding)	Deviation type	Example	Explanation of deviation (students)
Symbol priority (A)	Tampering rules (1)	$125 \times 8 \div 125 \times 8$ $=(125 \times 8) \div (125 \times 8)$ $=1000 \div 1000$ $=1$	125x8 is easier to calculate orally, so count 125x8 = 1000 on both sides of the division, and then 1000 ÷ 1000 equals 1
	First impressions (2)	$25+25 \times 8$ $=50 \times 8$ $=400$	Based on the "left to right, first up, then down" principle learned in the Chinese language
	Step by step (3)	$16 \div (2+8)$ $=16 \div 2 + 16 \div 8$ $=8+2$ $=10$	Because multiplication has multiplication distributive law, multiplication and division operations at the same level, so the division also can be used to divide the distributive law
Addition and subtraction column" problem (B)	Forgetfulness (1)	$258+367=515$ 258 $+367$ _____ 515	I forgot to write a small 1 in the tens place after adding the single digits to get 15, and then forgot to write a small 1 in the hundreds place when I added the tens place to get 11
	Borrow it and return it (2)	$1409 -1065=436$ 1491 -1065 _____ 436	The 1 in 1491 digits is not enough to subtract the 5 in 1065 digits, so borrow 1 from 9, 11-5=6. Then subtract 6 from 9 to get 3, 4 minus 0 equals 4, 1 minus 1 equals 0, and the answer is 436
Confusion (C)	Conceptual confusion (3)	The dividend is 125 and the divisor is 15, find the quotient $25 \div 125$	The dividend is the number to be divided, so it comes after and the divisor comes before
		The subtrahend is 68 and the minuend is 12, find the difference $12-68$	The subtrahend is the number being subtracted, so it comes after and the minuend comes before
Displaced numbers (D)	Mistaken number order (1)	$368+17$ $=386+17$ $=403$	"368" is written as "386" on the draft paper
	Missing numbers (2)	$720 \div 9=8$ $\phantom{9\sqrt{}}8$ $9\sqrt{720}$ $\phantom{9\sqrt{}}72$ _____ $\phantom{9\sqrt{7}}0$	In the previous calculation, it is possible to divide exactly, and it is not necessary to count the zeros in the single digit

Table 4.14 Learner deviation distribution table

Typical problem	Student ID	Participants	Ratio
A	1, 3, 5, 6, 7, 8, 12, 14, 15, 18, 19, 22, 23, 25, 26, 27, 28, 29	18	60%
B	1, 3, 5, 6, 7, 8, 11, 14, 15, 16, 22, 28, 29, 30	14	46.70%
C	1, 2, 12, 17, 21, 24, 25, 28	8	26.70%
D	4, 9, 11, 12, 14	5	16.70%
E	10, 13, 20	3	10%

(Note: "E" refers to "basic scientific type")

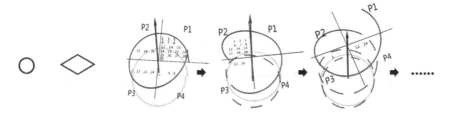

Figure 4.5 Personalized-cooperative learning road map operation

Table 4.15 Table of Classroom L students' selected times

Student ID	Selected times	Student ID	Selected times	Student ID	Selected times
9	14	4	6	20	2
17	13	7	5	18*+	2
19*+	12	29	5	25	2
26+	10	8	4	3	2
27	9	10*	4	14	2
6	9	11	4	22	1
30*+	8	16*	3	15	1
13	8	28	3	1	0
21*	7	24	3	5	0
2+	7	12	3	23	0

same group with, as a basis for subsequent grouping adjustments based on cognitive structure. Based on the number of times each student is selected, as shown in Table 4.15, four circles are used to represent the social relationships in the class, as shown in Figure 4.6. From inside to outside, they are: the central character circle (selected more than ten times), the sub-central character circle (five to nine times), the general character circle (two to four times) and the marginal character circle (zero to one times). (1) The number of students at the two extremes (circles 1 and 4) is low, and most students are in the middle circles (circles 2 and 3). (2) The proportion of central characters choosing each other is low, with only one pair of the four central characters choosing each other and preferring students in circles 2 and 3 as study partners. (3) Figure 4.7 shows the results of the survey on students' reasons for

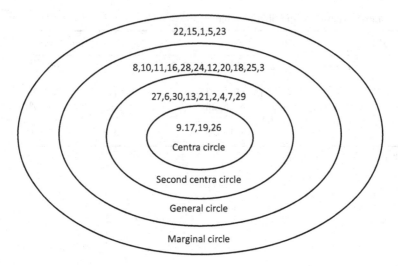

Figure 4.6 Map of Classroom L students' selected times

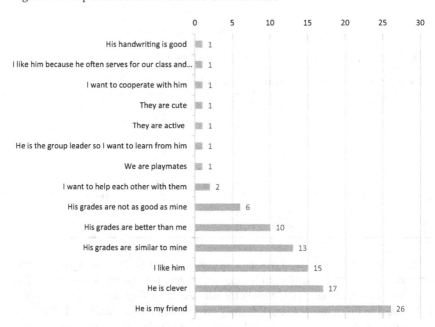

Figure 4.7 Reason map for learners to choose partners

choosing group study partners, where the dashed boxes are closed questions data and the others are open-ended questions. As can be seen from Figure 4.7, "whether they are good friends" is the highest, followed by "whether they are smart" and "whether they like them", while the three items related to grades (better than me, about the same and not as good as me) are at the bottom. This suggests that grades are not the most important factor in choosing a study partner.

Round 2: Group alignment based on cognitive structure

The study regrouped each round according to the operation route, and the specific grouping principles are as follows. (1) One group per five persons. (2) Adjustment based on the natural grouping of social relations, based on the order of school numbers, to reduce students' sense of difference. (3) The first and second rounds are grouped homogeneously according to the type of deviation. The remaining heterogeneous groups are as average as possible. Homogeneity makes the group focus on solving the problem of personalized cognitive biases in the front end of learning, and heterogeneity improves the complementarity between learners with different cognitive biases. (4) The third round allows students to freely combine and consolidate the improvement according to the previous two rounds of learning to test the effect of the above social skill guidance and application, as shown in Table 4.16. It clearly reflects the process of learners' cognitive bias reduction. Table 4.17 shows that only three groups appear fine-tuning phenomenon in the free combination, indicating that the grouping mode designed by teachers has been basically stable, and students are more accepting of the learning process in the first three weeks.

3. Teaching process

The teaching and learning process is organized according to Table 4.17, with a weekly cycle. Each activity and content is arranged for creative application based on the research base of the psychology of mathematics learning.

4. Classroom Structure

The arrangement of the classroom tables and chairs is changed and reorganized according to the needs of the above teaching activities, as shown in Figures 4.8 to 4.10. (1) Figure 4.8 shows the group structure of personalized-cooperative learning, with one square table per person and five tables presenting the group structure. (2) Each circle in Figure 4.9 represents a group, and the triangle represents the teacher, presenting a 3*2 array form, which facilitates the teacher's teaching and individualized instruction, and is named "Classroom Structure I". (3) The solid circles in Figure 4.10 represent the group that is presenting and leading the communication, with other groups around them, and the teacher instructing and guiding other groups around the presenting group, which is named "Classroom Structure II".

Evaluation method

The individual learner's academic performance is made up of four components in Table 4.18, forming a jigsaw structure, as follows. (1) Four members of the group each give a "cooperation" score for another peer; (2) five groups each give a "communication" score for the expression group; (3) the learner's own written

Table 4.16 PCL grouping table

Number	Typical problem	Students ID	Group nature
(1) The first week/the first round			
1	A	1,3,5,6,7	homogeneous
2	A	8,12,14,15,18	homogeneous
3	A	19,22,23,25,26	homogeneous
4	Five types	27,11,2,24,10	heterogeneity
5	Five types	28,16,17,4,13	heterogeneity
6	Five types	29,30,21,9,20	heterogeneity
(2) The second week/the second round			
1	B	1,3,5,6,7	homogeneous
2	B	8,14,15,22,28	homogeneous
3	B, C, D	29,12,25,2,4	homogeneous
4	E	9,10,11,13,16	homogeneous
5	E	17,18,19,20,21	homogeneous
6	E	23,24,26,27,30	homogeneous
(3) The third week/the second round			
1	C, E	1,2,3,4,5	heterogeneity
2	E	6,7,8,9,10	homogeneous
3	D, E	11,12,13,14,15	heterogeneity
4	E	16,17,18,19,20	homogeneous
5	E	21,22,23,24,25	homogeneous
6	E	26,27,28,29,30	homogeneous
(4) The fourth week/the third round			
1	E	1,2,3,4,5	homogeneous
2	E	6,7,9,10,18	homogeneous
3	E	11,12,13,14,15	homogeneous
4	E	8,16,19,20,23	homogeneous
5	E	17,21,22,24,25	homogeneous
6	E	26,27,28,29,30	homogeneous

test score; (4) the average of the written test scores of the five students in the group. (5) In summary, the individual performance reflects the results of personalized learning; the other three require the group members to work together and help each other in order for the individual to achieve better results, reinforcing the interdependence between learners.

Data analysis

Academic performance is the most visual evidence of effectiveness in empirical studies of classroom teaching and learning. ERP EEG data reflects the brain science evidence of learner-centred designs in promoting learner development; and the degree of correlation between learning styles and academic performance and the effect sizes characterize the role and extent of learning styles in learner-centred designs. The research is explained in detail in Chapters 3 and 4 and will

Table 4.17 Weekly teaching process

Learning time	Monday	Tuesday	Wednesday	Thursday	Friday
Teaching content	SS	SK+KS			KS
Teaching aim	Learn social skills, for PCLS ramming foundation	Study subject knowledge, and understand the learning strategies			Conclude learning strategies, and construct cognitive structure
Teaching strategies	Teaching, games, group communication	Lecturing of individualized instruction	Individualized instruction; Intra-group communication	Communication between groups	Lecturing, group communication
Theory basis	The students master the more social skills, learning team can achieve higher achievements (David, 2002)	① Teachers teaching combined with learners retelling exercise ② Learning strategies infused with subject knowledge. Both of these can improve academic performance, especially for intermediate and struggling learners (Fang & Guo, 2000)			Strategy training alone can improve academic performance in a short time (Liu, 2001)

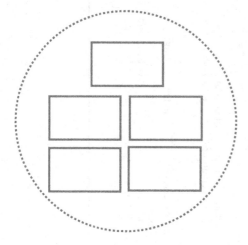

Figure 4.8 Group structure

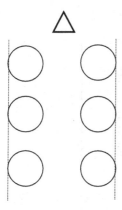

Figure 4.9 Teacher lecturing structure

not be repeated in this paper; data and analyses that need to be supported in the discussion will be cited directly. In this paper, the data and findings of the study that characterize learner interdependence and academic achievement, interpersonal relationships and psychological well-being specifically in relation to learning styles are explained in detail.

Visual data on academic performance

1. Comparison of academic performance in four types of classrooms

The mean grades and standard deviations of the four types of classrooms after different manifestations of the same variable in terms of control and intervention are

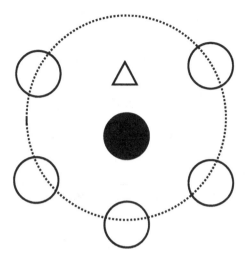

Figure 4.10 Inter-group communication structure

Table 4.18 Academic performance evaluation

Components of academic performance	Group interaction		Individual written test	
	Within the group	*Between groups*	*Individual performance*	*The average of group*
Performance ratio	10%	10%	70%	10%
Evaluator	Members in the group	The other team	Teachers	Teachers

Table 4.19 M-C-I-L classroom grade point average scale

Class	M	C	I	L
Academic grades (average)	83.21	88.37	78.39	94.67
Standard deviation	8.164	10.217	18.294	5.125

shown in Table 4.19. From the table, it can be seen that, in terms of the mean academic achievement dimension, the L classroom is the highest and the I classroom is the lowest among the four types of classrooms, with grades ranked L>C>M>I. In terms of standard deviation, the L classroom is the smallest and the I classroom is the largest, with grades ranked L<C<M<I.

The results of the two-by-two comparison of the difference in mean academic performance between the four types of classrooms are shown in Figure 4.11. As can be seen from Figure 4.11, Classroom L, which had the highest mean academic performance, had a higher mean academic performance of 16.28 points than Classroom I, which had the lowest, while Classroom L differed from Classroom

I Class	I Class			
M Class	4.82	M Class		
C Class	9.98	5.16	C Class	
L Class	16.28	11.46	6.3	L Class

Figure 4.11 M-C-I-L classroom academic performance mean difference scale

Table 4.20 M-C-I-L Classroom achievement retention rate for academically excellent students

Classroom	M	C	I	L
Ratio	94.25%	90.12%	84.36%	98.28%

M by 11.46 points, which is essentially the same as the difference of 12.02 in the exploratory experiment.

2. Academic achievement retention rate of academically gifted students

Some researchers have suggested that cooperative learning may be more effective for struggling students and affect the academic achievement development of academically gifted students, so the study focused specifically on the academic achievement retention rate of academically gifted students. According to Professor Takahashi Naozumi (2014) at the University of Tokyo, the three categories of academically gifted, intermediate and struggling students were divided 2:5:3, i.e. the top 20% of the test were gifted students, the middle 50% were intermediate students and the bottom 30% were struggling students. The study compared the pre- and post-test scores, and the retention rates of the four classroom categories of academically gifted students are shown in Table 4.20, ranked as L>C>G>I, which is consistent with the increase in the mean academic performance of the four classroom categories.

3. Changes in the performance of students in the three categories of excellence–moderate–poor

The study observed the academic achievement improvement scores of the three categories of students in the four types of classrooms, namely, students with academic excellence, students with moderate education and students with difficulty, based on the 2:5:3 theory, as shown in Figures 4.12. (1) In terms of the magnitude of improvement for the three categories of students in the same classroom, the L classroom had the largest difference and the G classroom had the smallest; the L classroom had the largest improvement for students with difficulty and the smallest for students with academic excellence; the other three types of classrooms all had the largest improvement for students with moderate education and

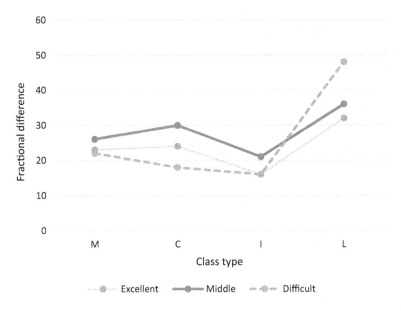

Figure 4.12 Distribution of the improvement in the performance of students in the three categories of excellent, moderate and poor

the smallest for students with difficulty. (2) For both the academically gifted and intermediate students, the four types of classrooms improved in the order of L>C>G>I. (3) For the struggling students, the four types of classrooms improved in the order of L>G>C>I.

Learners interdependent relationship between measurement data

The Learner Interdependence Relationship (LIR) is a quantitative representation of how learners and learners learn and relate to each other in three types of learning: competitive, individual and individualized-collaborative. The study used effect sizes as a measure to assess the impact of different learner interdependence relationships on academic achievement, interpersonal attractiveness, social support and self-esteem,[1] with the (+) effect sizes shown in Figure 4.13 and Figure 4.14.

As can be seen from Figure 13, all (+) effect sizes for LIR and academic achievement are greater than +.25, and therefore all are at the significance level. The L-I classroom reached +.89, indicating that the L classroom has a more significant level than the average multimedia classroom that currently exists.

Interpersonal attractiveness in Figure 4.14 refers to the psychological state of mutual liking, need and dependence between individual learners and their peers during the occurrence of learning behaviours, which is a distinct positive interdependence relationship. In this study, questionnaires and interviews with learners

I Class	I Class			
M Class	+.32	M Class		
C Class	+.65	+.40	C Class	
L Class	+.89	+.58	+.68	L Class

Figure 4.13 LIR and academic achievement effect sizes

I Class	I Class			
M Class	+.08	M Class		
C Class	+.28	+.31	C Class	
L Class	+.58	+.41	+.36	L Class

Figure 4.14 LIR and interpersonal attraction effect sizes

I Class	I Class			
M Class	+.18	M Class		
C Class	+.21	+.20	C Class	
L Class	+.70	+.61	+.43	L Class

Figure 4.15 LIR and social support effect sizes

were used to derive effect sizes between learner interdependence and interpersonal attractiveness. As can be seen from Figure 4.14, (1) C-I did not reach the significance level; (2) M-I, M-C, L-I, L-C and L-M all reached the significance level, with L-I having the highest significance level.

Social support in Figure 4.15 refers to teachers' and parents' affirmation, encouragement and trust in learners. Good social support contributes to academic achievement and healthy physical and mental development. The study conducted questionnaires and interviews with teachers, parents and students on social support to derive effect sizes for learner interdependence and social support. From Figure 4.15, it can be seen that (1) I-C, M-C and M-I did not reach the significance level, (2) L-C, L-I and L-M all reached the significance level, with L-C having the highest significance level.

Self-esteem in Figure 4.16 refers to a sense of self-worth that is generated and developed by learners during the learning process based on self-evaluation, as a result of an individual's self-evaluation of their social role, which is formed through social interaction and comparison. The study used learner psychometrics to derive effect sizes for learner interdependence and self-esteem. As can be seen from Figure 4.16, (1) M-C, I-C and I-M did not reach significance levels; (2) L-C, L-M and L-I reached significance levels, with L-C having the highest significance level.

Mathematical thinking visualization of diagnostic data

1. Diagnostic data on mathematical learning strategies

The study applied the Mathematics Learning Strategies Diagnostic System for Primary School Students to diagnose strategies in four types of classrooms (four

I Class	I Class			
M Class	+.17	M Class		
C Class	+.12	+.20	C Class	
L Class	+.56	+.31	+.43	L Class

Figure 4.16 LIR and self-esteem effect size

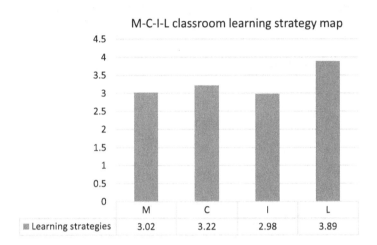

Figure 4.17 M-C-I-L classroom learning strategy map

classes), as shown in Figure 4.17. According to the figure, (1) among the four types of classrooms M-C-I-L, L was the highest and I the lowest, and the phenomenon that the difference between M and I was not significant was consistent with the ranking of academic achievement, again indicating the positive correlation between academic achievement and learning strategies. (2) The three effect sizes of LIR and interpersonal attractiveness, social support and self-esteem were not consistent with the ranking of learning strategies and academic achievement. This indicates that there is no absolute positive correlation between academic achievement, learning strategies and learning quality. (3) The L classroom was at the optimal level in all five of these areas, indicating that the L classroom performed best in both academic achievement and learning quality.

2. Diagnostic data on the cognitive structure of mathematics

The study applied the CSV-PDA, a visual diagnostic tool for children's cognitive structure, to the four types of classrooms (four classes), as shown in Table 4.21, where the trends in the four types of classrooms, M-C-I-L, are shown in Figure 4.18.

A synthesis of Table 4.21 and Figure 4.18 shows that: based on SOLO classification theory it can be seen that: (1) Classroom L had the lowest proportion of

Table 4.21 M-C-I-L Classroom cognitive structure distribution table (percentage)

Class type	M	C	I	L
Single point schema	13.3	10.0	30.0	3.3
Merge schema	50.0	53.3	40.0	40.0
Graphical schema	30.0	33.3	23.3	40.0
Multi-way schema	6.7	3.4	6.7	16.7

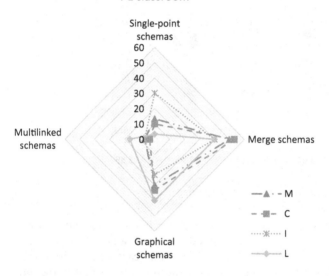

Figure 4.18 Distribution of cognitive structures in the M-C-I-L classroom

low-level cognitive structures and the highest proportion of high-level cognitive structures; Classroom I had the opposite; and the difference between the two types of classroom was significant. Classroom C was similar to Classroom M and was at an intermediate level. This phenomenon is consistent with the distribution of academic achievement and learning strategies, and illustrates the positive correlation between the three in the diagnostic study. (2) In terms of LIR and interpersonal attractiveness, social support and self-esteem, this is consistent with the learning strategies profile.

Learner's feedback data on learning styles

The study was conducted at the end of the four-week experimental intervention with a questionnaire (Appendix 3) and some student interviews (in the form of a classroom chat rather than a very formal interview as they were primary school students) to find out how students actually felt about the final group member-ship structure; this questionnaire is descriptive in nature and the typical questions selected for this paper and the results are as follows.

1. Students are generally satisfied with the PCL group structure

Figure 4.19 shows students' attitudes towards group members and the classroom structure (seating). 80% of students were Very satisfied and satisfied with the PCL group members and the classroom structure, 16% felt average and 4% felt less satisfied than before. The questionnaires and interviews revealed that for those who felt "average" and "dissatisfied", the main reason was not that they were not satisfied with the learning style, but that they were not satisfied with the group members, e.g. "A certain student is very bossy", "I would rather be in a certain group".

1. The PCL approach to learning is endorsed by most learners

Figure 4.20 shows the level of agreement with the PCL learning style, with 26 participants agreeing to "learning their own part" and "exploring with the teacher and classmates in a group", demonstrating the appeal of personalized learning and collaborative learning.

2. Multi-way interaction recognized by learners

The multi-directional nature of the interaction is more fully reflected in Figure 4.21, which shows the learners' preferred mode of interaction, with four options

▦ A.Quite satisfied ▦ B.Satisfactory ▦ C.Ordinary ▦ D.Unsatisfactory

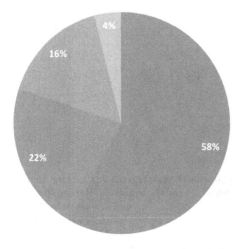

Figure 4.19 Learners' attitudes towards the PCL group structure

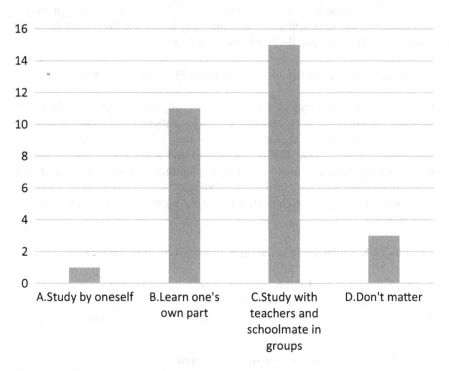

Figure 4.20 Learners' preferred learning styles

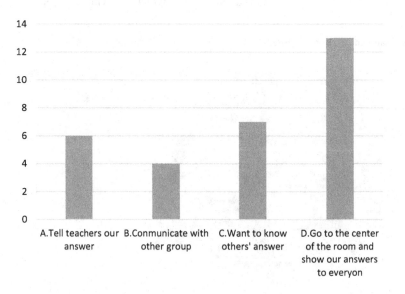

Figure 4.21 Learners' preferred method of interaction

encompassing both intra-group and inter-group communication. Option D, on the one hand, directly illustrates the effectiveness of the inter-group communication structure and, on the other hand, indirectly illustrates the learning effect of personalized learning and intra-group communication in enhancing learners' confidence.

1. Learners want teachers to be more deeply involved in the PCL learning process

Figure 4.22 shows the role and involvement that learners would like teachers to play in the PCL learning process. 74% of learners would like teachers to be present in the group on a regular basis and no learners would like teachers to be present at the podium, i.e. they would like teachers to be more deeply involved in the PCL learning process as "instructors" and "participants".

2. Learners are excited about the application of PCL in multiple disciplines

Figure 4.23 shows that 84% of the learners were very keen or able to apply PCL to other subjects such as language and English. Of the 12% of students who did not want to communicate, it was found that most of them were not disapproving of PCL, but were not satisfied with the group members for the same reasons as "overall satisfaction with the group structure". This suggests that the PCL experiment in mathematics has a certain degree of disciplinary applicability, although it needs to be validated in other disciplines. In subsequent experiments, it is necessary to further optimize the structure of group members and the content and

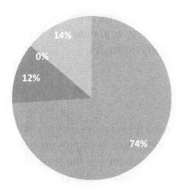

- A.Always come to the group to disscus with us
- B.The teacher stand by listening to us
- C.Stand on the podium and stay out of the group
- D.Casuarly

Figure 4.22 How learners would like teachers to participate

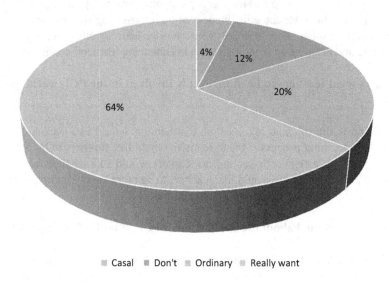

Casal ▨ Don't ▨ Ordinary ▨ Really want

Figure 4.23 Learners on the photo subject application promotion

methods of developing metacognitive strategies and social skills, and to work on improving the positive interdependence between members.

Conclusion

According to the above academic performance data and interdependent relationship between learners and academic performance, interpersonal attraction, the effect of social support and self-esteem are the most important to learners. The research can be compared and analyzed from different angles.

"Personalized-cooperation" learning could improve academic performance

Using various data on academic achievement in the four classroom types, the study can conclude that (1) Classroom L is the most effective in improving academic achievement, followed by Classroom C, and Classroom I is the least effective. This validates the effectiveness of moderate competition and suggests that individualized, collaborative learning is currently the most effective way of learning. (2) The L classroom was able to improve the academic performance of the three categories of students, namely the best, middle and low achievers, breaking away from the previous teaching reform which only benefited some clusters of learners. (3) The L classroom had the smallest standard deviation, the highest retention rate for students with high academic achievement, and the largest improvement for students with low academic achievement, which exceeded that for students with high and moderate academic achievement, while the I classroom had the opposite. This phenomenon indicates that the L classroom motivates all learners to work effectively with each other and promote each other; the I classroom lacks competition and supervision, and the retention rate of students with high academic achievement decreases, while students with low academic achievement are less self-motivated. (4) The standard deviation in M and L classrooms is close to that of the exploratory experiment, which verifies its effectiveness. (5) The mean academic achievement in Classroom C is higher than that in Classroom M, but the standard deviation is greater than that in Classroom M. The lowest improvement rate of students who are struggling indicates that the competition in Classroom C is too fierce, causing some students who are struggling to give up.

"Personalized-collaborative" learning effective for social skills improvement

From the data on learner interdependence and interpersonal attractiveness and social support in Figures 4.14 and 4.15, the study can draw the following conclusions. (1) The L classroom had the highest effect sizes for both and reached the significance level, indicating that the L classroom was effective in improving social skills. (2) The difference in academic performance between the C and I classrooms was 9.98 points, which is relatively significant, while the C-I effect size in Figure 4.14 was +. 08, which is close to 0, indicating that the interpersonal appeal of the two classrooms is very close and that learners do not agree with the atmosphere of either classroom. (3) The effect sizes for both M-I and M-C in Figure 4.14 do not reach significance levels, indicating that the multimedia classrooms that are currently widely available are also not very well accepted by learners. (4)The positive C-I in Figure 4.14 and positive I-C in Figure 4.15 indicate that classroom C is objectively more interpersonally attractive than classroom I. However, parents, teachers and students are subjectively more supportive of classroom I, which is consistent with our learning habits of not being good at collaboration and requiring independent work.(5) The significant L-C of +.70 in Figure 4.15 indicates that parents, teachers and students do not like overly competitive classrooms and deeper down they want learners to work together to achieve personalized development.

"Personalized-collaborative" learning is good for the quality development of learners

From the data on learners' interdependence and self-esteem in Figure 4.16, the study can draw the following conclusions. (1) M-C, I-C and I-M all reached significance levels, indicating that learners were more depressed and had less self-fulfilment in M, C and I classrooms. (2) L-C, L-M and L-I all reached significance levels, indicating that L classrooms promoted learners' psychological development, which is consistent with the EEG development in the L classroom in the exploratory experiment. (3) Academic achievement in the C classroom was second only to the L classroom, while the L-C effect size was the largest, suggesting that learners were pressured to achieve academic achievement in the C classroom due to competitive pressure, while simultaneous development of academic achievement and learner quality was achieved only in the L classroom.

Note

1　The effect size is calculated as (experimental group mean − control group mean) / control group standard deviation. It is related to X, r or t, the difference being that the effect size is not limited by the sample size, whereas the other statistics are limited by the sample size. If the effect size is +1.0, it is considered to be very effective for any kind of educational reform. This means that the average student in the experimental class reached a level that only 15% of the students in the control class would have reached. An effect size of +25 is usually considered significant.

References

Charles, M.R. (2016). *Instruction-design theories and models: The learner-centered paradigm of education*. New York and London: Routledge: 420–431.

Chen, J.G., & Yang, N.C. (2015). Learning sciences in the past decade: Development, reflections and innovations-an interview with processor Keith Sawyer. *Open Education Research, 21*(04), 4–12.

Cheng, L., Yang, Z.L., & Wang, X.F. (2007). A study on eye movements of different presentations of web-ads. *Psychological Science, 30*(3), 584–587.

David, H.J. (2002). *Theoretical foundations of learning environments* (Second Edition). Shanghai: East China Normal University Press: 8.

Fang, P., & Guo, C.Y. (2000). Research on the learning strategies in mathematics. *Psychological Development and Education, 16*(1), 43–46.

Feng, R., & Ren, Y.Q. (2009). The turning of learning research and the formation of learning science. *E-education Research, 30*(2), 23–26.

Hu, H., & Dong, Y.Q. (2016). The future trend of educational media research: To promote the learner-centered design. *Research on Modern Distance Education, 29*(6), 11–17, 38.

Hu, H., & Dong, Y.Q. (2017). How technology promotes deeper learning: An empirical study and theories construction about "personalized-cooperative" learning. *Research on Modern Distance Education, 30*(3), 48–61.

Hu, H., & Dong, Y.Q. (2017). How technology promotes learning performance: An empirical study based on three types of classes. *Research on Modern Distance Education, 30*(2), 88–94.

Liu, D.Z. (2001). *Study on learning strategies*. Beijing: People's Education Press: 326–335.

McCombs, B., & Whisler, J.S. (1997). *The learner-centered classroom and school: Strategies for increasing student motivation and achievement*. San Francisco: Jossey-Bass Publishers.

Wu, X.C., & Guan, L. (2010). *Cooperative learning and classroom teaching*. Beijing: People's Education Press: 355–360.

Xiang, D.M. (2008). *The study of multimedia instructional information representation design*. Chongqing: Southwest University: 8–10.

Xin, T., & Zou, H. (2000). *School psychology*. Beijing: People's Education Press: 68.

Yan, S.G. (2015). *Philosophy of education technology*. Beijing: China Social Sciences Press.

5 Components of deeper learning teaching content

Theoretical analysis of deeper learning teaching content

Marzano's cognitive objectives

Since the introduction of the concept of "deeper learning", it was explained in the early days by the advanced level of Bloom's taxonomy of cognitive objectives (usually analysis, evaluation and creativity) (Duan, 2012; Zhang & Chen, 2013; Zhang, Wu & Wang, 2014). Some scholars have suggested that deeper learning is not a direct extension of shallow learning, but another learning process that is fundamentally different from the beginning of learning, and that deeper learning is divided into two stages: "one is new knowledge understanding, and the other is internal migration and external expanding migration". "Problem solving" is an important mark of deeper learning (Liu & Wang, 2017). Based on this and the empirical data in Chapters 2 and 3, this understanding of the deeper learning process is also supported by the author: "Bloom's taxonomy of cognitive objectives simplifies the relationship between the nature of thinking and learning" (Li, 2010).

Marzano's taxonomy of cognitive objectives contains three systems: cognitive, metacognitive and self-cognitive. In terms of processing levels the cognitive system contains four levels: extraction, apprehension, analysis and application of knowledge, the metacognitive and self-cognitive systems correspond to levels 5 and 6 respectively; and in terms of the knowledge domain cognitive system contains declarative knowledge (information), productive knowledge (mental skills) and motor skills (mental-causal action processes). The cognitive system is mainly concerned with new knowledge comprehension and internal and external associative transfer. The metacognitive system runs through the entirety of the cognitive system and determines the level and depth of its operation, which contains two components: "what to do" and "when, where and how to do". "What to do" refers to the perception of the strategies needed to accomplish the task effectively; "when, where and how to do" refers to the ability to use monitoring mechanisms to ensure that the task can be completed successfully. The self-cognitive system is the individual learner's judgement of whether or not to engage in a new task and determines the depth of involvement, which can also be understood as "judgement and determination" and consists of four aspects: testing importance, testing

DOI: 10.4324/9781003278702-5

efficacy, testing affective responses and testing overall motivation. The self-cognitive system is more difficult to understand and some consider it to be metacognition, but Marzano considers it to be superior to metacognition and to be the valve through which metacognition operates (Sheng, 2008).

Based on an understanding of cognitive objectives, the reconstruction of class learning content should be based on this and should reflect the process of achieving cognitive objectives. The content of learning should be understood and interpreted from the perspective of the curriculum, and there are currently several perspectives: "planned teaching and learning activities" (Wu, 1986), "learning experiences" (Chen, 2001), "resources for student development" (Chen, 2003), "educated culture" (Huang, 1996), etc. It can be seen that the above-mentioned views describe the connotation of the curriculum from different perspectives, but they all show the "dynamic and static" character of the curriculum, but what is the carrier of the curriculum? It is undoubtedly the "learning content and its resources", i.e. "what to learn". The composition of learning content reflects the static nature of the curriculum, while the reconstruction of the curriculum reflects its dynamic nature, the two being twin representations of each other. Therefore, studying the composition and reconstruction of learning content in class is the process of reconstructing the curriculum.

The theory of ecological curriculum

The American scholar Goodlad (1979) proposed five levels of curriculum:

> the ideological curriculum, the formal curriculum, the perceived curriculum, the operational curriculum and the experiential curriculum.

Goodlad intercepts five important "cross-sections" in the trajectory of curriculum movement from ideal state "flow" to practice. "Each section is an important form of curricular presence, linked together into a chain of curriculum transformation". This idea of curriculum in motion and movement overcomes the one-sidedness of a static understanding, but its limitation is a linear way of thinking about curriculum. Jin Yule argues that the curriculum is a dynamic ecological curriculum, with complex connections between the various levels of the curriculum as two-way or in a network (2003). Accordingly, the study considers Goodlad's five-level curriculum as a dynamic ecosystem with a dynamic balance between the sub-curricula of the system. "Too much or too little attention to one aspect of the teacher, students, materials or environment can upset the 'ecological balance' of the class or other educational context" (Schubert, 1986).

The practice and balanced model

Based on the theory of ecological curriculum, the design and development of class learning content revolves around the interaction of "theory" and "practice", which Schwab's "the practice and balanced model" (1995) of curriculum design and development embodies. The model focuses on specific contexts, gaining insight and understanding of real situations and solving specific practical problems, reflecting its "practical" nature. It favours the elaboration of specific and diverse approaches in order to move the logical basis, content composition and representation means of the curriculum from theory to practice; from the analysis of teaching objectives to the diagnosis of learning starting points and contextual analysis; from normative pedagogical design to concrete action implementation programmer; from a top-down system of curriculum decision-making to bottom-up collective deliberation; from theoretical and textual norms to practice and creativity, etc.

Generative-orientation curriculum reconstruction

Curriculum reconstruction orientation refers to teachers' awareness of the nature of the curriculum reconstruction process and their behavioural performance in the process. Du Zhiqiang (2010) believes that there are two kinds of curriculum orientations suitable for deeper learning.

> One is the mutual accommodation orientation based on modern hermeneutics, which emphasizes not only the need to orient towards the formal curriculum but also the need to enter the teaching and learning context. The other is based on a constructivist approach, which believes that each learner should not wait for knowledge to be passed on, but should work on issues that occur naturally in class based on his or her unique experience of interacting with the world.
>
> (pp. 68-69)

The former emphasizes teachers' behaviours and the latter students' behaviours. In essence, there is no clear gap between the two, as they share common theoretical assumptions, such as the contextual and concrete nature of the curriculum, its constructive and generative nature, and so on. This is in line with the theory of ecological curriculum and "the practice and balanced model" model of curriculum development, which is why the study collectively refers to the two orientations as the "generative orientation". It emphasizes that the teacher, guided by the ideal curriculum, designs a comprehensible curriculum based on the activities, behaviours and learning resources of the class context, and the learner, guided by the teacher, generates a valuable experiential curriculum through "personalized-collaborative" learning (operational curriculum).

Components, structure and characteristics of deeper learning content

Mapping the deeper learning research framework to the learning content

Combined with the exploratory experiment on "major influences on deeper learning in primary mathematics" in Chapter 3 and the univariate validation experiments on "learning content and resources" and "personalized-collaborative learning" in

Chapter 4, a mapping table of "21st century competence", "deeper learning competence" and "technologies promote deeper learning (TPDL) for learning content" was derived, as shown in Table 5.1. As can be seen from the table, the composition of "learning content" in the TPDL empirical study basically corresponds to the "21st century competence" and "six dimensions of deeper learning", reflecting the competence requirements of deeper learning. Firstly, the cognition, interpersonal and individual domains correspond to the cognitive, metacognitive and self-cognitive systems of Marzano's taxonomy of cognitive objectives. Secondly, the cognitive domain mainly contains subject knowledge (SK) and strategies to knowledge (KS), i.e. the cognitive system; the interpersonal domain mainly contains social skills (SS), of which KS and SS can constitute the metacognitive system; thirdly, the individual domain is mainly the enhancement of KS and SS after in-depth reflection and application, i.e. the development process of the metacognitive system to the self-cognitive system. Fourthly, the cognitive structure (CS) contains the synthesis of the two previous systems, i.e. the self-cognitive system. The formation of the CS requires the accumulation of SK, KS and SS, in order to gradually generate accurate judgement, strong execution and deep reflection, etc.

Interpretation of the "4S" components

As can be seen from Table 5.1, the learning content in the TPDL consists of subject knowledge, strategies to knowledge, social skills and cognitive structure, collectively referred to as the "4S" components of learning content shown in Table 5.2.

As can be seen from Table 5.2, the four components are independent of each other and fit together into a unity that complements each other. Classical teaching

Table 5.1 Mapping of "21st century competence", "deeper learning Competence" and learning content

21st century competence domains (NRC)	Competence dimensions of deeper learning (AIR)	Learning content (TPDL)	
Cognitive domain	Dimension 1 Mastery of core academic content	Subject knowledge (SK)	Cognitive structure (CS)
	Dimension 2 Critical thinking and problem solving	Strategies to knowledge (KS)	
Interpersonal domain	Dimension 3 Effective communication	Social skills (SS)	
	Dimension 4 Working collaboratively		
Individual domain	Dimension 5 Learning to learn	KS+SS	
	Dimension 6 Will to learn		

Table 5.2 Interpretation of the "4S" learning content components

Elements	Definition	Examples	Teaching strategies
(SK)	Refers to the representation of subject knowledge points as a unit	Multiplicative distribution law; tree planting problems	Lecture method
(KS)	Refers to the learning strategies that correspond to subject knowledge	Special number multiplication strategies, e.g. 101*68 = (100+1)*68; the rule of calculation for planting trees at both ends of a road: (distance/length) + 1	Lecture method; discussion method; graphical method
(SS)	Refers to the action of interacting with others	E.g. behaviours in relation to others, such as accepting authority, communicating and cooperating; behaviours related to oneself, such as emotional expression, moral behaviours, positive attitudes towards oneself; behaviours related to tasks, such as participating activities, completing tasks, following directions, etc.	Anchoring method; discussion method; game method; situational acting; brainstorming
(CS)	Refers to the structure of the learner's knowledge, and the total conceptual content and organization that is expressed	Merging concept schemas; graphical concept schema	Discussion method; graphical method

focuses on the "subject knowledge" of the formal curriculum, with the other three components covered, but mainly by the conclusion and induction of learners themselves, without systematic development of materials and organization of learning activities. The four components form the following relationships. Firstly, SK is the core and fundamental content of learning, consisting mainly of declarative and productive knowledge, which is a basic requirement for mastering core academic content in deeper learning (dimension 1). Secondly, KS is a method and "additive" to the effective application of subject knowledge, significantly improving learners' critical thinking and problem solving skills (dimension 2). Thirdly, good SS are lubricant for these learning activities, creating effective communication (dimension 3) and collaborative working (dimension 4). Fourthly, the construction of good CS (complex graphs) is a symptom of the formation of higher-level thinking in learners and is a reflection of the development of deeper learning thinking. On the one hand, learners will be able to apply and transfer this content flexibly to achieve real-life problem solving, and on the other hand, they will gradually develop excellent metacognitive qualities and learn to learn (dimension 5), and will be able to monitor, regulate, reflect on and enhance their learning power (dimension 6) in due course. The teaching and learning arrangements for the four components will be explained in detail in Chapter 5.

Element structure like a mushroom

Based on the interpretation of the "4S" learning content elements and their relationships, a "mushroom" element structure was developed to further clarify the structure and relationships between the "4S" elements, shown in Figure 5.1. The diagram shows an element structure like a mushroom, which is explained as follows. First, SK is the core layer of the "mushroom stem" and becomes the main body of learning content. Second, KS is the peripheral layer of the "mushroom stem", which corresponds to SK and is integrated with it in the learning process to solve problems together. Third, SS plays the role of "fertilizer" and is distributed between the core and peripheral layers of the "mushroom stem", promoting the growth of the core and periphery through effective communication, discussion, participation and positive emotional interaction, etc. Fourth, CS is the "mushroom head", which grows under the influence of the previous three and is both the object and the internalized result of the learning process.

Generation of the "ecological flow" operational paradigm

Based on the theory of ecological curriculum and the "practice and balanced model" of curriculum development, the operational paradigm of the "4S" learning content in the actual classroom is summarized in the "ecological flow" paradigm. The term "ecological flow" originally refers to the functional flows of material metabolism, energy conversion, information exchange, value addition and subtraction, and biological migration that reflect the ecological relationships in an ecosystem (Baidu, 2017). The study uses this terminology to express the

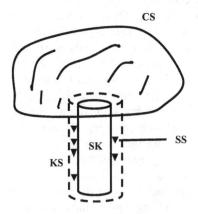

Figure 5.1 Structure of the "4S" elements

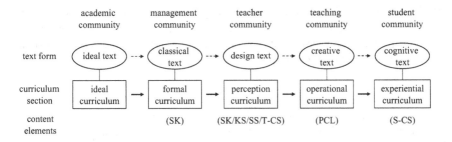

Figure 5.2 The "ecological flow" paradigm of curriculum operation

transformational state of Goodlad's five curriculum forms and their corresponding "4S" learning content, as shown in Figure 5.2.

As can be seen from Figure 5.2, this operational paradigm consists of two "data flows": "curriculum section" flow and their corresponding learning content elements, and "text form" flow corresponding to the course sections. Text forms are the textual expressions that correspond to the curriculum sections and serve as a guide for teachers and students in class operations, such as lesson plans, learning manuals, activity rules and process videos, which is explained as follows. (1) The representation of the ideal curriculum is the ideal text, which is initiated by academic institutions, curriculum experts and other academic communities. (2) Under the guidance of the ideal curriculum, the educational management and publishing departments form the educational management community, which compiles the classical text made up of SK. (3) In the school context, teachers and team members form a community of teachers who, through individual teacher perception and reflection, as well as team brainstorming and deliberation, develop a design text corresponding to the perception curriculum, which consists of SK, KS, SS and teacher-CS summarized by the teacher. (4) Teachers and students form a pedagogical community, implementing operational lessons and generating creative texts through "personalized-collaborative" learning (PCL). (5) Finally, the individual and community of students form the experiential curriculum through the learning process, producing the cognitive text, i.e. the student-CS.

Characteristics of the structure of learning content and its operational paradigm

Looking at the elements of learning content, its structure and its operational paradigm, the study summarizes them into five basic characteristics, which are explained as follows.

Generativity

There are many "chance encounters" and "generative excitement" in the way teachers and communities understand and reconstruct formal curriculum texts, as well as in the way they operate and reflect on them. At the same time, learners' differences in learning backgrounds, learning styles and learning needs can also produce "unexpected" lessons. Thus, the unanticipated nature of the three cross-sections requires the "ecological flow" to break out of the confines of the formal curriculum and become generative.

Individuality

In the operation of the "ecological flow" paradigm, the latter three sections are not "copies" of the formal curriculum, but are based on individual teachers' and students' life experiences, professionalism, family backgrounds and other factors, resulting in unique, or even different, ways of operation, behaviours and cognitive structures from others. It is a unique representation of the individual based on a particular context.

Implicit

In the learning process, teachers have a great deal of psychological wisdom that is difficult to express, such as the power of rebellion, passion, responsibility, cooperation and communication skills, etc. At the same time, students are influenced and developing implicitly. The experiences, intuitions, insights and emotions of teachers and students are deeply rooted in the process of design, creativity and cognitive behaviours, and are implicitly integrated into the structure of thinking.

Criticality

The teacher's comprehension and design of the formal curriculum is not only a positive interpretation, but also the use of his or her own accumulation, to accept and reject teaching materials according to the cognitive diagnosis of the learners and to analyze its strengths and weaknesses and give constructive modifications. At the same time to reflectively deconstruct, select, supplement and transform it, going beyond the formal curriculum to form a new form.

Foresight

There are unintended elements to the above "ecological flow", which is generated in a dynamic flow, and while they are not confusing, can be anticipated to a certain degree, such as the source of content, strategies and tools, PCL organizational strategies, class environment, etc. of the operational curriculum. They may not be "identical" to the empirical curriculum, but have a guiding and directive function.

Framework, strategies and values of deeper learning content reconstruction

Framework of reconstruction

After summarizing the process of learning content reconstruction in empirical studies, we have summarized the framework of the "Understanding – Discussing

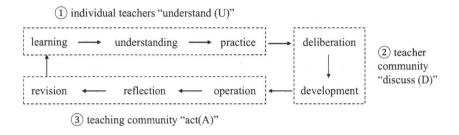

Figure 5.3 UDA curriculum reconstruction framework

– Acting (UDA)" curriculum cycle based on the theory of "ecological" curriculum, as shown in Figure 5.3. As can be seen from the diagram, (1) curriculum reconstruction is a cyclical structure. (2) Curriculum reconstruction consists of three subjects: the individual teacher, the teacher community and the teaching community, which correspond to three types of behaviour: "understand – discuss – act". (3) The "individual teacher" is the beginning of the structure, consisting of "learning", "understanding" and "practice", which are explained as follows. First, "learning" is when teachers learn the ideal curriculum and the formal curriculum and master the core academic content. Second, "understanding" is when individual teachers understand and add to the curriculum based on their learning. Third, "practice" is when individual teachers practice and reflect on the basis of their understanding, leading to an individual understanding of the curriculum. (4) The "teachers' community" is the middle end of the structure and consists of two parts: "deliberation" and "development", which are explained as follows. First, "deliberation" is a term borrowed from the "practice and balanced" model of curriculum development, and is composed of curriculum experts, teachers and researchers, key teachers and individual teachers, who work together to refine the curriculum through brainstorming, discussion and even debate. Second, "development" of learning materials such as learning activities, learning guides and digital learning resources to accompany the comprehension curriculum by teachers and resource developers, based on the design text of the comprehension curriculum. (5) The "teaching community" is the end of the structure and consists of three elements: "operation", "reflection" and "revision", which are explained as follows. First, "operation" means that the teacher and students operate the comprehension curriculum designed and developed in class to produce the creative curriculum. Second, "reflection" means that the teacher and students review and summarize the merits and problems of the creative curriculum from their own perspectives after the classroom teaching. Third, "revision" means that the teacher revises the comprehension curriculum and adapts the creative curriculum on the basis of the reflection of the teacher and students, and then moves on to the next cycle of reconstruction.

Strategies of reconstruction

Based on the empirical research and the structure of the UDA curriculum reconstruction framework, the research summarizes the reconstruction strategies as shown in Table 5.3.

The following conclusions can be drawn from Table 5.3. (1) The reconstruction strategies include seven strategies, such as dialogic understanding and brainstorming, according to the order of the reconstruction framework, and indicate the specific behaviours of teachers and students corresponding to each strategy,

Table 5.3 "4S" learning content reconstruction strategies

Reconstruction strategies	Definition	Teachers' behaviours	Students' behaviours
Dialogic understanding	It refers to the meaning generated by teachers and students in equal dialogue with the formal curriculum, where meaning exists in the intersection of the "horizon" of the classical text and the "horizon" of individual teachers and students	Linking knowledge into a system	Integrating into life situation
Brainstorming	It means that teachers and students are free to express their own ideas about "dialogic understanding" in their own communities, and that new understandings are developed	Free discussion	Free discussion
Curriculum deliberation	It refers to the process by which curriculum experts, researchers, key teachers and individual teachers review the multiple "understandings" from the "brainstorming" process, resulting in a meaningful "comprehension curriculum"	Reporting, reflecting, and revising	——
Class operation	It refers to teachers implementing "comprehension curriculum" in the classroom, which in turn generate "creative curriculum"	Teaching	Participating in teaching and learning activities
Conscious reflection	It refers to teachers and students consciously reflecting on the content and activities based on student feedback during and after the "classroom operation"	Accepting feedback; analyzing and diagnosing problems; criticizing and improving	Accepting guidance; participating actively; criticizing and giving feedback
Activity adaptation	It means that teachers and students continually adapt their teaching or learning behaviours in real time or in the next round, based on their "conscious reflection"	Adapting teaching content and activities	Adapting ways of thinking and participating
Theoretical refinement	It refers to the theoretical summary of the above process by teachers and students	Keeping a teaching journal	Keeping a learning journal

providing realistic operability for their implementation. (2) The systematic "flow" of the seven strategies reflect five characteristics of "4S" learning content structures and their operational paradigms, such as "generativity" and "individuality". (3) The seven strategies form a closed structure in the reconstruction framework, in which "dialogic understanding" and "theoretical refinement" reflect the "understanding" of individual teachers and students; "brainstorming" and "curriculum deliberation" reflect the "discussion" of the teacher community; "classroom operation", "conscious reflection" and "activity adaptation" reflect the "action" of the teaching community. (4) The process of reconstructing learning content is itself a process of professional development for teachers and learning for students. For example, the requirement for students to give critical feedback in "conscious reflection" is itself a training for students in "critical thinking and problem solving", which is also a requirement of the framework of deeper learning practices.

Application value

The process of reconstructing the "4S" learning content described above is not simply a matter of selecting, adding or deleting learning content, but of teachers and students understanding, constructing and generating its meaning, and has the following three practical implications. (1) The reconstruction of learning content is the process of generating a curriculum that moves from classical to practical. It transforms the curriculum from a "classical text" to a "cognitive text" and is an effective practice for teachers' professional development, promoting the development of learning qualities such as coordination, cooperation and criticism, and improving academic performance. (2) The reconstruction of learning content provides a meaningful learning vehicle for "teaching and learning". This process changes the stagnant, boring and abstract nature of the "classical curriculum", activates its relevance to life situations and problem solving, and systematically integrates the learning content that students need in the process of growth and development. (3) The reconstruction of learning content is a guarantee that deeper learning will occur for learners. Deeper learning is not just a "brutal" improvement in academic performance, but a process that promotes the harmonious physical, psychological and qualitative development of the learner. It requires, on the one hand, the improvement of academic performance while increasing performance levels and, on the other hand, the promotion of healthy development of the learner's body and happy growth of the nervous system, leading to the development of good learning qualities.

A portrait of deeper learning class

Deeper learning class roles

Learners

Deeper learning focuses on the "learner-centred" approach. In practice, it is necessary to diagnose learners' cognitive biases, learning styles and other individual attributes, and at the same time to develop learners' motivation to learn.

Specifically, learners should be accurately analyzed in terms of their current level of knowledge, learning content, learning activities and attitudes, in order to prepare for personalized deeper learning. First, in terms of current knowledge, learners' cognitive biases, learning styles and other individual attributes should be diagnosed, so that students are likely to reach their learning goals. Second, in terms of learning content, learners' cognitive starting points should be combined with appropriate forms of expression, so that learners can effectively assimilate and adapt to the learning content and continuously form new cognitive starting points. Third, in terms of learning activities, they should be designed on the basis of learners' experiences and cognition, and individual and group activities should be effectively combined to achieve the overall development of learners' cognitive and interpersonal domains. Fourth, in terms of attitudes, learners' motivation should be effectively mobilized through the creation of an environment in which learning activities can be carried out in a full and dynamic mood.

Teachers

In deeper learning, teachers should have a deep understanding of learners' cognitive processes, select, reconstruct and design teaching content in depth, and participate in learning activities in depth, as follows.

Firstly, they should have a deep understanding of learners' cognitive processes, guide learners' individual cognition at any time and adjust learners' cooperative environment. Secondly, they should carry out "understanding-based teaching design" according to learners' individual learning conditions, scientifically design "4S" learning content and promote learners' deep understanding of learning content and active participation in learning activities. Thirdly, we should deeply intervene in the organizational structure of learning in the way of "guidance, participation and supervision" to achieve "two-way interaction between teachers and students", which will enable learners to move from being "marginal participants" to "central subjects", and at the same time achieve the professional growth of teachers themselves.

Learning objectives

According to the cognitive requirements of deeper learning, it is important to improve the academic performance of learners and to promote the development of deep understanding, problem solving, critical innovation and other thinking.

In addition, the development of students' deeper learning skills in the cognitive, interpersonal and personal domains is to be considered as a pedagogical goal of deeper learning. In the cognitive domain, the importance of mastering core subject knowledge and developing students' higher-order thinking and critical thinking skills in teaching and learning should be the primary pedagogical goal in order to promote better mastery of core subject knowledge and develop students' critical thinking. These include how to relate learning to the real world, how to find and use information, how to solve problems and think critically, how to identify facts, and how to reason and analyze problems. In the interpersonal domain, the development of effective communication and teamwork skills is an important goal. In the personal domain, the development of perseverance and learning to learn is an important goal, including the development of self-efficacy, resilience, perseverance, self-directed learning, self-management and self-motivation, and the gradual development of a lifelong learning perspective.

Learning content

Learners are expected to learn the "4S" learning content reconstructed by teachers and to use the "S-DIP" approach to digital resource representation. Firstly, teachers should have a good grasp of subject knowledge and teaching materials, and design the "4S" content of the unit accurately according to the 21st century competence domains and the competence dimensions of deeper learning: subject-based content (SK), learning strategies (KS), social skills (SS) and cognitive structure (CS). Secondly, the "S-ACIG" deeper learning process model should be used to characterize learning resources. Finally, the "4S" content should be developed according to the principles of deeper learning resources.

Learning styles

"Personalized-collaborative" deeper learning in class combines personalized, collaborative and competitive learning approaches in an authentic classroom. It has six basic elements: cognitive diagnosis, active interdependence, process participation, multi-directional conversation, individual responsibility and social skills. There are five types of collaborative group structures: single centre, no centre, double centric, pyramidal and parallel. It is important to note that deeper learning may take the form of linear personalized learning or collaborative learning that spirals around personalized learning. However, only through collaboration and conversation, while maintaining the core elements of the learner, can meaning be constructed, and only when the teacher, learning partner, curriculum and resources fit deeply into the above unity can personalized-collaborative learning truly happen.

Learning process

Deeper learning is not an advanced stage based on Bloom's Taxonomy of Educational Objectives, but rather a "start-to-finish" deeper learning process based on Marzano's Taxonomy of Educational Objectives, embodied in the "S-ACIG" deep processing process, as shown in Figure 5.4.

Figure 5.4 illustrates the cognitive process in the following six ways.

(1) The cognitive process is the whole process of schema construction, with each stage pointing to different learning content, learning styles and forms of resource representation, with different functions.

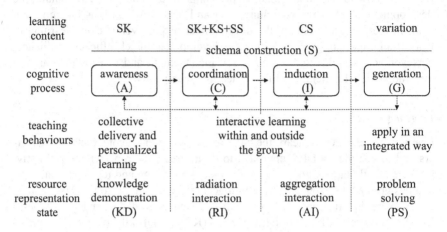

Figure 5.4 "S-ACIG" deeper learning design model

(2) The "awareness" stage is the entry point for learning, i.e. the process by which learners engage, perceive, experience and understand the learning content through PCL activities. In this phase, the SK content is studied, using collective delivery, personalized learning, knowledge demonstration, classroom presentations, content analogies and other forms of digital learning resources, with an emphasis on the memorization and understanding of declarative knowledge.

(3) The "coordination" stage is based on internalization, in which learners develop multiple understandings, doubts and even misunderstandings, and need to select, reorganize and reflect on multiple cognitions in order to begin to construct their own cognitive structures. In this stage, the interactive learning approach is used both within and outside the group in order to ensure the effectiveness of the cognitive aspects of selection, restructuring and reflection; and to ensure the smooth running of this approach, the SK, KS and SS components are studied. SK is used as a vehicle to promote the active construction and development of deeper learning qualities such as collaboration, discussion and critique. The resources are mainly represented by "radiation interaction", which facilitates effective discussion, brainstorming and contextualization based on anchor-based teaching.

(4) The "induction" stage reflects on and organizes the cognition that has been gradually unified during the "coordination" stage, and has two functions. The first is to form a rational cognitive structure. The second is to integrate and select different strategies to solve the same problem based on a scientific cognitive structure, thus forming an optimal pathway and preparing for "automation". Therefore, at this stage the learning content is mainly focusing on CS, which helps learners to begin to consciously construct cognitive structures, using "aggregation interaction" resources.

(5) The "generalization" stage gradually develops stable schemas that can be transferred to different contexts and problem solving situations, and in the process, existing schemas are constantly revised and improved. The resources for this stage are mainly problem situations, which learners apply in an integrated way to develop variation, thereby improving problem-solving skills and developing design and creative thinking.

(6) The four stages of cognition are shown in the solid line in the diagram as a classic developmental process, with each stage returning and cycling through the dotted line depending on the learner's individual learning diagnosis and feedback. This also reflects the superiority and operability of "personalized-collaborative" learning.

Technology enabling deeper learning

Based on a review of the empirical research process and an analysis of the deeper learning (mathematical) mechanism, the research summarizes the practical route to deeper learning, which will be explained in detail in the next section. Based on the intelligent and physical technologies used in this route, the technology enablement of the deeper learning process is analyzed, as shown in Table 5.4, to further understand the mechanics of deeper learning.

The following conclusions can be drawn from Table 5.4. (1) The deeper learning practice route consists of seven steps and each step corresponds to the corresponding actor, learning content, intelligent technology and physical technology. (2) Based on the deeper learning practice route, technology enables mainly five aspects, such as learning content presentation and perception. (3) Intelligent technology is primarily a strategy for designing and organizing learning activities, and physical technology is used to support the implementation of intelligent technology. (4) The knowledge awareness stage, where technology mainly presents learning content and facilitates learners' perception. (5) The cognitive starting point diagnosis stage, where technology mainly improves the accuracy and convenience of diagnosis and provides a basis for personalized learning. (6) The curriculum selection and reconstruction stage, where technology mainly facilitates the composition of learning content and its digital resource representation to fit the properties of individual learners or clusters. (7) The three phases of activation, acquisition and deep processing of knowledge can be supported by technologies such as blockchain and mixed reality. On the one hand, they guarantee the personalization of the learning process and allow learners to participate physically in the learning situation, and on the other hand, they form a learning community, allowing learners to interact in a distributed manner in a learning situation with ecological characteristics and realize the socialization of learning. (8) The learning assessment phase, where technology is mainly reflected in the monitoring of learning performance and the continuous adjustment of learning strategies. In summary, technology enablement is a combination of physical and intelligent technologies, which is characterized by stages, precision, convenience and effectiveness.

Table 5.4 Mapping of technology enablement of deeper learning

Deeper learning practice line	Subject	Learning content	Intelligent technology (design)	Physical technology (support)	Technology enablement
Knowledge awareness	Learners	SK	Presentation and perception	Electronic whiteboard; smart terminals; digital resources	Representation and perception
Cognitive starting point diagnosis	Teachers	Cognitive starting point thinking quality	Second order diagnosis thinking visualization	Second order diagnostic test questions; thinking visualization PDA; educational data analysis	Precise diagnosis
Curriculum selection and reconstruction	Teachers (Resource Developer)	"4S" content; "S-DIP" representations	"UDA" curriculum Reconstruction technology; "CRF" resource development technology	Software for content selection and reconstruction and digital resource development	The fit between "content", "resource", and "learner"
Activation of prior knowledge	Teachers and learners	Prior linked knowledge	"Personalized-collaborative" learning (PCL)	Blockchain technology; AI; VR; AR; MR; educational data analysis	Personalization; socialization; ecologization; Embodied participation; distributed interaction
New knowledge acquisition	Learners	"4S" content; "S-DIP" representations	PCL		
Deep processing knowledge	Learners	"4S" content; "S-DIP" representations	"S-ACIG" deep processing		
Assessment for learning	Teachers and learners	Academic performance; quality of thinking	Diagnostic test; thinking visualization	Diagnostic test questions; thinking visualization PDA; educational data analysis	Performance monitoring

Attributes of deeper learning class

The study presents a more comprehensive theoretical, methodological and operational paradigm of technology-enabled deeper learning in primary school mathematics through the processes of empirical research, data analysis, model induction and mechanistic analysis construction. It is long in duration and multi-dimensional in content, and still treats the deeper learning class as a "cross-section". Guided by the CTCL paradigm, the study designs a figure of the deeper learning class in order to understand its nature in a holistic manner, as shown in Figure 5.5.

As can be seen from Figure 5.5, the deeper learning class can be viewed from eight perspectives. First comes the learner, which is the central expression of deeper learning being "learner-centred". In practice, individual attributes such as cognitive biases and learning styles need to be diagnosed, and learners' motivation to learn needs to be developed. The second is teachers' quality. Teachers should have a deep understanding of learners' cognitive processes, select, reconstruct and design teaching content, and participate in learning activities in depth. The third is

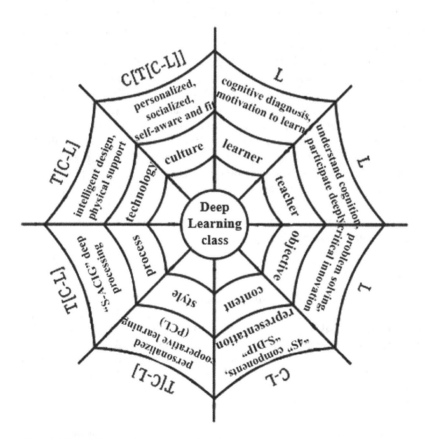

Figure 5.5 Attributes of deeper learning class

learning objectives, which are primarily based on improving learners' academic performance, improving learning performance and promoting the development of learners' thinking in terms of deep understanding, problem solving and critical innovation. The fourth is learning content, where learners are expected to learn the "4S" learning content reconstructed by the teacher and digitally represent it using the "S-DIP" approach. The fifth is the learning style, which is a conscious, active, multi-party collaborative process of personalized learning and collaborative interaction that fits the individual learner. The sixth is the learning process, which is not based on the advanced stage of superficial learning in Bloom's Taxonomy of Educational Objectives, but on a "start-to-finish" deeper learning process based on Marzano's Taxonomy of Educational Objectives, embodied in the "S-ACIG" deep processing. The seventh is the learning technology, which is designed, organized and implemented using intelligent technology, supported by physical technology. The eighth is the learning culture, which, through the deeper learning process described above, culminates in a deeper learning class culture. It is about social dependence and interaction in personalized learning; learners are highly self-aware and have a high degree of fitness to the learning content and learning style. It is evident that the deep class does not mean the difficulty degree of class but the situation, based on the depth of the cognitive starting point of the learner, i.e. the depth of the coordinated development of the individual learner and the learning community.

At the same time, according to the CTCL research paradigm, the deeper learning class can be understood and examined as follows. Firstly, the learner, the teacher and the learning objectives, fully embodying the attribute of "L", reflect the full attention of educational research to the learner. The second is the unity of the learning content and the learner, expressed as "C-L", which reflects the learner's deep understanding and relevance to the learning content. The third is the unity of learning styles, learning processes and learning technologies, which is manifested in the intervention of technology on learners, i.e. "T[C-L]", reflecting the view that "technology is the learner's way of being". The fourth is the culture of learning, i.e. "C[T[C-L]]", which ultimately forms a new learning culture in the learning process, further promoting the generation of a deeper learning class and the development of learners' quality.

References

Baidu (2017). Retrieved April 28, 2017, from http://baike.baidu.com/link?url=t6odnK7 5juH72418MeGfr4r5nWgOEjLYPwiuiDNnHADUqYlmWYISfKTJfURG4JaidJo JcQUHrDK3M88pp4kO0562YjSgDelTQRG0yDVT-GZ6gd79HdAW-didSegy1KiW.
Chen, S.J. (2001). *Curriculum and teaching.* Guilin: Guangxi Normal University Press.
Chen, Y.Q. (2003). Curriculum as student development resource: A new perspective for understanding the essence of curriculum. *Curriculum, Teaching Material and Methods, 23*(11), 10–14.
Du, Z.Q. (2010). *Research on comprehension curriculum.* Beijing: Guangming Daily Press.
Duan, J.J. (2012). E-learning research on strategies to promote deep learning in e-learning environment. *China Educational Technology, 33*(5), 38–43.

Goodlad, J.I. (1979). *Curriculum inquiry: the study of curriculum practice*. New York: McGraw-Hill book company.

Huang, F.Q. (1996). New exploration of curriculum essence. *Theory and Practice of Education, 16*(1), 21–25.

Jin, Y.L. (2003). *The idea and innovation of new curriculum reform*. Beijing: People's Education Press.

Li, J.H. (2010). *The introduction of the new taxonomy of educational objectives*. Shanghai: Shanghai Education Press.

Liu, Z.Y., & Wang, Z.J. (2017). The empirical study of behaviour engagement influence on deep learning: Exemplified with video learning in virtual reality (VR) environment. *Journal of Distance Education, 35*(1), 72–81.

Schawab, J.J. (1995). *Curriculum development in the postmodern era*. New York: Garland Publishing.

Schubert, W.H. (1986). *Curriculum: Perspective, paradigm, and possibility*. New York: Macmillan.

Sheng, Q.L. (2008). Foster high-level ability of problem-solving: The systemic explanation of Marzano's taxonomy of cognitive objective. *Open Education Research, 14*(4), 10–21.

Wu, J. (1986). *Teaching theory*. Changchun: Jilin Education Press.

Zhang, H., Wu, X.J., & Wang, J. (2014). Study on the evaluation theoretical structure building of deep learning. *China Educational Technology, 35*(7), 51–55.

Zhang, Y.Q., & Chen, Y.Q. (2013). Learning scientific horizon in deep learning oriented information teaching mode change. *China Educational Technology, 36*(4), 20–24.

6 Digital resource development for deeper learning

Theoretical analysis of deeper learning digital resources development

Schema

A schema is a representational approach that integrates concepts, propositions and representations, and refers to an organized knowledge structure that organizes fragmented stimuli, information and data and their relationships to form a cognitive structure. Schemas include individual schemas, self-schemas, group schemas, role schemas and event schemas, which represent the cognitive structure of different subjects or objects respectively. Mind mapping is an effective visualization tool for schemas.

Cognitive load theory

The most important factor in cognitive processing is "cognitive load", which refers to "the state of mental load and mental effort felt by an individual in the course of a job, assignment or task" (Sun & Li, 2017). It consists of the following three assumptions (Jeroen & Van, 2005). Firstly, the human information processing system consists of two channels, visual and auditory, in which information is selected and presented to short-term memory. Secondly, the information capacity of short-term memory (working memory) is limited, and meaningful learning requires extensive cognitive processing in short-term memory. Thirdly, the processed information is sent to long-term memory, the capacity of which is almost unlimited. It is evident that short-term memory, or working memory, has a limited number of units to process information, but can be "expanded" by expanding the amount of information contained in each unit. The most basic method of capacity expansion is to adopt a "structural" form, organizing the necessary associated information into "blocks", i.e. schematic representations, so that it is possible to condense a lot of independent information into more than one block and enter working memory, i.e. to reduce the cognitive load of the same amount of knowledge through a schematic representation of resources.

DOI: 10.4324/9781003278702-6

A resource-based view of education informatization

Professor Lai Jiahou puts forward the "life-environment view" of education informatization. He divides the "life-environment view" of education informatization into five levels of discussion, one of which is the resource view of teaching informatization. This theory believes that due to its inherent characteristics and advantages, information technology can provide rich learning resources to facilitate students' learning, mainly containing the following three main ideas (Li, 2002). Firstly, each media has its own characteristics and advantages, and it cannot be said that a certain media is all-powerful and can replace others; the application process should take into account the strengths and weaknesses of the "diversity" of resources. Secondly, resources should have the characteristic of "mobility", which means that human activities are dynamic, not static, and that the construction of educational resources should be integrated into human activities. Thirdly, it emphasizes that resources are "shared". In the learning process, teachers and students interact, communicate and work together to complete the construction of meaning. In this process, the sharing of resources should be encouraged, in which the participation of each learner generates new resources.

Cognitive process of deeper learning

In the process of researching deeper learning technologies in class, the cognitive process of deeper learning was analyzed, and the "S-ACIG" deeper learning cognitive process model was constructed, as shown in Figure 6.1. (1) The cognitive process of deeper learning is the whole process of schema construction and consists of four stages: "awareness", "coordination", "induction" and "generalization". (2) Any stage of "coordination", "induction" and "generalization" can return forward and circulate depending on the individual learner' situation. (3) The "awareness" stage is the entry into learning, i.e. the process by which learners engage, perceive, experience and understand the learning content through PCL activities. (4) The "coordination" stage is based on "awareness", in which learners develop multiple understandings, doubts and even misunderstandings, and need to select, reorganize and reflect on multiple cognitions in order to begin to construct their own cognitive structures. (5) The "induction" stage is a period of reflection and organization of the cognitions gradually unified in the "coordination" stage. This stage has two functions: firstly, to form a rational cognitive structure, and secondly, to integrate and select different strategies to solve the

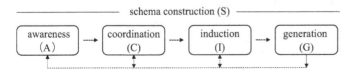

Figure 6.1 "S-ACIG" deeper learning cognitive process

same problem based on a scientific cognitive structure, thus forming an optimal path and preparing for "automation". (6) The "generalization" stage gradually forms a stable schema that can be transferred to different contexts and problem solving situations, and in the process, the existing schema is constantly revised and improved.

In summary, the construction of digital resources for learning and teaching should be closely focused on the cognitive process of learning, and the process of constructing learners' schemas and cognitive structures is that of cognitive development and the occurrence and progression of learning activities. The "cognitive load" theory clarifies the design of digital resources through schema representation and "blocking". The resource-based view of education information technology emphasizes the characteristics of digital resources; the deeper learning cognitive process provides the core clues for the dynamic design and phased application of digital resources. The study is based on the above schema, cognitive and digital resource perspectives for the representation and development of deeper learning resources.

Methods for the representation of deeper learning resources

Representation state of deeper learning resources

Representation state is that of deeper learning resources mapped according to the "operational paradigm of ecological Flow" of learning content, and is the relatively stable representation level and form of digital resources at a certain time in the cognitive process. This representation is in a state of continuous flux. A state is a relative stability, not a definite "stage" or "level", corresponding to the process of learning content and curriculum generation. The main purpose of using "state" in the study is to distinguish them from "stages" or "levels". Closely following the cognitive process of deeper learning and the cues of learning content, the representational states of deeper learning resources are shown in Figure 6.2.

As can be seen in Figure 6.2, the resource representational state flows with the cognitive process and maps to the learning content, fully reflecting

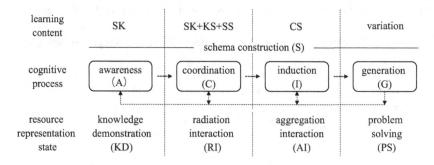

Figure 6.2 "S-DIP" representational state of deeper learning resources

the reconstruction of the learning content and its integration with the digital resources. This is explained in terms of cognitive processes as follows. (1) The resources are built around the schema (S) process, which corresponds to the "4S" learning content in the first section of this chapter, and are at different levels in different cognitive processes. The core vocabulary of the states – demonstration, interaction and problem – was chosen and named the "S-DIP" representation state of deeper learning resources. (2) The "awareness" stage focuses on "SK" content, using digital learning resources in the form of knowledge demonstration, lesson presentations and content analogies, emphasizing the memorization and understanding of declarative knowledge. (3) In the "coordination" stage, the "radiation interaction" representation is used for the effectiveness of the cognitive aspects of selection, restructuring and reflection, with the main learning components "SK", "KS" and "SS". "SK" is used as a vehicle to promote the active construction and development of deeper learning qualities such as collaboration, discussion and criticism and to facilitate the effective implementation of activities such as discussion, brainstorming and contextual performance based on anchor-based teaching. (4) The "induction" stage is dominated by "CS", which helps learners to begin to construct cognitive structures consciously, using "aggregation interaction" resources. (5) The "generalization" stage provides "problem situations", where learners are trained in variation through integrated applications to improve problem-solving skills and develop design and creative thinking.

Methods for the representation of deeper learning resources

Based on the characteristics of the learning content and the representational state of the resources at each stage of the cognitive process, and in conjunction with the forms of resource existence and application paradigms in the empirical studies, the study summarizes the methods for the representation of deeper learning resources. Table 6.1 maps the instructional media and their accompanying resource forms used in the classroom deeper learning process according to their representational states and explains their methods and processes of supporting teaching and learning. (1) Classical teaching media are combined with information technology devices, such as blackboard and online platform interaction using tablet operation. (2) Static and dynamic resources are used alternately, such as text, animation, games, etc. (3) The process of resources supporting teaching and learning is matched with learning content and learning styles, such as the integration of subject content, comprehension strategies, and social skills through collaborative approaches such as brainstorming, games, contextual performances, etc. (4) Teaching media and corresponding resources are operated in a "flow" of resource representations.

Table 6.2 analyzes the characteristics of the teaching media and resources used in the study according to the dimensions of the characteristics of the teaching media (He & Li, 2003). It is clear from the table that different media and resources have different characteristics, and that the actual teaching process should be

Table 6.1 Mapping of resource representational states, instructional media and resource forms

Resource representational states	Teaching media	Resource forms	How to support teaching
Knowledge demonstration	Blackboard; presentation screen	Text; blackboard writing; micro-video (presentational resources)	Systematic presentation of learning content in the form of text, blackboard writing, images, etc. through group instruction, personalized learning etc.
Radial interaction	Tablet; online platform	Micro-videos; animations; and games (interactive resources)	A collaborative approach to integrating subject content, comprehension strategies and social skills through discussion, brainstorming, games and contextualization
Aggregate interaction	Tablet; thinking visualization PDA	Mind maps (guidance resource)	Guide learners to summarize subject knowledge through discussion, diagramming, diagnosis and revision
Problem situations	Presentation screens; online platform	Text; contextual questions; animations (training resources)	Transfer of diagrams, problem solving and creative thinking through contextual questions, variation training, etc.

adjusted and selected in real time according to the learners' situation, the learning content and the learning environment.

Tables 6.3 summarizes the digital resource representation methods used in empirical research for deeper learning content by visual representation methods (Zhu, 2013) based on knowledge classification and provides corresponding case studies for revision, testing and further extension in practice. The specific forms of the resource representation methods are explained as follows.

(1) The "SK" learning knowledge section adopts three main forms of representation: "concept map", "graphical method" and "target decomposition". The "concept map" is used to form a meaningful network structure of scattered and isolated factual knowledge, such as elementary arithmetic and laws of operations, through various relationships and finally forms a "block class". The "graphical method" uses visuals to reveal the relevant elements of simple problem solving and their relationships. The "target decomposition" is a typical approach to problem solving in cognitive skills, where each operational stage has a clear goal and leads to a final problem solution; in primary school

Table 6.2 Characteristics of teaching media and resources

Type characteristics		Tablet	Online platform	Text	Black-board writing	Micro-video	Animation	Games	Mind mapping	Contextual questions
Presentational power	Spatial	✓				✓	✓	✓	✓	✓
	Temporal		✓	✓	✓	✓	✓	✓	✓	✓
	Movement		✓		✓	✓	✓	✓		✓
Reproducibility	Immediate	✓				✓	✓	✓		
	Afterwards		✓	✓			✓		✓	✓
Engagement	Affective			✓	✓	✓	✓	✓	✓	
	Behavioural	✓		✓	✓	✓				✓
Controllability	Easy	✓						✓	✓	✓
	Difficult		✓							

Table 6.3 Table of methods for characterizing deeper learning resources

Learning content	Knowledge category	Specific form
SK	Algorithm and elementary arithmetic The law of arithmetic and simple arithmetic Problem solving	Concept map; graphical method; target decomposition
KS	Correspondence strategies	Iceberg model
SS	Individual expression skills Member communication skills Teamwork skills	Metaphor; four-section comic; synaesthesia
CS	Schema representation	Mind map
variation	Contextual questions	Montage

    mathematics, elementary arithmetic and application problems are all part of problem solving, but they are presented in different ways.

(2) "KS" is the counterpart of "SK", where "SK" is explicit and "KS" is invisible. In order to facilitate learners' understanding and deeper exploration of the relationship between the explicit and the invisible and the strategies they use, the study mainly used is the "iceberg model". It actually divides the components of a thing into two aspects: the visible and the invisible. The iceberg model is used to characterize the relationship between the visible and invisible elements of the same thing and their transformational characteristics.

(3) The "SS" focuses on enhancing learners" individual expression skills and their ability to coordinate communication and cooperation among team members, using metaphors, four-section comics and synaesthesia. The metaphorical approach is a rhetorical technique that allows learners to perceive, imagine and experience the mental processes of communication and cooperation under the suggestion of analogues, such as the activities in game simulation. A four-section comic is an ancient form of "picture-telling" representation that uses four images – a beginning, a development, a climax and an ending – to give an unintended outcome. Learners experience interpersonal skills in a fun and surprising way. Synaesthesia refers to the psychological phenomenon of interaction between senses, where the stimulation of one sense triggers another, e.g. contextual simulations trigger multiple organs of the learner through visual metaphors, underscoring, etc., thus stimulating their emotional resonance.

(4) The "CS" cognitive structures are visualized in the learner's brain using mind maps, for example, showing the nature of "integer arithmetic", including concepts, relationships and application topics, thus forming a three-dimensional and systematic schematic structure.

(5) The variation training focuses on providing different contextual questions to facilitate transfer. The study adopts a "montage" approach, where a series of images are "assembled" in different ways to produce different effects, providing learners with different contextual questions.

Characteristics of deeper learning resources

According to the synthesis of the representation states and methods of deeper learning resources, six main characteristics are elaborated as follows.

Diversity

Seven resources are presented in Table 6.3 and nine representation methods are presented in Table 6.3, showing the diversity of deeper learning resources and that the study is still only a glimpse. Diversity can richly represent the complexity of the "4S" knowledge component while meeting the needs of learners for multi-sensory access.

Fluidity

Resources are not static, but change dynamically with the progression of the main cognitive process, effectively supporting the development of the learner's cognitive process.

Sharing

Although each learner has their own personalized learning resources based on their cognitive diagnosis, there are individual expression, discussion and collaboration within and outside the "cluster",[1] and the sharing of resources increases their utilization and effectiveness.

Interactivity

In the process of resource sharing, there is a wealth of interactive behaviours between humans and machines, teachers and students, including the transfer of knowledge, the collision of ideas, the exchange of emotions and the occasional inspiration.

Generativity

In the process of interaction, as resources are transferred, understood and perceived, learners create new ideas, methods and strategies in their critical thinking, thus generating new resources, where creative thinking sprouts and develops.

Contextual

The above types of activities are not fragmented and isolated, but are problem solving in the face of real situations, promoting the development of learners' ability to learn by example.

Development model of deeper learning resources

Principles of deeper learning resource development

Based on the representation states and methods of deeper learning resources, the study proceeds to the development of digital learning resources, and the following five principles are observed in the process of resource development.

Blocking factual knowledge to reduce cognitive load

Factual knowledge is characterized by fragmentation and isolation, and its data and information are often trivial and informative, making it difficult to identify its relationships directly, thus increasing the cognitive load on learners. Therefore, in the process of resource development, designers need to find the intrinsic logical relationships and "structure" them to form a blocked system, so as to reduce the cognitive load, facilitate the assimilation and adaptation of new knowledge to the "original cognitive structure", and ultimately construct a new schema.

Making cognitive skills procedural to reflect cognitive processes

Cognitive skills are sequences of cognitive processes, which form a complex "production system" that forms a complex psychological mechanism through several "conditions (C) – actions (A)" production models. This system forms inter-relationships through a "transact-SQL". Resources are developed to visualize this procedural process, allowing learners to clarify the complex psycho-cognitive processes and prepare them for "automation".

Modelling problem solving to enhance "automaticity"

Problem solving is an advanced form of cognitive skills of discrimination, concepts, rules and advanced rules, including the intellectual skills of using knowledge for problem solving and the process of continuous adjustment using metacognitive strategies, which is essentially a thinking construction process. Therefore, in deeper learning, support resources should help learners to model their thinking, so as to facilitate systematic thinking about the relationship between various levels and elements of the problem on the basis of understanding the cognitive process, and finally form "expert knowledge" to "automate" the problem.

Integrating strategic knowledge to realize "knowledge-strategy integration"

Strategic knowledge is the "twin" of subject knowledge, it is the lubricant of problem solving and it goes hand in hand with subject knowledge but is most likely to be overlooked by teachers and students or not applied fluently even if understood.

Therefore, it is important to dig deeper into the "KS" knowledge and integrate it with the "SK" in the resource development process to achieve "knowledge-strategy integration". The "iceberg model" in the resource representation is designed to emphasize the importance of "digging deeper" into the underlying strategies and integrating them with the representational knowledge.

Making emotional knowledge sensible to produce
"emotion-situation-action" resonance

The learning process is not just about cognition, but about the harmonious development of knowledge, emotion and situation; personalized-collaborative learning requires the support of individual expression, communication and emotional integration, and is also a way of developing these interpersonal skills. Resource development is then not just a process of transferring knowledge and understanding, but the coordinated development of learning qualities, which are important expressions of deeper learning. Resource development should then use a variety of techniques to resonate with learners' multiple sensory channels such as "emotion-situation-action" with techniques such as metaphor and synaesthesia being used in Table 6.3.

Development model of deeper learning resources

In the process of deeper learning resource development and application it can be seen that it mainly focuses on the following three aspects in the cognitive process: firstly, the fit of content selection and restructuring; secondly, the diversity and rationality of resource representation; thirdly, the feedback and correction of learners' learning effects. Therefore, the study summarizes the development model of deeper learning resources as the "CRF model", as shown in Figure 6.3.

As can be seen from Figure 6.3, the deeper learning resource development process consists of the following five stages.

The first stage is content selection and restructuring, which consists of four main aspects. (1) Resource development starts from subject content "SK" selecting; not all learning content has to be developed into digital learning resources, but mainly focuses on the classical cognitive processes that need to be visualized. (2) Based on the selection of "SK", a deeper exploration of the corresponding "KS" is carried out, and "SS" are selected and reorganized to fit with them. (3) The integration of "SK" and "KS" is on the basis of the above. (4) In both one-way and two-way processes, attention must be paid to the relevance of the findings of empirical research – that "technology design" rather than "technology itself" facilitates learning development.

The second stage is the analysis of the teaching objectives, which is based on the clustering of learners' cognitive diagnoses in order to stratify and categorize the "4S" content selected and reorganized.

The third stage is the selection of the representation method and the design of the situation, which is based on the characteristics and content of the different

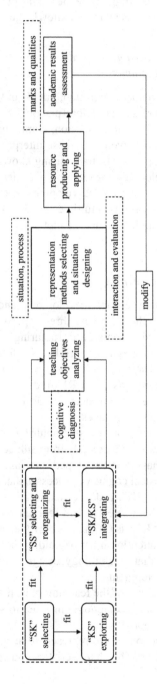

Figure 6.3 "CRF" deeper learning resource development model

clusters. In this process, the focus should be on the design of four aspects: problem situations, cognitive processes, interaction methods and evaluation mechanisms.

Fourthly, based on the technological design, the resources are produced and pedagogically applied.

The fifth is the feedback and modification stage, based on the feedback of learners' marks and learning quality to further modify and improve the resources and accumulate classical materials for the large-scale promotion of deeper learning.

The connotation of deeper learning resources and application strategies

The connotation of deeper learning resources

The study accepts Professor Zhong Zhixian's idea of systematic learning resources (2001), which believes that "learning resources are a system that includes five categories: people, materials, tools, implementation and activities". Based on the operational content of the empirical study, the deeper learning systematic resource view was constructed, as shown in Table 6.4.

From Table 6.4, the connotation of deeper learning resources can be understood as follows. (1) Deeper learning resources are a dynamic operating system in which the elements collaborate and work together. (2) A deeper learning resource system consists of four elements: "people", "content", "materials" and "learning activities". In this study, "people" refer to teachers, learners, parents and those involved in school education; "content" refers to "4S" learning content; "materials" refer to digital resources, texts, tablets, online learning platforms, etc.; "activities" refer to various activities within the scope of PCL, such as games, brainstorming, etc. (3) The main mechanism of the deeper learning resource system is to externalize or visualize the learner's cognitive processes and thus facilitate the internalization of knowledge and the construction of individual schemas (cognitive structures), which is an internal and external state transducer. (4) Deeper learning resources are characterized and exist in an "S-DIP" progression of states that develop in tandem with cognitive processes. (5) Learning resources are an effective tool to support the smooth implementation of PCL and ultimately improve learning performance.

Table 6.4 Deeper learning resource system

Core view	Components	Operational mechanism	Expression	Main purpose
Deeper learning resources are a systematic operating body	People, content, materials and activities	A state transducer for the externalization of cognitive processes and the internalization by the learner	A vehicle to support the progression of the learner's cognitive processes	To support PCL implementation and to improve learning performance

Application strategies for deeper learning resources

Based on the six characteristics of deeper learning resources and the application methods in the empirical study, the study believes that deeper learning resources should focus on their systemic, cognitive and dynamic nature in the application process, and specifically contains three application strategies.

Establishing a systematic view of learning resources and constructing the operational mechanism

The systemic view of learning resources is a guiding strategy for the application of deeper learning resources. It requires abandoning the instrumental view of learning resources, developing a deeper understanding of what the "system" is, establishing a systemic mindset and being able to understand the role and position of the learning resource system within the learning system and its relationship with other systems. On this basis, we will build a deeper learning resource system and grasp the mechanism of its operation, so that it can play a good supporting role in the deeper learning system.

Focusing on learners' cognitive process and understanding their development mechanism

Understanding learners' cognitive processes and their developmental mechanisms is a mechanistic strategy for the application of deeper learning resources, which requires teachers or instructors to have a deep understanding of learners' cognitive processes, which is the guideline for the stages and ways of applying learning resources, and which is the mechanism needed to be observed in the design, development and practice of learning resources.

Dynamically applying learning resources and timely controlling their production status

It is a practical strategy of deeper learning resources application to dynamically apply and control in a timely manner their production status. It requires that learning resources be allowed to "flow" during the operation of the deeper learning system, be reasonably selected and implemented in the learning activities according to the cognitive laws in practice, and be adjusted and reasonably controlled according to the dynamic resources generated by teacher-student, student-student and human-computer interaction in the learning process.

Note

1 Cluster: A biological term for an organism that has homogeneous characteristics and is concentrated in a particular environment. This article refers to learners with the same or similar cognitive diagnostic outcome attributes.

References

He, K.K., & Li, K.D. (2003). *Theory and practice of instructional media*. Beijing: Beijing Normal University Press.

Jeroen, J.G., & Van, M. (2005). Research on cognitive load theory and its design implications for e-learning. *Educational Technology Research and Development, 53*(3), 5–13.

Li J.H. (2002). Create the spirit of students and teachers to the life of the informationization environment - "life environment view" of education informatization. *e-Education Research, 23*(2), 3–10.

Sun, C.Y., & Li, S.L. (2017). *Cognitive load theory and its use in teaching*. Beijing: Tsinghua University Press.

Zhong, Z.X. (2001). *Introduction to distance education: principles and methods of pedagogy*. Beijing: Higher Education Press.

Zhu, Y.H. (2013). *Based on the knowledge classification research of visual representation*. Unpublished doctoral dissertation. Nanjing Normal University, China.

7 Teaching method of deeper learning
"Personalized-cooperative" learning

Analysis of "personalized-cooperative" learning theory

Development context of learning style

Cooperation, competition, and individualization are the three main ways of working in human society, as well as the three main ways of learning that are common in the school education process (Wu & Guan, 2010). As far as social production is concerned, individualization is the most basic mode of production, cooperation is the core element of contemporary society, and competition is a means to promote continuous social progress. However, competition in contemporary society is team competition based on cooperation. As far as school education and classroom learning are concerned, only the idea of "based on individualized efforts, centered on cooperative learning, and promoted development with moderate competition" can lead the actual teaching in order to effectively promote the development of individual students and school groups. However, traditional classrooms in my country emphasize competition and individualized learning. "Completing homework independently" is a typical embodiment of this idea. These two learning methods are characterized by the mutual dependence between learners: individualized learning means that there is no mutual dependence between learners, and the learning content and evaluation are completed separately; their knowledge comes from two channels: one is the teacher—students, the other is students—learning resources. Competitive learning means that there is a negative dependence between learners. Anyone's success means the failure of others. The pros and cons have been debated. Therefore, researchers began to attempt to build a positive interdependence relationship between learners' "cooperative learning". At the same time, with the development of intelligent learning terminals and the rise of big data and learning analysis technologies, researchers have begun to pay attention to "personalized learning", which is based on individual learners or clusters of cognitive starting points, learning interests, learning styles and other individual factors , create a smart learning environment and design learning activities.

The individual is the basic unit of individualization, and individualization is the manifestation of the individual. The difference between personalized learning and individualized learning is very different: one is that personalized learning emphasizes the individual differentiation of learners, including learning style,

DOI: 10.4324/9781003278702-7

learning attitude, learning motivation and many other factors; individualized learning only emphasizes the individual's Existing form. One is that personalized learning emphasizes the individual differentiation of learners, including learning style, learning attitude, learning motivation and many other factors; individualized learning only emphasizes the individual's Existing form. The third is that personalized learning does not completely deny the element of cooperation, and it also hopes to establish a positive relationship of mutual dependence among learners (Chen & Yang, 2015). However, in current classroom teaching, when teachers pay attention to individualization, they often ignore the cooperation between learners, and when they pay attention to cooperative learning, they often ignore the individual differences between learners. Since purely competitive learning has been abandoned by the academic world, the research focuses on cooperation and personalized learning.

Cooperative learning

Cooperative learning was first advocated and implemented by the famous American educator David Koonts in the 1970s, and has developed into one of the most respected teaching theories today. Cooperative learning is the general term for a series of methods to organize and promote classroom teaching. D.W. Johnson & R.T. Johnson defined the concept of cooperative learning and divided cooperative groups into three basic types: formal cooperative groups, informal cooperative groups and grass-roots cooperative groups. The basic principles of cooperative learning are: positive mutual dependence, everyone's responsibility, fair participation, and simultaneous interaction (Kagan, 1994). At the same time, cooperative learning also pays attention to individual learners, pays attention to the impact of group goals and group evaluation or rewards on student achievement, and emphasizes the significance of individual responsibility to the failure of small groups (Slavin, 1985).

Nowadays, cooperative learning has been widely used in the teaching of various subjects, and different teaching modes have emerged according to the different characteristics of subjects and courses. Among them, Leaning Together (LT) is the most applicable, for all grades and all disciplines. Small Group Achievement Division (STAD) and Small Group Games Competition (TGT) are suitable for general teaching techniques at most disciplines and grade levels. Team Assisted Individual (TAI) is specially suitable for teaching machine in grades 3-6 grade. Cooperative Literacy Integration (CIRC) is specially suitable for teaching reading and writing in grades 3-6. Group Investigation (GI) is a general plan for organizing classes to use different cooperative learning strategies in certain subjects General plan; Structure Approach (SA) (Spencer Kagan) and Jigsaw (JIGSAW) focus on independent group learning, and the learning materials can be subdivided and adapted to different age groups(Aronson, 1978; Johnson & Johnson, 1994).

It can be seen that the research on cooperative learning methods has been quite mature, and a relatively complete system has been formed from the definition of concepts, theoretical foundations to implementation strategies. Studies have shown that cooperative learning is more effective than competitive learning and independent learning. From formal cooperation groups, informal cooperation groups, and cooperation-based groups, to class-level and school-level cooperation, there is guidance on student cooperation, as well as guidance on teacher cooperation in teaching (Johnson & Johnson, 2004).

Personalized learning

Personalized learning is based on learners' individual differences, emphasizing that the learning process should adopt appropriate methods, means, strategies, content, processes, evaluations, etc. in accordance with their individual characteristics and development potential, so that learners can obtain full freedom in all aspects (Zheng, 2015). It is composed of five closely related basic elements: learning assessment, effective teaching, course selection, school management, and extracurricular development and support.

Regarding the research of personalized learning, scholars at home and abroad are quite different. Most of the foreign research focuses on the development of personalized learning (teaching) algorithms, technologies and systems, including adaptability and personalized learning systems based on students' cognitive characteristics can be applied (Chang et al., 2015). The personalized learning system using the decision tree analysis method is proven to effectively improve academic performance by constructing a personalized learning path (Lin et al., 2013); through the decision support system to recommend suitable courses for students, personalized learning curriculum planner in the college English learning style. The trial effectively improves students' listening, speaking, reading and writing skills in English (Jeong et al., 2012). In comparison, domestic scholars mainly discuss personalized teaching (learning) models from the theoretical and practical levels, focusing on applied practice and effect evaluation, and rarely involve technology development. Including goal-driven personalized learning models (Zheng, 2010) and personalized learning models from the perspective of neo-constructivism; supported by emerging teaching models, personalized teaching models based on flipped classrooms (Wang, 2014), personalized learning models based on Web environments, etc (Zhong, 2012; Hao, 2012). Some scholars have constructed a subject-based personalized learning model, among which personalized learning of college English has attracted much attention (Wang & Dong, 2011; Yang, 2011).

It can be seen from this that in personalized learning, learners can select the required learning resources and services according to their learning interests and needs, according to their learning progress and pace, and search, select and organize information through various tools and services, thereby completing the processing of information and realizing the absorption and innovation of knowledge.

In summary, we can draw the following conclusions: (1) in the study of learning methods, there is a phenomenon that only focuses on one learning method and ignores other methods. Paying attention to personalized learning often ignores the importance of cooperation, and at the same time ignoring the individual differences of learners; (2) in terms of research methodology, domestic research emphasizes speculation but ignores empirical evidence and cannot obtain quantitative empirical support. It attaches importance to theoretical models. Constructing and ignoring the summary of specific teaching strategies makes it difficult to translate theories into teaching practice, and it is difficult to provide operable programs for frontline teaching. To this end, this research focuses on learners' deeper learning in classrooms, integrates the respective advantages of the three learning methods of individualization, cooperation and competition in real classrooms, implements empirical research on "personalized-cooperative" learning with competitive characteristics, and conducts theoretical studies.

Elements and structure of "personalized-cooperative" learning

Elements of "personalized-cooperative" learning

Based on the literature discussion, the research summarizes the basic elements of personalized-cooperative learning based on the teaching content and teaching behaviours in the empirical research, as shown in Table 7.1.

From Table 7.1, we can see that there are six types of teaching behaviours in empirical research. Through the transformation from "behaviour" to "theory", they correspond to the six basic elements, as follows:

Cognitive diagnosis: the CTCL research paradigm emphasizes exploring the cognitive biases of learners in order to understand the cognitive structure of individual learners or clusters, so as to provide appropriate learning content and resources for personalized learning and provide a basis for cooperative learning grouping, as a starting point for learning. In empirical research, learners' cognitive biases are divided into five basic types. The method of diagnosis has been described in detail in Dr. Jing Wang's research (Wang & Dong, 2012; Wang & Dong, 2013; Wang & Dong, 2014).

Active interdependence: based on the results of cognitive diagnosis, teachers will guide and instruct the groups to form a well-coupled group and encourage members to use their own different resources (different cognitive structures) to assume corresponding roles. Harmony and responsibility can not only give play to individual advantages and promote individual development but also promote the growth of the community, and finally move each from the "edge" to the "centre", iterative cycle, and form a new learning community. The empirical research and discussion explained in detail the grouping strategy of forming positive interdependence. In the effect feedback, 80% of the learners expressed satisfaction with this structural relationship. The specific cognitive structure is discussed in detail in the next section.

Process participation: the learning process is a sequence of events that can be identified over a period of time, instead of traditional group. Where only the "cooperative learning" is seen. Teachers should enter the group learning process as instructors or participants. While guiding knowledge, they should observe the learners' use of the emphasized or designated cooperative skills, and give

Table 7.1 Mapping of PCL teaching behaviours to essential elements

Teaching behaviour	Essential elements	Paraphrase	Function
Cognitive starting point diagnosis	Cognitive diagnosis	Understand the cognitive structure of individual and group learners	Starting point detection
Group guidance and instruction	Positive interdependence	A canine relationship is formed among the group members, who play different roles to maintain their personalities and share resources	Structural coupling
"Behaviour-theory" transformation ⟹			
Teachers supervise and participate in group activities	Participation in the process	The teacher enters the learning community as a mentor or participant during group operation	Teaching and learning make progress together
Communication within and between groups ⟹	Multi-directional session	Through self-reporting, discussion, retelling, competition and other strategies to promote individual learners and learning community meaning construction	Construction of meaning
Metacognitive strategy training	Individual responsibility	Develop learners' ability of monitoring, feedback, adjustment and reflection	Activate the symbiotic
Social skill training	Social skills	Develop interpersonal skills among learners	Lubrication system

feedback to students through direct or indirect methods, and finally achieve the stage that "teach-learn" complement each other. 74% of the learners in the empirical study hope that teachers will step off the stage and deeply participate in the learning process of PCL. This point is a transformation of teachers' roles and functions. It is not only a requirement for current teachers, but also a guide for future teachers' training.

Multi-directional conversation: in empirical research, both the learning process and learning evaluation include intra-group and inter-group communication, allowing learners to promote the meaning construction of individuals and groups through self-reporting, discussion, retelling, and competition. In empirical research, most learners expressed their expectations for the above-mentioned multi-directional interaction from different dimensions.

Individual responsibility: research develops learners' monitoring, feedback, adjustment and reflection abilities through the cultivation of metacognitive strategies. Individual responsibility can activate the learner's internal learning motivation and then activate the vitality of the learning community, and finally can help realize the symbiosis and development of the individual and the group.

Social skills: these are the lubricant for the coordinated operation of the learning system, enabling learners to understand and trust each other, communicate with other members correctly and clearly, accept and support each other, and resolve conflicts constructively. In empirical research, the "T-chart" strategy is used to arrange special teaching time to promote the development of learners' social skills.

In summary, the six elements fit and promote each other, reflecting the modern teaching ideas of learning and teaching from different perspectives. (1) From the perspective of the teaching design process, it includes the starting point, process and result of learning. (2) From the perspective of the learning process, it embodies the sequence of events such as the structural relationship between the individual learner and the community, the way of interaction and the construction of meaning. (3) From the perspective of learning results, it emphasizes academic performance, learning motivation, social responsibility, teamwork and other abilities. (4) From the perspective of learning system performance, the six-element cooperation reflects the "pulley effect". If teachers can improve the use of one or more of the six elements in a more precise way, the performance of the system will be doubled.

The structure of "personalized-cooperative" learning

The well-coupled structure of learning groups is a guarantee for the effective development of PCL learning activities – this is the point that is the least concerned with or the most difficult to operate in current personalized learning and cooperative learning. The research summarizes the empirical research through classroom observations, questionnaires and interviews. The mutual dependence of group members and their structural characteristics in the group are explained through descriptive research as shown in Table 7.2.

Table 7.2 PCL team structure

Structure type	Structure shown in figure	Structural features	The overt behaviour
Single centre type		The group structure is centred on one learner, surrounded by a juxtaposed relationship among other learners	The centre performs the "action authority", assigns roles to members, and interacts with other learners. At the same time, other learners interact with each other, and the group has a unified opinion
No centre type		There is no central member in the group structure, and all learners are in parallel relationship	There is a phenomenon of accidental flow of "exercising power". Group roles are formed consciously. Learners interact randomly with each other and finally reach an agreement through various arguments
Double centre		The group structure is centred on two learners, surrounded by juxtaposed relationships among other learners	After reaching an agreement through interaction, the two central participants jointly perform the "exercise authority", assign roles to members, and interact with other learners. At the same time, other learners interact with each other, and the group has a unified opinion
The pyramid		The teams present a hierarchy, branching off at level 2 and then developing separately in parallel	The first layer has only one "leader", who is "high above" and performs the "highest executive authority", and only interacts with the second layer. The second layer performs the "secondary executive authority" and interacts with the next layer. Learners in the branch structure have no interaction, and group opinions may differ under the general framework
The parallel type		The groups present a parallel structure, with a hierarchy within the parallel branches	The group is consciously divided into parallel development, and each branch structure has a "leader" who performs the "exercising power" within the branch structure. There is interaction within the branch structure, and the group may have multiple opinions

(Note: solid lines indicate substantial interaction, and dashed lines indicate only formal interaction)

Based on the data in the empirical research and the summary in Table 7.1, the research is explained from the following four aspects. (1) There are at least five learner relationship structures in the PCL learning process. (2) The five structures are all developed around the "right to act", which shows that the "right to act" is the core element of the PCL study group and reflects the organizational structure characteristics of social relations. (3) In the empirical research, the consensus rate of the self-organization structure based on social relations in the first stage and the organizational adjustment based on the cognitive structure in the second stage reached 78%, which once again reflects the social relationship characteristics of "things gather in groups and people are divided into groups". There is a correlation between the cognitive structure of learners and social relations; (4) The characteristics of "right to act" in the above explanation and its relationship with other learners, the correlation between cognitive structure and social relations, and the structures can be seen in Table 7.3. Large-scale empirical research is needed on the amount of effect between them, and conclusions can be drawn only through the analysis of big data. The research will be further in depth in follow-up research.

The connotation and model of "personalized-cooperative" learning

Representation status of the four types of learning methods

The research is based on the data of exploratory experiments and the teaching behaviours, questionnaires and interviews in the "learning methods" confirmatory experiments, combined with literature discussion, and summarizes the representation status and existence methods of the current typical four types of learning methods, as shown in Table 7.3.

Based on the data in the empirical research and the summary in Table 7.3, the research is explained from the following four aspects. (1) The competitive learning, multimedia classroom, and personalized-cooperative learning in the table correspond to the C classroom and M classroom in the empirical study. In the Learner-Center Class, personalized learning has not yet been reflected in empirical research, and it is analyzed based on relevant literature. (2) In the empirical research, most of the (+) effect of learner interdependence (LIR), academic performance, interpersonal attractiveness, etc. reached +.25 or more, showing its greater influence. Among them, the performance value of the L classroom is the best, which fully shows that the design of the "learning method" (personalized-cooperative learning) variable is conducive to the improvement of learners' academic performance, which is in line with the "learning method" and "academic performance" in the exploratory experiment. The greatest correlation is consistent. (3) Through the "dependent variables" analyzed in the empirical research (academic performance, interpersonal attractiveness, social support, learner self-esteem, etc.), it can be seen that L classroom improves learners' scores and learning quality.

Table 7.3 Representation states of four types of learning styles

Characterization of dimension		Competitive learning	Multimedia classroom	Personalized learning	Personalized-cooperative learning
Learning goals and motivation		Surpass others	Improve their grades and try to cooperate	Interest	Interest, responsibility, surpassing yourself
Learning strategies		Independent learning	Discussion, inquiry, etc (direction may not be clear)	Independent learning	Independent study, retelling, discussion, presentation, etc. (very clear direction)
The learning process	Information exchange mode	"Teacher–student" collective, one-way	"Teacher–student" collective, one-way, individual "teacher-student", "student-student" effective two-way	"Teacher-student" individual, effective bidirectional	"Teacher-student", "student-student" collective, individual, effective bidirectional
	Peers give and receive help	None	Existence (not necessarily clear)	None	Existence (very clear)
	Self-reflection	Weak	Weaker	Stronger	Strong
	Peer feedback	None	Existence (not necessarily clear)	None	Existence (very clear)
	Challenges and arguments	None	Existence (not necessarily clear)	None	Existence (very clear)
	Advocacy and commitment	None	Almost no	None	Existence (very clear)
	Trust and Anxiety	Distrust, anxiety	Partial trust, existential anxiety	None	Trust, little anxiety
	Learning performance	Low	Medium	On the average	High
Learner relationship		Competition	Competition and moderate cooperation	Not clear	Cooperative and friendly
The study result		Score	Grades, learning quality (not necessarily clear)	Grades, learning quality (part)	Grades, learning quality

Design prototype of "personalized-cooperative" learning

According to the theories in the empirical research, the former is more suitable for the teaching of well-structured basic knowledge points, and the latter is more suitable for the teaching of open application knowledge points. In order for the two to be applied in a balanced and coordinated manner in the classroom situation, the design needs to adopt a connected, dynamic, and holistic continuum thinking method to prevent the phenomenon of dual opposition and the loss of the other. In classroom situational teaching, these two interactive structures are a continuum in the entire classroom activity system; the problematic nature of the learning content determines which interactive structure to choose. The research is based on the problem-centred classification framework of progressive teaching methods provided by Hokanson and Hooper (Hokanson & Hoops, 2004), which constitutes a continuum of problematic curriculum content and learning activity design, and the "individualization of empirical research". The summary of the collaborative learning design prototype is shown in Figure 7.1. In Figure 7.1, the symbols used in empirical research are used to indicate the corresponding relationship, where "△" means "teacher", "□"means "student", "○" means "study group formed by □", "●" means "a group that is hosting an interaction between groups", and "◇" means "problem". The meaning of "SK, KS, CS" has been explained in detail in the research glossary of exploratory experiments, so I won't repeat it in this article.

This framework uses "problems" as clues to describe the interaction between teachers, learners and learning content (problems), and the "structure and methods of learning activities" that exist in this interaction, constructing "teaching behaviour" and "teaching behaviour". The three continuums of "classroom structure" and "cognitive level" are specifically explained as follows. (1) The teaching behaviour continuum describes the teaching process in empirical research, mainly including collective delivery, personalized learning, intra-group interaction and inter-group interaction, as well as the five stages of comprehensive application. (2) The classroom structure continuum uses "problems" as clues to describe the structure and methods of learning activities corresponding to teaching behaviour. (3) The cognitive level continuum describes each of the two continuums mentioned above. The learning goals and cognitive development levels corresponding to learners at this stage mainly include initial knowledge and acceptance, memorization and comprehension, application and analysis, synthesis and evaluation, and creation and challenge. In actual classroom situational teaching, not every class has to complete these five levels, nor does every learner have to reach these five levels; it is the complete level of learning unit or topic teaching. According to the learning content and individual characteristics of learners, teachers can slide on the two double-arrow tracks to adjust the learning level to suit the learning content and learners' needs.

The continuum of classroom structure is the focus of this research, taking "problems" as clues, and the specific explanations are as follows. (1) Receiving teaching in zero-problem space. In the initial stage of learning, students have no

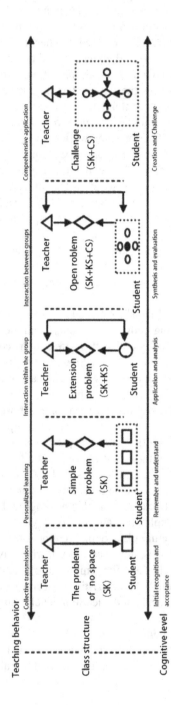

Figure 7.1 PCL design prototype

problems in solving, and teachers impart basic knowledge SK to learners one-way. For disciplines with strong rules such as mathematics and language, it is necessary for teachers to provide learners with the necessary basic information at this stage, and it is also the basis for learning to occur. On this basis, the cognitive bias and cognitive structure of learners can be diagnosed. (2) Individualized teaching for simple problem solving. In the stage of cognitive diagnosis, the teacher provides simple questions directly related to the content according to the learners' cognitive structure. Learners use strategies such as imitation and repetition to remember and comprehend the SK knowledge that they did not understand in stage 1. Teachers also play a one-way guiding role. (3) Expansion of interaction within the group for problem solving. At this stage, learners are mainly encouraged to use the acquired SK knowledge to solve new comprehensive problems composed of multiple simple problems that are indirectly related to the content. Stage 2 can be answered directly with SK knowledge, while in stage 3, the application process and strategy of SK knowledge need to be considered. Therefore, at this stage, through group member interaction and teacher participation in group guidance, learners begin to accept and summarize KS knowledge, and begin to integrate and apply SK knowledge. (4) Inter-group interaction for open problem solving. This stage mainly encourages learners to integrate the knowledge of KS and SK in stage 3, they can solve more complicated and applicable problems by inferences and then form a learner's individual CS structure through combination, reflection and adjustment strategies. At this stage, learners interact with other groups on the basis of intra-group interaction, and teachers are deeply involved in this process. The information between teachers and students is no longer one-way transmission but two-way communication. For example, students' strategies can also promote teachers' own thinking, summarization and professional development. (5) Comprehensive application of various strategies to solve challenging problems. At this stage, learners have fully mastered SK knowledge, and they are mainly encouraged to reconstruct KS knowledge and CS structure to solve the problem of inferior structure. The teacher basically does not participate in the early stage of problem solving, and the learners conduct inter-group discussions through personalized thinking, and then exchange between groups to form a problem-solving plan, and then the teacher deeply participates in verifying the scientificity and feasibility of the plan, and advances it in depth. The interaction and development between teachers and students, and between students and students, ultimately form a good learning quality.

The connotation and model of "personalized-cooperative" learning

Based on the empirical data analysis and literature discussion, the research summed up the elements, structure, representation status and design prototypes of personalized-cooperative learning. So how can we understand personalized-cooperative learning, and what is the whole picture? On the basis of the above, the research summed up a personalized-cooperative learning model, as shown in Figure 7.2, to understand its connotation in depth. As can be seen from

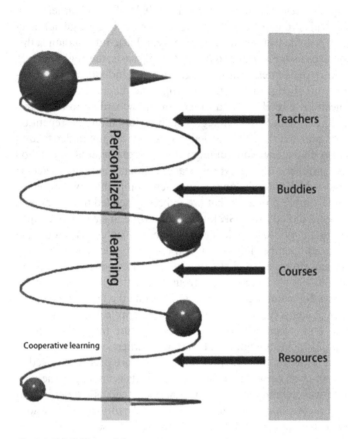

Figure 7.2 PCL model

Figure 7.2, the PCL model consists of four parts: one is straight-up personalized learning, which means that learning based on the learner's individual interests, motivations, needs, styles and other characteristics is the core; the second is the spiral of personalized learning. Rising cooperative learning means that the development of learning requires teamwork and multiple interactions; the third is the gradually larger ball on the spiral curve, which means the learner's gradual development process. The above three are not isolated but an organic unity that fits each one, indicating that the learning process does not rise in a straight line. Only by maintaining the core elements of the learner, through collaboration and conversation, can the construction of meaning be realized. The fourth is the outer four elements, which means that only when teachers, school partners, courses and resources fit the above unity in depth, personalized-cooperative learning can really happen. The structure, characteristics, design and development strategies of courses and resources will be elaborated in other parts of the research.

In summary, personalized-cooperative learning has the following connotations: (1) it takes personalized characteristics as the core and cooperative interaction as a means; (2) the positive mutual dependence between students is its stable structure; (3) teachers' in-depth guidance and participation are its driving force; (4)the content and structure of the course are in line with the cognitive structure of learners.; (5) the resource representation conforming to the cognitive law and meeting the needs of the learners in quantity are its carrier. This understanding of personalized-cooperative learning is a comprehensive interpretation of the "learning method" of "learner-centred design" and an explanation of the relationship between learning methods and teachers, learners, learning content, and learning resources.

The implementation strategy and value of "personalized-cooperative" learning

Starting point

Starting point refers to diagnosing the cognitive structure and individual needs of learners. The learner's characteristics such as the structure, type and orientation of cognition, as well as individual interests, motivations, needs and styles are the starting point of learning, the starting point of instructional design and the basis for the development of instructional activities. The second-order diagnostic method is an effective tool for evaluating the cognitive starting point of learners. Teachers, teaching researchers, and researchers can cooperate to develop diagnostic tools for specific subjects and content. On this basis, with the power of computer software technology developers, the cognitive starting point diagnosis system is developed to realize cognitive diagnosis automation and can collect a large amount of data to analyze learners' cognitive starting point status and development rules, and provide a large-scale learning transformation, based on empirical data.

Process

Process refers to scientific organization and construction of an active and interdependent learning structure. The learning process is an analysis of the "black box" of the learning system that only focused on learning results in the past. On the basis of accurately grasping the characteristics of learners (clusters), a correct understanding of the elements and structure of personalized-cooperative learning, scientifically organize the relationship between members, master the evolution process of content-based classroom structure in PCL design prototype, effectively design, select and implement teaching behavior, and finally promote the change of learning mode in classroom situation, and truly improve learning efficiency.

Content

Content refers to ingenious selection and reconstruction of subject knowledge, strategies and social skills. Learning content is the object of learning, the carrier for the development of learner's quality, and the tool and key for learners to enter society. Therefore, subject knowledge (SK) is the core, but not the only one. The corresponding learning strategies (KS) and social skills are the "additives" that promote the understanding, transformation and application of subject knowledge, and the "lubricants" that ensure the effective operation of learning systems and social organizations. The existing textbook structure is organized and arranged in accordance with the knowledge logic system, rather than the learner's cognitive laws. Therefore, the learner-centred design paradigm requires teachers to skillfully select subject knowledge, learning strategies and social skills, and reconstruct the content organization system and its representation methods, and vigorously develop digital learning resources that conform to learners' cognitive laws.

Involvement

Involvement refers to teachers and learners deeply participating in the learning process and activities. The learner is the subject of learning, and the active and interdependent organizational structure is conducive to the motivation and responsibilities of the learner, who then participates in the learning process deeply. This does not mean that the teacher "stands by the side". The function and role of the teacher changes from one of "collective transfer of knowledge" to one of guidance, "participation and supervision" in the organization of learning. The way in which the organization interacts changes from a predominantly "one-way" teacher-student approach to a predominantly "two-way" teacher-student and student-student approach. The role of learners in the learning community has gradually shifted from the "periphery" to the "centre". In this process, teachers are also the advancement of their own professional development and finally achieve the purpose of teaching each other.

Performance

Performance refers to jigsaw evaluation that improves efficiency and develops learner quality. The assessment approach of the learner-centred design paradigm adopts a jigsaw structure, emphasizing the combination of individual written examination and group interaction, the combination of learning results and the learning process, the combination of learning individuals and learning organization, and promotes the simultaneous development of learning efficiency and effectiveness, academic performance and learning quality growing together. The empirical research includes four parts: individual scores and group averages in written examinations, and intra-group and inter-group evaluations in group interactions, each accounting for a certain percentage. In actual teaching, teachers can appropriately adjust the structure of the puzzle evaluation content, method and proportion according to factors such as the learner's situation, teaching content and stage.

Culture

Culture refers to classroom organizational structure changes that trigger the germination of learner-centred learning systems. The application of learner-centred design in the classroom situation has triggered changes in the organizational structure of the classroom, leading to the adjustment and conversion of the roles and behaviours of teachers and learners, and the development of learning efficiency and quality. If this change occurs in every classroom, it will inevitably require the content and structure of teaching materials (learning content) in the social learning system (school), the layout of schools and classrooms, the network learning pattern (learning environment), and the representation and organization of learning content (learning resources). Teacher and student roles (teaching behaviour), assessment mechanism (learning evaluation) and other learning and teaching related factors have been innovated. Then, in this process of change, managers (administrative leaders and policy makers at all levels and types), researchers (theoretical research and practical instructors), service providers (education companies, school logistics, etc.) and frontline teachers will be required. Changes in the thinking and behaviour of people such as parents and learners will also design the interests of the above-mentioned groups of people. Therefore, follow-up research will focus on the coordination and transformation strategies of the relevant interests of the learning system, promote the generation of a social learning system (school) characterized by "learner-centred design", and form a new learning culture, which will further enhance learning efficiency and effectiveness. Quality reflects the iterative development law of the learning system.

References

Aronson, E. (1978). *The jigsaw classroom*. Thousand Oaks, CA: Sage Publishing Company, 208–210.

Chang, T.W., Kurcz, J., & Moushir, M. (2015). El-Bishouty, Kinshuk, Sabine Graf. Adaptive and personalized learning based on students' cognitive characteristics. *Lecture Notes in Educational Technology*, (8), 77–97.

Chen, J.G., & Yang, N.C (2015). Learning sciences in the past decade: Development, reflections and innovations: An interview with processor Keith Sawyer. *Open Education Research*, *21*(4), 4–12.

Hao, Z.H. (2012). Exploration of personalized learning model based on web2.0. *Journal of Yunnan RTV University*, *33*(2), 17–20.

Hokanson, B., & Hoops, S. (2004). Levels of teaching: A taxonomy for instructional design. *Educational Technology*, *44*(6), 14–22.

Jeong, H.Y., Choi, C.R., & Song, Y.J. (2012). Personalized learning course planner with e-learning DSS using user profile. *Expert Systems with Applications*, *23*(3), 2567–2577.

Johnson, D.W., & Johnson, R.T. (1994). *Leading the cooperative school*. Edina, MN: Interaction Book Company, 56–68.

Johnson, D.W., & Johnson, R.T. (2004). *Cooperative learning*. Beijing: Beijing Normal University.

Kagan, S. (1994). *Cooperative learning*. San Juan Capistrano, CA: Kagan Cooperative Learning, 236–237.

Lin, C.F., Yeh, Y.C., & Hung, Y.H. et al (2013). Data mining for providing a personalized learning path in creativity: An application of decision trees. *Computers & Education*, *38*(12), 199–210.

Slavin, R.E. (1985). *Team-assisted individualization. Learning to cooperate, cooperating to learn.* New York: Springer: 177–209.

Wang, J., & Dong, Y. (2011). Personalized learning and reform of college English "3+1" teaching mode. *Journal of Jilin Normal University of Engineering Technology, 27*(10), 23–5.

Wang, J., & Dong, Y.Q (2012). On high school students' cognitive status before learning information technology: Research on psychology in learning information technology based on CTCL(1). *Journal of Distance Education, 30*(5), 56–62.

Wang, J., & Dong, Y.Q. (2013). The development of cognitive assessment tool for high school students' naive deevs about information technology: Research on psychology in learning information technology based on CTCL(2). *Journal of Distance Education, 30*(1), 67–72.

Wang, J., & Dong, Y.Q. (2014). Investigation of high school students' conceptual change in information technology: Research on psychology in learning information technology based on CTCL(3). *Journal of Distance Education, 30*(4), 14–29.

Wang, X.Y. (2014). Based on flip the personalized teaching mode of classroom inquiry. *Education information in China, 19*(3), 12–15.

Wu, X.C., & Guan, L. (2010). *Cooperative learning and classroom teaching.* Beijing: People's Education Press, 355–360.

Yang, X.F. (2011). College English teaching reform in the exploration and practice of personalized teaching mode. *Journal of Hubei University of Economics: Humanities and Social Sciences Edition, 8*(5), 182–183.

Zheng, Y.X. (2010). Under the information technology support goal-driven personalized learning model. *E-education Research, 31*(7), 89–92.

Zheng, Y.X (2015). Research on teaching method for college students' personalized learning from the perspective of new constructivism. *Journal of Distance Education, 33*(4), 48–58.

Zhong, Z.R. (2012). Based on the personalized learning model construction and application of Web2.0 environment. *China Educational Technology,* (8), 107–110.

8 Observation of learning-brain

Observation of learning and teaching behaviour and visualization of learning-brain

We have found that along with the trend towards information and intelligence in teaching and learning contexts, the observation and analysis of learning and teaching behaviour has undergone significant changes in terms of the scale of data collection, the data patterns of the samples and the methods of behavioural analysis. Technologies such as educational data mining and learning analytic provide effective ways to analyze deeper learning. The methods of behavioural analysis of learning and teaching are moving from a predominantly artificial to an automated approach, and the means of behavioural analysis are moving from a predominantly subjective to an objective analysis. From the previous coding analysis based on observations in the classroom to machine learning based on feature extraction, the analysis of teaching behaviour is gradually weakening the influence of subjective factors, and the role of technology in assisting analysis is becoming more and more obvious.

Behaviour analysis originated from feature extraction

The traditional characterization of behaviour in the classroom is mostly based on the behaviour in the classroom itself, the answers to questions in the classroom, etc., which are strongly subjective in nature. With the continuous innovation of technology, machine learning originated from feature extraction is gradually becoming mainstream and is mostly based on learner analysis platforms to meet the personalized learning of students. Deeper learning classifies different features by dividing them into five deeper learning factors and analyzes the behaviour in different learning contexts and platforms. The researcher can use the necessary technology or tools to obtain data on the behaviour of the teaching subjects, mainly including the learning data of resources, the data of media operation, the data of interactive communication and the data of practice assessment. In addition, the development of biometric technologies has led to the possibility of acquiring signal data on the physiology of the learning process. Researchers can use facial recognition systems and wearable devices to capture learners' facial

DOI: 10.4324/9781003278702-8

expressions, body postures, eye movements and EEG signals to analyze learners' emotional states, concentration levels and thinking dynamics to inform scientific and personalized teaching interventions. After the researcher has collected data on behaviour, the data is cleaned and collated as necessary, the information on the behaviour of multiple forms of data and different subjects of teaching is aggregated and statistically categorized from multiple sources according to certain categories or patterns. The pre-processed data on behaviour is eventually stored in a sample database.

Subject analysis originated from cognition

The intelligent approach to analysis has led to an expansion of the level of analysis from characterizing the external behaviour of the subject to exploring their implicit cognitive state. The findings move from the superficial generalization of teaching patterns and classroom styles to the analysis of internal and external motivations such as motivation, psycho-emotional and strategic approaches. This allows us to understand the learning patterns and process mechanisms of learners and to facilitate the process of precise teaching and curriculum reform. However, due to the complexity of the field of practice in education, it is difficult to effectively interpret teaching and learning behaviour by following only generic ideas of analysis of data. Therefore, researchers of deeper learning need to incorporate educational concepts and expert experience into data-driven teaching behavioural in the process of analysis, prompting the organic integration of domain knowledge and data models to form behavioural analysis models for specific teaching problems. The basic idea is to start with the educational scenario and the educational problems that need to be addressed. A system of indicators is selected from existing pedagogical research findings that are relevant to the teaching context. The relevant characteristics of the sample of representations are then extracted from the behavioural data of the teaching subjects. Experts assess the characteristics of the sample and select discriminatory characteristics as variables for behavioural analysis. The mapping among the categories of teaching behaviour and the characteristics of the sample data are established to form clear and unambiguous rules for the measurement.

Brain cognition

Firstly, the brain is plasticity. The human brain is a dynamic and changing living organism. It interacts with its environment on a moment-to-moment basis. Under the stimulation of an appropriate learning environment and learning experiences, brain neurons as well as synapses continue to build connections and strengthen the brain's synapses, thus influencing a person's cognition, emotions and behaviour. Through learning and training, the brain can be functionally trained. When knowledge changes from static single character symbols to vivid, diverse and interesting visual, auditory, kinaesthetic and other information to stimulate the brain, it activates more brain areas and causes excitation of brain cells, which in turn creates more complex and higher level neural circuits. They are involved in cognitive processes such as perception, attention, memory and thinking, and facilitate the deeper processing of information from the absorption tract, thus controlling human decision-making, behavioural choices and problem solving. Secondly, positive emotions can drive cognition. Brain science has proven that emotions have an impact on various aspects of cognition such as attention, thinking, memory, decision-making, etc. When stimuli of emotional events are present, attention and intuition towards emotional content are enhanced, and positive emotions enhance one's memory. The left side of the brain has a rational, logical, abstract nature and is known as the "language brain", which exercises control of spoken language, word and number recognition, problem solving, etc. The right brain, known as the "picture brain", is perceptual, intuitive, visual and autonomous in nature. It tends to process spatial perception, reasoning, situation recognition, etc. The left and right brains are able to work in tandem and communicate and connect with each other to achieve information exchange and interactive functions. If the left brain processes content, the right brain can make contextual connections to the content, thus forming a holistic cognition. Furthermore, multichannel perception creates a multi-sensory cognitive pathway that effectively engages the human mind in cognitive processing. The unique information of the world can be provided to us by different senses, yet our perception of the world is not a jumble but a multi-sensory unified experience. When multi-sensory learning is engaged, more neuronal networks are linked into more distinct neural structures that can be accessed through more sensory channels (Guo Ruifang, 2005). The kinaesthetic and tactile senses may be stimulated by the taster experience, constantly searching for connections, building models of knowledge, expanding the level of knowledge and constructing it in three dimensions. The information acquired is processed in a holistic mesh from more cognitive paths, dynamic, contextual and complex, which in turn enhances cognitive efficiency.

Knowledge visualization

Knowledge visualization refers to the massive access to the learning space and visual space through pictures, images, videos etc. It is necessary for learners to understand, acquire and generate knowledge by "reading pictures", where knowledge forms are visually represented by means of illustrations. In the process of graphic interaction, the left and right brains are effectively engaged in learning, and the functions of the left and right brains are brought into full play. The right brain tends to process information such as graphic images and space. The left brain, on the other hand, is involved in the connection and understanding of various types of knowledge, such as engaging in logical reasoning, analysis and synthesis and other activities of thinking. The formation of new cognitive pathways and ways of thinking is a great enrichment to the understanding and learning of texts in symbolic languages (Zhao Guoqing, 2004), and others, in their analysis of what types of knowledge to visualize, argue that the essence of knowledge visualization is the transformation of implicit knowledge of individuals into explicit knowledge that can act directly on the human senses (that can be touched, seen, heard and manipulated). The combination of illustrations and text melds all types of thinking, targeting different types of knowledge and allowing learning to develop holistically, in three dimensions and in a multidimensional way.

Thinking visualization

The visualization of thinking lies in the visualization of the learner's thought process and expression of ideas. In this process, it is possible to discover what the scholar is really thinking (what) and how he or she is thinking (how); observations can be made from the scholar's words, expressions, body movements, etc. Learners can also be guided through thinking diagrams (circle diagrams, flag diagrams, double bubble diagrams, tree diagrams, bracket diagrams, flow diagrams, compound flow diagrams, bridge diagrams) for overall presentation. Through the constructive process of diagramming, sorting out cognitive structures and expanding cognitive ideas can effectively increase the depth and breadth of thinking and promote more logical and organized thinking. The use of mind maps can effectively target divergent thinking for training. Sorting through networks of subject knowledge and processing knowledge in a refined and hierarchical way allows for a better understanding and mastery of knowledge.

Visual diagnosis of mathematics learning strategies for primary school students

Learning strategies are an important factor influencing deeper learning. The development of a visual diagnostic system for primary school students' learning strategies in mathematics is useful for understanding the distribution of learning strategies among individual learners and groups, and for providing data to support personalized learning and cooperative grouping in small groups.

Learning strategies and deeper learning

Learning strategies are an important part of mathematics education research. They are mental operations directed towards cognitive goals and are an important part of learners' problem solving. It is also an important way of promoting the cognitive development of learners, as the American child psychologist Siegler argues, that the development of rules can be used to explain children's cognitive development (Siegler, 1997a). Carole and Jerrifer, and Carr and Jessup have found that a major source of children's cognitive ability is the use of strategies to solve problems (Carole & Jerrifer, 1988; Carr & Jessup, 1997). It is evident that the study of learning strategies is an important part of promoting cognitive development. Research has also shown that there is a significant positive correlation between motivation, learning strategies and academic achievement, e.g. Lei and Zhang have shown that superficial low levels of motivation will lead to superficial, negative learning strategies (Lei et al., 2015; Lei & Zhang, 2014; Zhang

& Guo, 2014; Zhang & Yang, 2015; Zhang, 2012). The learning strategies used by students with deeper motivation also tend to be a high level and proactive. At the same time, Wang and Liu (Wang & Liu, 2014a, b) revealed that there is a clear causal relationship between motivation and academic achievement. This causal relationship occurs precisely through the mediation of learning strategies, i.e. motivation affects academic achievement indirectly by influencing learning strategies. A study by Liu et al. (Liu et al., 2014) also showed that motivation explained up to 24% of learning strategies. The study by Wan and Zheng (Wan & Zheng, 2014) also suggested that students' internal and external motivation are mutually reinforced in their learning, and both have a significant impact on learning strategies. Learners mostly adopt narrowly targeted, rote learning strategies driven by a superficial motivation of fear of failure. Learners who are motivated by intrinsic interests, on the other hand, tend to adopt deeper refinement strategies to maximize the meaning of the learning content. The former brings about erratic and poor learning outcomes, while the latter has a stable and positive effect on learning outcomes (Biggs, 2001; 2012; 2014). It can be seen that the development of learning strategies in a psychological sense facilitates increased motivation, improved learning methods and thus academic achievement. It is an important factor influencing the occurrence of deeper learning, and it is necessary and essential to include it in the study of techniques of deeper learning in the classroom.

Diagnostic scales for learning strategies in primary mathematics

Professor Liu Dianzhi, a leading researcher in learning psychology at Soochow University, developed a questionnaire for assessing learning strategies in primary school mathematics and obtained permission to use the instrument for the diagnosis of learning strategies. The questionnaire (Appendix 1) is a self-report style five-point scale to assess primary school students' level of mathematical learning strategies, with 40 questions, including three sub-questionnaires.

Metacognitive strategies include planning, monitoring and regulating, and evaluating and reflecting on strategies that students use in their learning of mathematics, with 11 questions covering those areas: 1, 5, 9, 13, 17, 21, 25, 29, 31, 33, 35. There are 22 questions on cognitive strategies, including two sub-dimensions with six questions on basic cognitive strategies (questions: 2, 6, 10, 14, 18, 22) and 16 questions on specific cognitive strategies (questions: 3, 7, 11, 15, 19, 23, 26, 28, 30, 32, 34, 36, 37, 38, 39, 40). Among them, basic cognitive strategies refer to general strategies in primary school mathematics, such as paying attention to the mathematical content highlighted by the teacher and self-questioning to test the effectiveness of mathematical learning. Cognitive strategies refer to learning strategies that facilitate the learning of specific idiosyncratic problems in primary school mathematics, including the learning of mathematical concept formulae, calculation, problem solving and geometric knowledge.

The support-seeking strategy has seven questions and contains two sub-dimensions for the four questions of the get-help strategy (questions: 4, 12, 20, 24) and the three questions of the self-help strategy (questions: 8, 16, 27). Get-help strategies refer to learning strategies in which students use external resources to solve problems in mathematics. Self-help strategies refer to learning strategies in which students achieve their goals through their own efforts.

To avoid the tendency of respondents to pretend to be good, the following expression was used in the guide: "Everyone has their own customs to practice in mathematics learning. To find out what your classmates usually do, you are invited to answer the following questions". At the same time, in order to ensure the reliability of the subjects' evaluations as far as possible, the phenomenon of moderate responses was prevented to the greatest extent possible. The five levels are set in the order of "I am not at all like this", "I am mostly not like this", "I am sometimes like this", "I am mostly like this" and "I am totally like this". In addition, to ensure the reliability of the assessment, each strategy was introduced with the words "I will" and "I always", e.g. "I will make up a collection of questions that I get wrong in my mathematics homework and exams".

Overview of the diagnostic system

Functions of the administrator account

The administrator account has the following five main categories of permissions.

This is a system of administrator login. As the administrator's entry point to the system, logging in is the most basic but particularly important aspect. By distinguishing between roles, it is possible to effectively ensure the differentiation of different permissions for different roles, thus ensuring the security and validity of the back-office data.

As shown in Figure 8.1, the system is divided into five dimensions, which are gender, class, school, region and the general settings subsystem.

In this query of the gender dimension, you can click on "Gender breakdown" on the left menu or "Gender comparison trend" on the right to jump to the gender

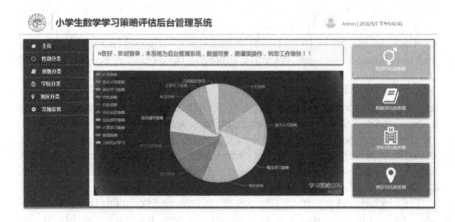

Figure 8.1 Running screen of the back-office management system

breakdown view. In the gender dimension, the administrator can view a trend graph of the distribution of all persons currently participating in the test by gender. The effect is shown in Figure 8.2.

The distribution of learning strategy was visualized separately according to the two dimensions of mean score and variance of academic performance. Managers can easily view the gender distribution; and the system provides the status of several visualizations for a better user experience. Administrators can click on the feature image at the top right of the trend graph to see different views of the same data. You can take the comparison chart of the mean scores of gender as an example and click on the "Switch bar chart" image button in the top right corner to get the effect as shown in Figure 8.3, the stacking effect as shown in Figure 8.4, the effect of the individual items of gender as shown in Figure 8.5 and the raw data as shown in Figure 8.6.

In this query of class dimension, the administrator can view a comparison trend graph of the strategies of the students participating in the test in the class dimension. And you can view the comparison trend graph for two or more classes that the administrator wants to compare. In Figure 8.7, it shows the comparison graph for three classes.

When you move the mouse over the axis point of the corresponding strategy trend graph, the screen will automatically display the raw data for the different schools under that strategy in a prompt box for the "planned strategy" effect of the variance comparison. As with the gender dimension, you can click on the function button in the top right-hand corner of the trend chart to see the status of

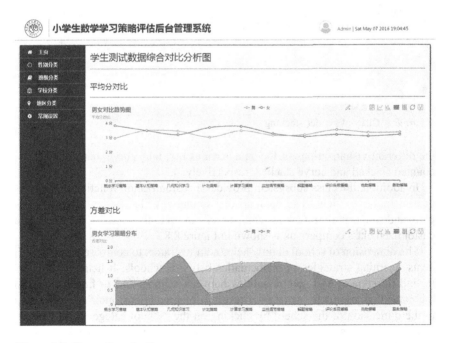

Figure 8.2 Chart of gender line

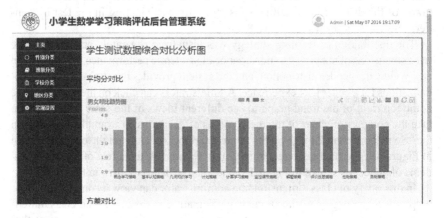

Figure 8.3 Chart of gender bar

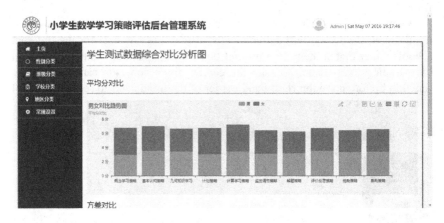

Figure 8.4 Chart of gender stacking

the different visualizations of the data, such as bar, line, curve, bar stacked, discounted stacked and curve stacked, respectively.

In addition, the class subsystem provides a customization function that allows administrators to view trend comparisons among any classes they wish to compare, and supports simultaneous comparisons of up to five classes, the effect of a customized class comparison is shown in Figure 8.8.

The dimension of school mainly helps administrators to compare trends in students' learning strategies in mathematics between schools. It helps researchers to find differences and commonalities between schools and to find patterns in the data. It is useful for your own research or predictions, etc. You can jump to the dimension of the school by clicking on the "school category" on the left. The default is to show the most recent comparison between the five latest of the schools, as shown in Figure 8.9. If there are less than five participating schools,

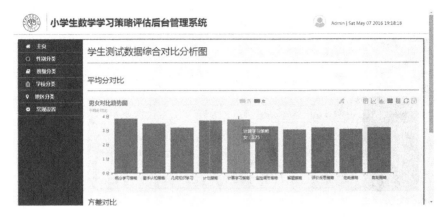

Figure 8.5 Chart of gender single

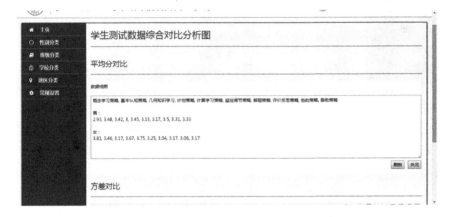

Figure 8.6 Graph of raw student test data

the vacant schools will be shown as blank bars or translucent far dots. With the customized comparison of schools, administrators can select the school data they want to compare in detail, again by clicking on the different buttons on the trend graph to view a visualization of the graph in different states.

The regional dimension mainly compares the distribution of learner strategies in different regions, as shown in Figure 8.10. The visualization status is the same as the class dimension.

What follows are the functions of the user account. The user opens the home page of the website and the login page appears. Once logged in, users can see the results of the questionnaire they have filled out. If you are new to the site, you will need to "register".

When the user clicks on "Register Now", the page redirects to the registration page. On the registration page, you can set the following information: username

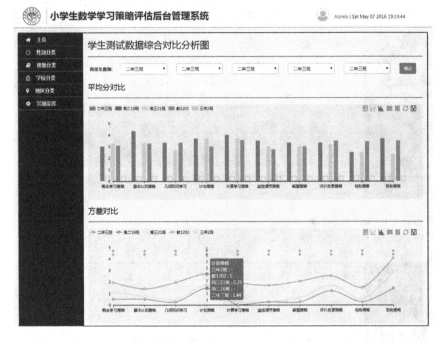

Figure 8.7 Chart of class comparison

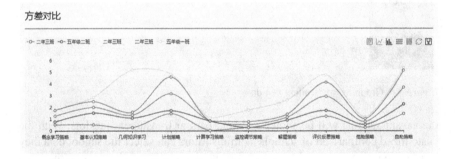

Figure 8.8 Comparison chart for custom classes

and password. Information such as gender, school, class, region, etc. will only be selected by the user by clicking on the drop-down menu. After successful registration, the user is granted login access to the site and can log in and perform the test, as shown in Figure 8.11.

The first page of the user measurement is the requirement to fill in the questionnaire and then "Go to test", as shown in Figure 8.12.

The assessment questionnaire is filled in and then it jumps to the first subquestion on the test page, as shown in Figure 8.13. When there is no time limit set

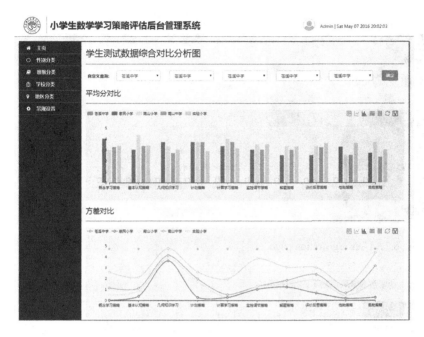

Figure 8.9 Comparison chart for custom schools

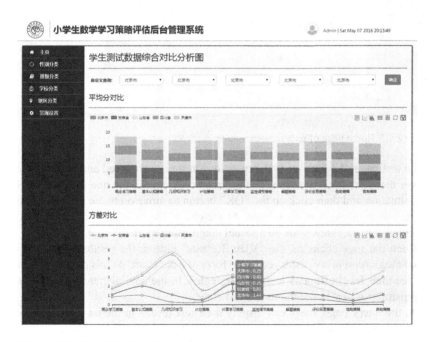

Figure 8.10 Chart of regional comparison

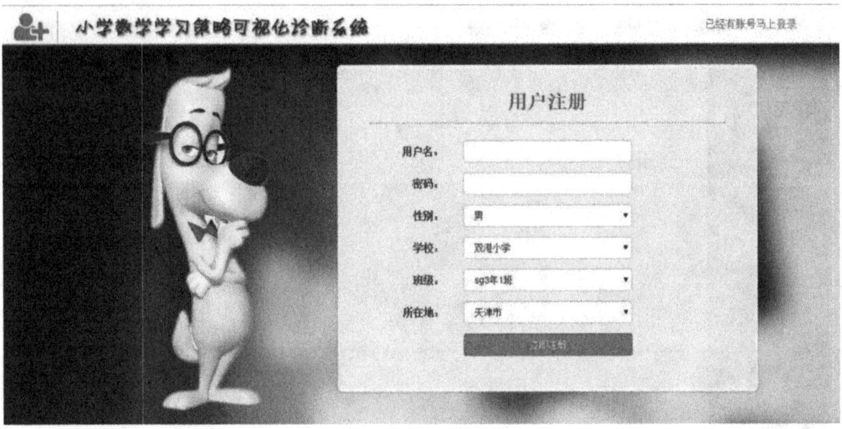

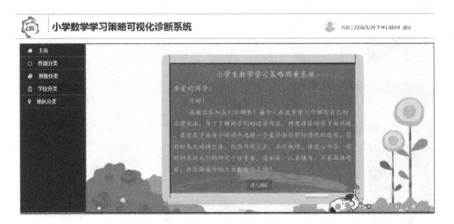

Figure 8.11 User registration page

Figure 8.12 Home page of user measurements

on the test page, the user reads the questions at their own speed and chooses the answer that suits their situation. The user can only choose the one that best suits their situation and then click on the "OK" button to move on to the next question until the 40th question is completed. At the end of the evaluation of the learned strategies, you can view your own visual diagnostic report.

When the user clicks on the "View Results" button, the results of the individual measurement are displayed in the form of a bar chart. At this point, the user will see their level of maths learning strategies. In the administrator system, the administrator will also see the user's test status.

On the query page, users can display their test results in the bar, line and pie charts, just like on the admin page. At the top right of the display, there is a line of buttons for the conversion of functions, for example ⌁. When the user clicks

Figure 8.13 Page of user measurement

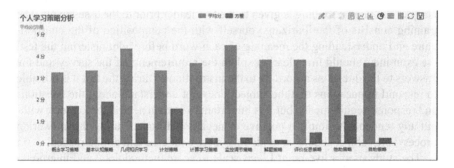

Figure 8.14 User enquiry page

on the button in the top right corner of the trend graph, for example 🖥, they will see the test results displayed as a curve effect graph and be able to query their raw data. Please click on the button in the top right corner to get the original view, and the ability to save and print.

The author developed a visual diagnostic system for primary school students' learning strategies in mathematics and obtained the software copyright.

Diagnostic design and implementation

Diagnostic issues

The study diagnoses the strategies of learning mathematics of primary school students in four cities, S, W, K and C, representing the four regions of East China, Central China, Southwest China and Northeast China respectively. The following questions are to be answered: firstly, what is the current distribution of primary school students' mathematics learning strategies between cities (regions) and how do they differ; secondly, whether there are differences in mathematics learning strategies between boys and girls; and thirdly, what differences exist between grades.

Diagnostic subjects

The study identified primary schools in the four cities with levels at the higher, middle and the lower end of the scale as one-third of the total of each, and selected students in grades 3, 4 and 5 from these. These students were generally able to understand the assessment questionnaire correctly and also had some accumulation of learning strategies.

Diagnostic implementation

Measurement process

The study was conducted in a multimedia room for group administration. The main test is conducted by the teacher of mathematics of the class to avoid unfamiliarity of the pupils; training is given to the test leader prior to the assessment. The training consists of familiarizing yourself with the composition of the questionnaire and understanding the meaning of each word before administering the test. the examiners should first clearly explain the requirements of the survey and the answers to the questions according to the instructions. During the test it is possible to respond to questions that the subject does not understand about the questions and response requirements, but it is important to remain neutral throughout, without any tendency to imply a positive or negative attitude. During the answering process, the subject should be made to answer with ease and not be rushed.

The study used a five-point Likert scale to score methodology and interpretation, with each question item followed by a five-point scale of "I am not at all like this", "I am most of the time not like this", "I am sometimes like this", "I am most of the time like this", and "I am completely like this", which were scored as "1", "2", "3", "4" and "5" respectively. All questions are scored positively, with higher scores. A mean score of 1 indicates very poor mastery of strategies, a mean score of 2 indicates poor mastery of strategies, a mean score of 3 indicates average mastery of strategies, a mean score of 4 indicates good mastery of strategies, and a mean score of 5 indicates very good mastery of strategies. The diagnostic system for primary school students' learning strategies in mathematics automatically generates a report for visual analysis. A total of 4125 questionnaires were distributed and 3837 valid questionnaires were returned, with an efficiency of 93%, including 1132 in city of S, 956 in city of C, 1007 in city of W and 742 in city of K.

Data analysis

Status of primary school students' use of mathematics learning strategies

The number of questions in each dimension of the scale of mathematics learning strategies is different. We calculated the mean score for each dimension and obtained the mean score and standard deviation (arithmetic square root of the variance). The overall status of mathematics learning strategies is shown in Figure 8.15, which leads to the following conclusions: (1) The overall mean score of mathematics learning strategies for primary school students in the four cities is 3.38, which is between "average" and "good". (2) In descending order, the scoring on each dimension was metacognitive strategies (3.63), cognitive strategies (3.51) and support-seeking strategies (2.99), with support-seeking being the lowest, especially self-help strategies (2.75) which were mostly "poorly mastered strategies", i.e. the majority of the self-help strategies (2.75) were "poorly mastered", i.e. "I hardly know". (3) The specific learning strategies scored in descending order were: strategies for monitoring and regulation, strategies for evaluating and reflecting, strategies for problem solving, strategies for learning geometry, strategies for learning computation, strategies for basic cognition, strategies for planning, strategies for conceptual learning, strategies for other help and strategies for self-help.

The following conclusions can be drawn from Table 8.1: (1) the correlations between metacognitive strategies, cognitive strategies and support-seeking strategies were highly significant ($p<0.001$). In particular, the correlation between metacognitive strategies and cognitive strategies was $r=0.850$ and $r>0.8$, which is highly correlated. This is in line with some psychological studies that people with high metacognition also have high cognitive levels, and metacognition and cognition are mutually reinforcing and influencing each other (Liu & Huang, 2005). (2) The Pearson correlation coefficient between metacognitive strategies and support-seeking strategies was 0.543, $0.5<0.599<0.8$, which was moderate and highly significant ($p<0.001$). (3) The Pearson correlation coefficient between cognitive strategies and support-seeking strategies was $0.613,0.5<0.631<0.8$, which was moderately correlated and highly significant ($p<0.001$).

A comparison of the mathematics learning strategies of primary school students in the four cities is shown in the chart below. From Figure 8.16, it can be seen that (1) students in the city of S district scored higher on the mean of metacognitive strategies and cognitive strategies than the other three districts. (2) City of K scored significantly higher on average than the other three regions on support-seeking strategies. (3) City of C has the lowest of all three strategies. The higher scores on metacognitive strategies in the city of S are related to the fact that primary schools in the city of S have been providing mental health education for primary and secondary school students since the 1980s and enjoy a high reputation in the city and the country. As early as 1998, the Municipal Education Committee of city of S issued the "Mental Health Education Plan for Primary and Secondary Schools in the city of S (1999–2001)". In the plan, the Municipal Education Commission of the city of S calls for the implementation of mental health education in primary and secondary schools by means of comprehensive penetration, activity classes on mental health education, and psychological counselling and guidance (Shen, 2013). In 2012, the city set up a centre for the development of mental health education for students and became a research base for mental health education for students. It focuses on the high-end post-service

	Meta-cognitive strategies			Cognitive Strategies					Support seeking strategies		Average
	Planning strategies	Monitoring and regulation strategies	Evaluation and reflection strategies	Basic cognitive strategies	Conceptual learning strategies	Computational learning strategies	Problem solving Strategies	Geometric knowledge Learning Strategies	Get-Help Strategies	Self-help Strategies	
M	3.46	3.82	3.63	3.48	3.46	3.53	3.60	3.55	3.16	2.75	3.38
SD	0.994	1.053	0.866	1.098	1.176	0.945	0.965	1.024	0.997	1.100	0.672

Figure 8.15 Overall use of mathematics learning strategies by primary school students

Table 8.1 Correlation analysis of metacognitive strategies, cognitive strategies and support-seeking strategies

		Metacognitive strategies	Cognitive strategies	Support-seeking strategies
Metacognitive strategies	**Pearson correlation**	—	.850**	.543**
	Significant (bilateral)	—	.000	.000
Cognitive strategies	**Pearson correlation**	.850**	—	.613**
	Significant (bilateral)	.000	—	.000
Support-seeking strategies	**Pearson correlation**	.543**	.613**	—
	Significant (bilateral)	.000	.000	—

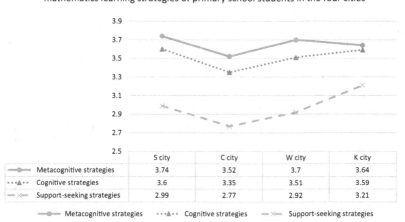

A line gragh of the specific distribution of the mean scores of mathematics learning strategies of primary school students in the four cities

	S city	C city	W city	K city
Metacognitive strategies	3.74	3.52	3.7	3.64
Cognitive strategies	3.6	3.35	3.51	3.59
Support-seeking strategies	2.99	2.77	2.92	3.21

Metacognitive strategies Cognitive strategies Support-seeking strategies

Figure 8.16 Line graph of the specific distribution of the mean scores of mathematics learning strategies of primary school students in the four cities

training of mental health education professionals in schools to enhance the professionalism of psychology teachers.

From Table 8.2, Figure 8.17 and Figure 8.18, it can be seen that the overall level of students' use of strategies for learning mathematics in the city of S was higher than that in the other three cities, and the overall level of students' use of strategies for learning mathematics in the city of C was lower. When the students' mathematics learning sub-strategies are ranked from highest to lowest in each city, it can be seen that the planning strategies are, in order: City W, City S, City K and City C. The monitoring and regulation strategies are, in order: City W, City S, City K and City C. The evaluation and reflection strategies are, in order, City W, City K, City S and City C. The evaluation reflection strategies are, in order: City S, City K, City W, City C. The basic cognitive strategies are, in order: City S, City W, City K, City C. Conceptual learning strategies in order: City K, City W, City S, City C.

Table 8.2 Use of specific strategies for mathematics learning by students in the four cities

	City S		City C		City W		City K	
	M	SD	M	SD	M	SD	M	SD
Planning strategies	3.59	0.998	3.33	1.012	3.60	0.966	3.37	0.840
Monitoring and regulation strategies	3.85	1.028	3.72	0.962	3.89	0.946	3.87	0.881
Evaluation and reflection strategies	3.76	0.821	3.50	0.858	3.61	0.814	3.67	0.714
Basic cognitive strategies	3.57	0.830	3.33	0.861	3.53	0.829	3.53	0.706
Conceptual learning strategies	3.53	0.942	3.25	0.945	3.54	0.945	3.59	0.773
Computational learning strategies	3.70	0.897	3.41	0.933	3.44	1.002	3.59	0.798
Problem-solving strategies	3.74	0.882	3.47	0.898	3.49	0.922	3.70	0.730
Geometric learning strategies	3.75	1.010	3.35	1.034	3.45	1.043	3.73	0.816
Get-help strategies	3.25	0.853	2.92	0.895	3.05	0.876	3.48	0.805
Self-help strategies	2.72	1.006	2.62	0.916	2.79	0.954	2.94	0.899

Computational learning strategies in order: City S, City K, City W, City C. Problem solving strategies are, in order: City S, City K, City W, City C. Geometric knowledge learning strategies are, in order: City S, City K, City W, City C. Other helper strategies in order: City K, City S, City W, City C. Self-assisted strategies are, in order: City K, City W, City S, City C. The standard deviations in Figure 8.22 show that city of K has the smallest individual student sex differences of the four cities, and the other three cities have essentially similar individual student sex differences.

Analysis of the variance in the overall level of mathematics learning strategies affecting primary school students is shown in the table below. A multi-factor ANOVA was conducted on the three factors of region, grade and gender to produce the results in Tables 8.3. It shows that the main effects of district ($p<0.05$) and gender ($p<0.01$) were significant, and the main effects and interactions with other aspects were not significant.

Analysis of the differences in the dimensions of strategies for learning mathematics by region is shown in this table. The results are shown in Table 8.4. There were significant differences in metacognitive strategies, cognitive strategies and support-seeking strategies between students in city of S and city of C. There were significant differences in support-seeking strategies between students in city of S and city of K. There were significant differences in metacognitive strategies between students in city of C and city of W. There were significant differences in support-seeking strategies between students in city of C and city of K. There were significant differences in support-seeking strategies between students in city of W and city of C. There were significant differences in support-seeking strategies between students in city of C and city of K. There were significant differences in support-seeking strategies between students in city of W and city of K. There is a significant difference between the city of C and the city of K in terms of cognitive strategies and support-seeking strategies.

A gender-differentiated analysis of primary school students' strategies for learning mathematics is shown in this table. Another factor influencing primary

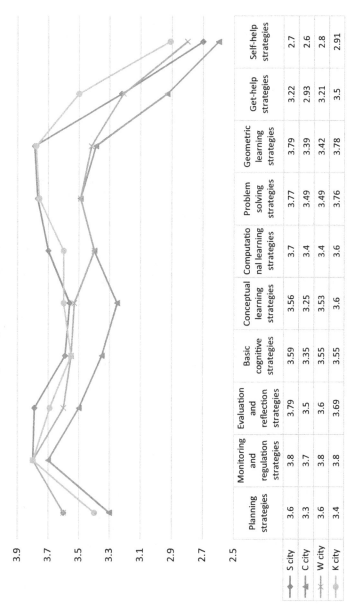

Line graph of average scores of specific mathematics learning strategies for primary school students in four cities

	Planning strategies	Monitoring and regulation strategies	Evaluation and reflection strategies	Basic cognitive strategies	Conceptual learning strategies	Computatio nal learning strategies	Problem solving strategies	Geometric learning strategies	Get-help strategies	Self-help strategies
S city	3.6	3.8	3.79	3.59	3.56	3.7	3.77	3.79	3.22	2.7
C city	3.3	3.7	3.5	3.35	3.25	3.4	3.49	3.39	2.93	2.6
W city	3.6	3.8	3.6	3.55	3.53	3.4	3.49	3.42	3.21	2.8
K city	3.4	3.8	3.69	3.55	3.6	3.6	3.76	3.78	3.5	2.91

S city   C city   W city   K city

Figure 8.17 Line graph of average scores of specific mathematics learning strategies for primary school students in four cities

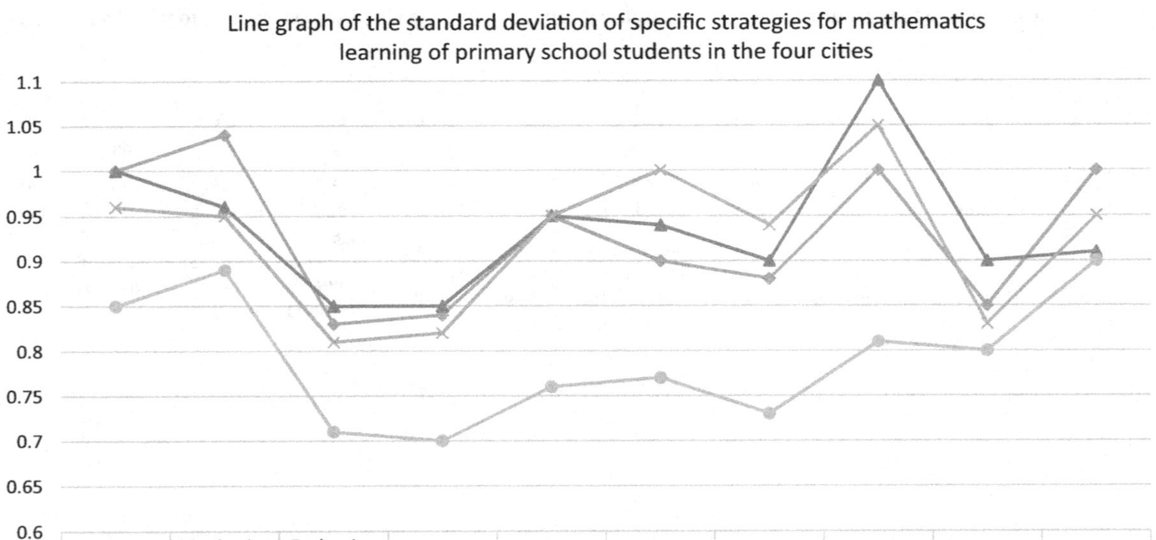

Line graph of the standard deviation of specific strategies for mathematics learning of primary school students in the four cities

	Planning strategies	Monitoring and regulation strategies	Evaluation and reflection strategies	Basic cognitive strategies	Conceptual learning strategies	Computational learning strategies	Problem solving strategies	Geometric learning strategies	Get-help strategies	Self-help strategies
S city	1	1.04	0.83	0.84	0.95	0.9	0.88	1	0.85	1
C city	1	0.96	0.85	0.85	0.95	0.94	0.9	1.1	0.9	0.91
W city	0.96	0.95	0.81	0.82	0.95	1	0.94	1.05	0.83	0.95
K city	0.85	0.89	0.71	0.7	0.76	0.77	0.73	0.81	0.8	0.9

S city — C city — W city — K city

Figure 8.18 Line graph of the standard deviation of specific strategies for mathematics learning of primary school students in the four cities

Table 8.3 Multi-factor analysis of variance (ANOVA) on mathematics learning strategies of primary school students

Sources of variation	SS	df	MS	F	Sig.
Region	3.606	3	1.202	2.750	0.042**
Grade	2.512	2	1.256	2.874	0.057
Gender	4.113	1	4.113	9.411	0.002**
Region * Grade	0.395	2	0.197	0.451	0.637
Region * Gender	1.559	3	0.520	1.189	0.313
Grade * Gender	0.034	2	0.017	0.039	0.962
Region * Grade * Gender	0.256	2	0.128	0.293	0.746

Table 8.4 Comparison of significant differences between districts in mathematics learning strategies for primary school students

	S-C	S-W	S-K	C-W	C-K	W-K
Metacognitive strategies	0.005**	0.747	0.102	0.021**	0.272	0.219
Cognitive strategies	0.001**	0.213	0.657	0.063	0.003**	0.399
Support-seeking strategies	0.040**	0.384	0.000**	0.309	0.000**	0.000**

**. Correlation is significant at the 0.05 level (two-tailed)

Table 8.5 Analysis of gender differences in learning strategies for male and female students (M+SD)

	Metacognitive strategies	*Cognitive strategies*	*Support-seeking strategies*
Boy	3.55+0.792	3.43+0.789	2.91+0.767
Girl	3.72+0.727	3.60+0.713	3.07+0.742
F	10.305**	9.145**	8.994**
Sig.	0.001**	0.003**	0.003**

school students' strategies for learning mathematics was gender, so further analysis was conducted on the gender factor where the main effect differential was significant. As shown in Table 8.5, girls generally scored higher than boys on all strategies. As can be seen from the standard deviations, the individual differences were higher for boys than for girls. There was also a highly significant difference between boys and girls for all three strategies ($p<0.01$).

As shown in Table 8.6, girls also scored higher than boys on each of the sub-strategies. In terms of standard deviation, the individual differences were higher for girls than for boys, except for the self-help strategies. In all other sub-strategies, boys had higher individuality differences than girls. Among these strategies, there was no significant difference between boys and girls only for the computational learning strategies, the other-assisted strategies and the self-help strategies. There were significant differences between boys and girls in all other strategies.

Table 8.6 Analysis of gender differences in mathematics learning sub-strategies between boys and girls

	Boys		Girls		Differences	
	M	SD	M	SD	F	Sig.
Planning strategy	3.35	0.999	3.57	0.919	9.809	.002**
Monitoring and regulation strategies	3.75	0.998	3.91	0.903	5.582	.018**
Evaluation and reflection strategies	3.55	0.838	3.71	0.775	8.023	.005**
Basic cognitive strategies	3.39	0.853	3.57	0.769	9.288	.002**
Conceptual learning strategies	3.40	0.952	3.53	0.873	4.205	.041**
Computational learning strategies	3.50	0.927	3.57	0.899	1.117	.291
Problem-solving strategies	3.53	0.882	3.67	0.856	4.688	.031**
Geometric learning strategies	3.48	0.996	3.64	0.986	5.108	.024**
Get-help strategies	3.10	0.933	3.22	0.833	3.867	.050
Self-help strategies	2.72	0.922	2.78	0.973	0.606	.437

In order to more intuitively see the distribution of male and female students in each learning strategy, the strategy scores of male and female students are drawn as a line chart, as shown in Figure 8.19.

Case study-two primary schools in city of S as an example

Through the analysis and comparison of the results of the tests of strategies for students' learning of mathematics in the four cities, it was concluded that the city of S scored the highest among the four cities; also, the city of S was the highest in the PISA test, which both validates the validity of this diagnosis and illustrates the relationship between learning strategies and academic achievement from one perspective. Based on this, the study focuses on the analysis of the diagnostic in primary schools A and B, grades 3 and 4, in the city of S.

Both primary schools A and B in the city of S, where the focus is on, are of medium standard in the area. Primary school A was selected from grades 3 and 4 and 222 questionnaires were distributed, 109 to grade 3 and 113 to grade 4. 222 valid questionnaires were actually returned, with an effective rate of 100%. 98 from grade 3 and 92 from grade 4. Questionnaires of 190 were distributed to primary school B. Questionnaires of 185 were actually returned, with an effective rate of 97.5%.

1. Inter-school variability in strategies for students' learning of mathematics

The results of the comparison of mathematics learning strategies of year 3 students in Primary Schools A and B are shown in Tables 8.7. The mean score of Primary School A was significantly higher than that of Primary School B. There was no significant difference between the two schools in metacognitive and cognitive strategies, but there was a significant difference in support-seeking strategies ($p<0.01$). In terms of standard deviation, the individual differences in

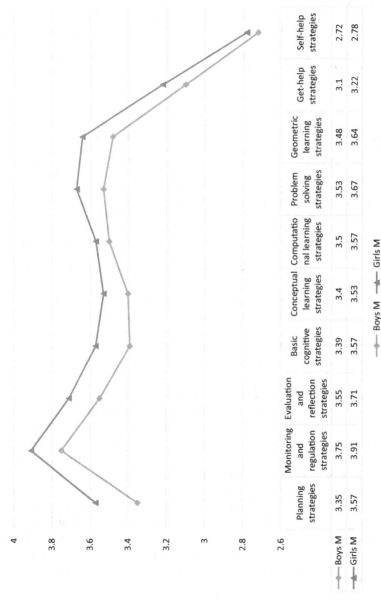

Line graph of maths learning strategy scores for boys and girls in four cities

	Planning strategies	Monitoring and regulation strategies	Evaluation and reflection strategies	Basic cognitive strategies	Conceptual learning strategies	Computatio nal learning strategies	Problem solving strategies	Geometric learning strategies	Get-help strategies	Self-help strategies
Boys M	3.35	3.75	3.55	3.39	3.4	3.5	3.53	3.48	3.1	2.72
Girls M	3.57	3.91	3.71	3.57	3.53	3.57	3.67	3.64	3.22	2.78

Boys M — Girls M

Figure 8.19 Line graph of maths learning strategy scores for boys and girls in four cities

Table 8.7 Differences in mathematics learning strategies between schools A and B

	School	M	SD	P
Metacognitive strategies	School A	3.8206	.86426	0.348
	School B	3.7216	.87726	
Cognitive strategies	School A	3.8112	.88062	0.470
	School B	3.5986	.88629	
Support-seeking strategies	School A	3.1770	.94470	0.002**
	School B	2.8297	.90336	

Table 8.8 Differences in specific mathematics learning strategies between schools A and B

	Primary school A		Primary school B		Difference
	M	SD	M	SD	P
Planning strategy	3.68	1.04	3.65	1.02	0.815
Monitoring and regulation strategies	3.90	1.00	3.78	1.12	0.335
Evaluation and reflection strategies	3.88	0.92	3.74	0.91	0.196
Basic cognitive strategies	3.67	0.96	3.55	0.91	0.291
Conceptual learning strategies	3.84	1.64	3.57	1.00	0.080
Computational learning strategies	3.82	0.98	3.66	0.97	0.176
Problem-solving strategies	3.82	0.96	3.61	1.02	0.084
Geometric learning strategies	3.91	1.02	3.61	1.06	0.017**
Get-help strategies	3.33	1.05	3.12	0.95	0.082
Self-help strategies	3.02	1.08	2.54	1.12	0.000**

metacognitive and cognitive strategies were slightly higher in Primary B than in Primary A, while the differences in support-seeking strategies were smaller in Primary B than in Primary A.

To better understand the scores of the two schools on each sub-strategy, they were further analyzed as shown in Table 8.8 and their mean line graphs are shown in Figure 8.20.

As can be seen from Table 8.8 and Figure 8.20, Primary School A scored higher on average than Primary School B on specific mathematics learning strategies. This is related to the fact that Primary School A started mental health education for primary school students back in the 1980s. As a result, Primary School A generally scored higher than Primary School B on metacognitive strategies, and there was a significant correlation between metacognitive and cognitive strategies. Students with metacognition also scored higher on cognitive strategies. In terms of standard deviation, the individual differences in monitoring and regulation strategies, problem solving strategies, geometry learning strategies and self-help strategies were slightly smaller in Primary A than in Primary B. There was a significant difference ($p < 0.05$) in geometry learning strategies and a highly significant difference ($p < 0.001$) in self-help strategies between primary schools A and B.

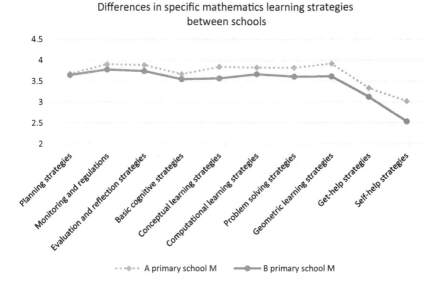

Figure 8.20 Differences in specific mathematics learning strategies between schools

Table 8.9 General status of mathematics learning strategies for students in grades 3 and 4

	Grades 3		*Grades 4*			
	M	*SD*	*M*	*SD*	*F*	*P*
Metacognitive strategies	3.82	0.86	3.96	0.73	1.651	0.200
Cognitive strategies	3.81	0.88	3.93	0.76	1.221	0.270
Support-seeking strategies	3.18	0.94	3.24	0.84	0.298	0.585

2. Differences in mathematics learning strategies between grades

A total of questionnaires of 222 were distributed to three classes in each of grades 3 and 4 in Primary School A. There were 109 questionnaires for grade 3 and 113 questionnaires for grade 4. The actual number of valid questionnaires collected was 222, with an effective rate of 100%. The general status of mathematics learning strategies for year 3 and 4 students was obtained, as shown in Table 8.9.

As can be seen from Tables 8.9, students' mean scores on the use of mathematics learning strategies were, in descending order, metacognitive strategies, cognitive strategies and support-seeking strategies. Students scored higher on metacognitive strategies than on cognitive strategies and support-seeking strategies, and scored three points above the threshold for metacognitive strategies, cognitive strategies and support-seeking strategies. Grades 4 mean scores were higher than grade 3 mean scores. There were no significant differences between grades 3 and grades 4 in metacognitive strategies, cognitive strategies and support-seeking strategies.

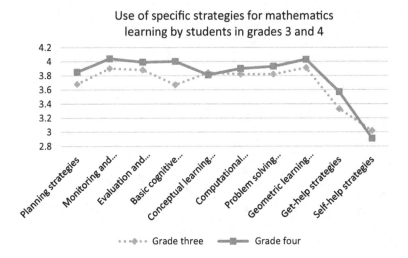

Figure 8.21 Use of specific strategies for mathematics learning by students in grades 3 and 4

To better understand the scores of year 3 and 4 on each of mathematics learning sub-strategies, we can see from Figure 8.21 that year 3 students scored slightly higher than year 4 students on the conceptual learning strategy and the self-help strategy. All other strategies were used at a lower level than the fourth graders. There was a significant difference in the basic cognitive strategies between grades 3 and grades 4 students ($p=0.043$, $p<0.05$).

As shown in Figure 8.22, in terms of standard deviation, there is a large variation in the conceptual learning strategies of year 3 students, mainly due to the fact that the thinking of students in the early years is still characterized by concrete images. In grade 3, students are exposed to more difficult and abstract concepts, which can be difficult to understand, so there is more variability between students. In contrast, grade 4 students have greater individual differences in basic cognitive strategies. Basic cognitive strategies refer to general strategies in primary school mathematics, such as paying attention to the mathematical content emphasized by the teacher and asking themselves questions to check the effectiveness of their mathematical learning. Grade 4 has entered the upper primary stage. The learning has been progressively enhanced. Students are required to master more generic strategies for learning mathematics, and in this context, individual differences between students gradually increase.

3. Differences in mathematics learning strategies and gender

As can be seen from Tables 8.10: (1) girls generally scored higher than boys on mathematics learning strategies in the two primary schools in S surveyed. (2) It can be seen from the standard deviation that the individual differences in mathematics

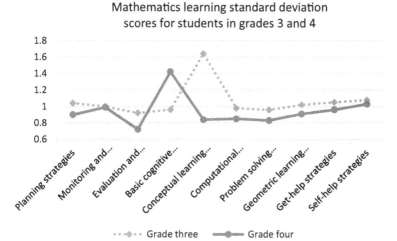

Figure 8.22 Mathematics learning standard deviation scores for students in grades 3 and 4

Table 8.10 Gender differences in learning strategies between girls and boys (M+SD)

	Metacognitive strategies	*Cognitive strategies*	*Support-seeking strategies*
Boys	3.72+0.861	3.75+0.876	2.96+0.936
Girls	3.93+0.806	3.75+0.851	3.09+0.855
F	4.207	0.501	1.251
Sig	0.016**	0.607	0.287

learning strategies of boys are higher than that of girls. (3) Of the three strategies, only the metacognitive strategy was significantly different (p<0.05).

As can be seen from the specific sub-strategies in Table 8.11 and Figure 8.23, boys scored slightly higher than girls in all sub-strategies except for strategies concept learning. In all other sub-strategies, girls scored higher than boys. In terms of standard deviation, in Figure 8.24, the individual differences were higher for girls than for boys, except for the strategies of evaluating reflective thinking, problem solving and learning geometry. For the other sub-strategies, the individual differences were higher for boys than for girls. For the other sub-strategies, the individual differences were higher for boys than for girls.

Of these sub-strategies, there was only a significant difference between boys and girls in the monitoring and monitoring strategy (p<0.01). There were no differences between boys and girls in any of the other strategies. Monitoring and regulating strategies are the responses of the cognitive subject to the monitoring and regulating activities of the individual cognitive activity, which can constantly evaluate the quality information of the cognitive activity, identify cognitive

Table 8.11 Gender differences in mathematics learning sub-strategies between girls and boys

	Boys		Girls		Differences	
	M	SD	M	SD	F	Sig.
Planning strategies	3.64	0.999	3.79	0.992	1.607	0.202
Monitoring and regulation strategies	3.71	1.144	4.09	0.902	7.526	0.001**
Evaluation and reflection strategies	3.79	0.854	3.91	0.882	1.605	0.202
Basic cognitive strategies	3.68	1.285	3.73	0.850	0.868	0.420
Conceptual learning strategies	3.76	1.330	3.65	0.983	1.197	0.303
Computational learning strategies	3.77	0.946	3.78	0.944	1.179	0.309
Problem-solving strategies	3.75	0.933	3.75	1.006	0.301	0.741
Geometric learning strategies	3.78	1.004	3.83	1.052	0.445	0.641
Get-help strategies	3.22	1.005	3.36	0.898	1.554	0.213
Self-help strategies	2.70	1.103	2.83	1.095	0.680	0.507

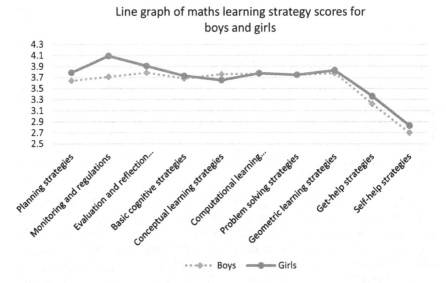

Figure 8.23 Line graph of maths learning strategy scores for boys and girls

deviations, and adjust the plan and choose the appropriate strategy to complete the task effectively (Liu, 1999). The differences in monitoring and regulation strategies between boys and girls were highly significant and consistent with the cognitive profile of 10-12 year olds. This is related to the different characteristics of self-awareness, emotions and volition of boys and girls. Research shows that girls are significantly more developed than boys in the areas of self-esteem, self-education and planning, and independence, while boys are not good at self-monitoring and are easily disturbed by external temptations (He, & Liu 1996).

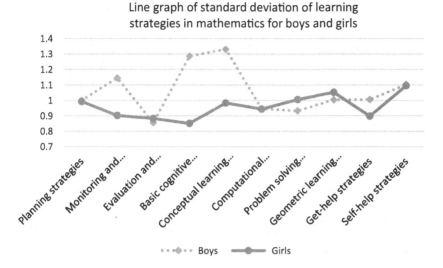

Figure 8.24 Line graph of standard deviation of learning strategies in mathematics for boys and girls

Conclusions of the study

Through the analysis of the above data, the study concluded the following: (1) the regional differences in learners were not significant. Regions with a better foundation can be selected as representatives for the experiments in this study; (2) there are gender differences in learners, with girls outperforming boys; (3) there are significant differences in the distribution of learning strategies, and the study should be conducted according to the questions on learning strategies; (4) the mathematics learning strategy scale has high validity and can be used for pre and post-test and latency measures in this study.

Visual diagnosis of primary school students' cognitive structures in mathematics

Cognitive structures are forms of representation of thinking, which is the human brain's generalization and indirect reflection of objective reality. Thinking is the basic form of activity of the human brain and is an elevated form of mental activity.[1] Mathematical thinking usually refers to the ability to think mathematically, the ability to think and solve mathematical problems using methods such as reasoning, analysis, induction, synthesis, abstraction and generalization. Thinking is abstract and is the brain's processing and reflection of objective reality. The question of how to represent the thinking in the learner's mind and how to better support and help the learner's learning in relation to his or her cognitive structure has become an issue of research and practice in thinking visualization techniques.

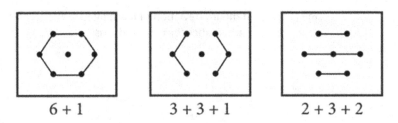

$$6 + 1 \qquad 3 + 3 + 1 \qquad 2 + 3 + 2$$

Figure 8.25 Students' card point combinations

Overview of the diagnostic system

Source of the problem

Supported by the Silicon Valley Education Fund,[2] YouCubed at Stanford University is transforming education and learning in mathematics and providing free and affordable mathematics resources and professional development content for K–12 educators and parents[3] (Boaler, 2008, 2014; Tang & Ma, 2014;). The project is led by Professor Jo Boaler. The author was involved in the design of the project's activities and their translation into Chinese. Among these interesting activities, a short six-minute video of Professor Jo Boaler teaching using dots on cards got the author thinking. In that activity, the combination of the seven dots as seen by the students is shown in Figure 8.25. You can see that each student sees maths differently. So why does everyone see maths differently when faced with the same seven dots? Is it possible to explore students' mathematical thinking processes in a meaningful way through "card dots"? The author tries to use computer and internet technology to manipulate the students' combined structure of the seven dots using PDA, which can visualize children's cognitive structure and at the same time store the displayed graphs in a certain coded form, forming big data for visualization of children's cognitive structure and providing visual mapping and improvement strategies for education and teaching.

Fundamentals of product design and development

1. THINKING VISUALIZATION TECHNIQUES

Thinking is internal to human cognition, not to behaviour. Thinking is more or less invisible and difficult to observe directly. Mental representation and mental arithmetic are the basis of the modern study of thinking. The view is that thinking is a series of activities that are internally symbolic. It leads to the production of novel and valid ideas or conclusions. Symbolic activity refers to the thinker's representation of external events, not just an objective reflection of the external driven by intuitive experience or the reproduction of long-term memory (Liu & Shui, 2002). Thinking is abstract and requires some form of representation of the thinking process, which is why visualization techniques have been developed. These use diagrams or combinations of diagrams to present methods, paths, ways and patterns of thinking and include two main types of diagramming techniques (mind maps, flowcharts, concept maps) and software techniques that generate diagrams directly (Mind manager, Free mind, X mind, etc.). The research uses graphics as a vehicle to combine the strengths of both types of technology to represent the states and characteristics of children's thinking in a game. The cognitive structures in the study are one of the key ways in which children's mathematical thinking is represented.

2. DIAGRAMS, MATHEMATICAL DIAGRAMS AND REPRESENTATIONAL DIAGRAMS

In the actual problem-solving process, it is necessary to find the information in long-term memory that is needed to correspond to the problem in order to be able to solve it. This "problem-responsive information" is the cognitive structure of the mind. The individual takes the incoming new information and reorganizes it by extracting the contents of the cognitive structures from memory. It is then integrated into a meaningful context to facilitate problem solving (Brown et al., 1989). A schema is a cognitive structure that exists in memory and contains the functions of selecting and filtering information, reasoning and predicting (Michael & Mark, 2015). Schema theory provides a cognitive psychological basis for the existence and application of mathematical schema.

A mathematical formula can be a simple mathematical symbol or expression such as "+", "-", sin, cos, etc., or an expression such as "1+1=2", "a+b=c", etc. "a+b=c", etc. Mathematical schema, as a fundamental part of students' mathematical cognition, are stored in the cognitive structure in the form of blocks of knowledge for recall. In learning activities and in certain physical contexts, learners organize their experiences intuitively to form representational schemata. In the process of learning mathematics, representational schemata are mainly a combination of concept-related properties and mental pictures, which provide the vehicle for mathematical schemata (Wang, 2007). In layman's terms, when children understand that 2+3=5, "2+3=5" is the mathematical equation. In a real-life situation, a child is given two matchsticks on the left and three matchsticks on the right, making a total of five matchsticks, and is then guided to understand how the concept of 2+3=5 corresponds to these five matchsticks in relation to the number of matchsticks and to link them together. This builds his representational schema and makes it concrete in his mind. When children understand that 3+2=5, again using the example of matchsticks, three matchsticks are placed on the left and two matchsticks are placed on the right. By counting, children will again see that there are still five matchsticks. When given concrete meaning, children can easily understand that 2+3=5 and 3+2=5 are equivalent, just in different positions. As can be seen, representational schemata provide a bridge between mathematical schemata and figurative objects, offering children the possibility of visualizing mathematical thinking with realistic operations.

3. THE CLASSIC "NINE-DOT-PROBLEM" PROBLEM
IN COGNITIVE PSYCHOLOGY

The classic "nine-dot-problem" in cognitive psychology is also the model used in many gesture passwords for smartphones today. There are a total of 986,400 passwords with at least two dots. In psychology, the subject is asked to draw four consecutive straight lines without repetition to connect all the dots, and the pen must not leave the paper until the nine dots are connected. Conventional thinking suggests that the line should be drawn within the square of nine dots. Unconventional thinking, on the other hand, breaks out of this square and extends the view beyond it. However, Weisberg and Alba implied that some subjects could draw the line outside the square and only 20% were able to understand the problem as shown in Figure 8.26 (Michael & Mark, 2009).

Why do many people confine their vision to the square? According to Piaget's schema doctrine, a stimulus is given to the subject by the outside world. As each subject has a different internal schema, the schema in turn has a selective and filtering effect. Individuals tend to select familiar schemata to reflect on the object based on their existing experience, while filtering out those that are rusty or useless. These familiar schema help individuals to solve many routine problems and are the most solid part of their cognitive structure. In the "nine-dot-problem", the vast majority of subjects could see at first glance that it was a square (pictorial perception). It can be shown that the mathematical schema of a square is so solid in existing schema of subjects that they can automatically filter it and then try to go beyond the boundaries to the outer areas of the square. It is a process of externalizing cognitive structures from the inside out, a mental picture of the organization of cognitive structures that are inherent in experience within a certain activity and physical environment, i.e. a representational model. Because of the filtering effect of the schema, when researchers suggest that lines can be drawn in the outer regions, only a small number of people are able to operate outside of the solidified mind.

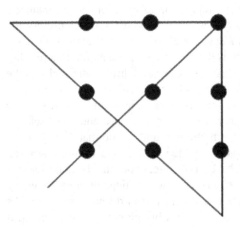

Figure 8.26 Nine-dot-problem linking method

This can be seen in the visualization of children's mathematical thinking. It is because the nine-dot-problem reflects the cognitive aspects of shapes that we can use the nine-dot-problem model to allow students to explore their structures by "connecting and drawing" their thinking; at the same time, the dot problem as a visual mathematical model in primary school mathematics is also very important for students' understanding of arithmetic. The dots in the nine-dot-problem can be used to establish correspondence with numbers, making it easier for students to carry out mathematical operations. The structure of the nine-dot-problem can trigger students to divide it into many different parts and produce a variety of methods. There is great value in encouraging students to diversify their algorithms. In summary, the nine-dot-problem reflects children's graphical cognitive structure and can also be used as a visual model to aid arithmetic understanding. It is not only the nine-dot-problem that has this function, but also the five-dot-problem, seven-dot-problem, twelve-dot-problem and twenty-dot-problem, which can be set up in a hierarchical manner from easy to not so easy, in order to explore students' thinking about the combination of graphical and mathematical operations. In this way, we can identify whether students' cognitive structures are strong or weak or not yet established, and use strategies to help them build their own good mathematical thinking structures based on the knowledge networks that they demonstrate. The CSV-PDA system was developed using a moderately difficult seven-dot-problem, as the subject of the study is children's thinking.

Composition and functions of diagnostic PDA products

A PDA, or Personal Digital Assistant, is a digital tool that helps us work, learn and play primarily on the move. The PDA in this study, called CSV-PDA (Cognitive Structure Visualization), consists of two parts, software and hardware. The software is in the form of an APP and contains two versions, Android and Web. It can be installed on any mobile smart terminal corresponding to the system and operated digitally; the hardware is completed by a microcontroller package with seven main lights and 18 auxiliary lights; communication between the two takes place via Bluetooth. When different graphics are constructed on the app, the microcontroller will respond by different colours to the structure and transformation of the graphics. The hardware part focuses on triggering children's interest and enhancing the playfulness of the PDA. The learners' attention is focused on the hardware toy, thus allowing their mathematical thinking to be visualized in the game rather than through traditional mathematical questions; the software part is collected through data to the server. The system automatically generates a map of the individual learner, class, grade, gender and other dimensions. It objectively reflects the state of the cognitive structure distribution of learners, thus providing a basis for activities such as adaptive allocation and intervention of resources for personalized learning and guidance of grouping for cooperative learning.

Diagnostic design and implementation

Diagnostic questions

The researcher visualized the cognitive structure of the same subjects in the diagnosis of strategies for learning mathematics. It allows answering the following questions: firstly, what is the current state of the cognitive structure of primary school students in mathematics between cities (regions) and how it differs; secondly, whether there are differences in the cognitive structure of mathematics between boys and girls; and thirdly, how the cognitive structure differs between grades.

Diagnostic subjects

The study was selected to study the same subjects in the diagnosis of strategies for learning mathematics in order to discover the relationship between learning strategies, cognitive structure and academic achievement on the one hand, and because the students have accumulated a lot of knowledge at that stage

Diagnostic implementation

1. IMPLEMENTATION TIME

The study was carried out one week after the diagnosis of the learning strategies, so that on the one hand the learners' developmental changes were not significant enough to correspond effectively to the learning strategies, and on the other hand the interval of one week reduced the disruption to the learners.

2. THE APPLICATION ENVIRONMENT

The diagnostic environment was the multimedia classroom of the primary school. The test platforms used were as follows: city of S used the school's standard electronic schoolbag (Lenovo Miix2), and the other cities used PCs in the school's computer room, all using Google Chrome and supporting HTML5 touch screening operations.

3. APPLICATION FLOW

Figure 8.27 shows a panoramic view of the entire application of the children's mathematical thinking visualization product. The product operates in an internet environment, with students using one device (or e.schoolbag, or mobile phone). A web page or Android application is opened, and the teacher is guided to perform the appropriate actions on the device and submit the data to the PC database via the HTTP protocol. The teacher can view all statistics on the PC. Students can view data from the individual backend on their own devices. Bluetooth is only available for one-to-one connections. The students took turns experiencing

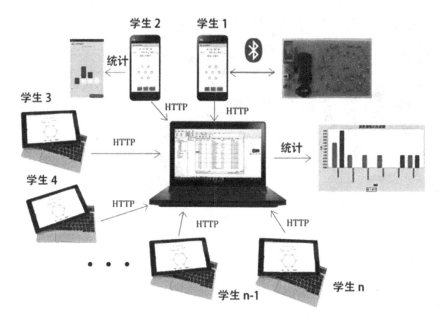

Figure 8.27 Panorama of CSV-PDA applications

Figure 8.28 Map of the measurement site (1)

the maths toy. The evaluation site is shown in Figure 8.28 and the procedure is described below.

Teachers organize students into multimedia classrooms by grade level and instruct them to open the hyperlinks to the pages of the e-book package and the mobile app.

Figure 8.29 Map of the measurement site (2)

The teacher instructs the students to fill in their school ID and tells them the rules for filling in their numbers, e.g. for year 5, class 8, the school ID would be "5108". Age and gender are selected from the drop-down list.

The teacher asks: "Good afternoon, students! Today we are going to do activity. How many dots are there in the pattern that you see on the screen?" Students are all able to respond with 7 dots.

> In what ways did the students see the seven points and how did they address them? The teacher requests students to connect the dots on the screen with your ideas and raise your hand when you have finished.

The reason why the teacher does not demonstrate the sample to the students here is that sample diagrams can be effective in facilitating the formation and refinement of diagrams. This would have limited students' thinking and discouraged them from playing freely.

"All students have drawn very well, now what about drawing patterns for everyone and filling in your calculations or your own ideas for calculating these points inside the 'calculate one'".

After confirming that the students have completed the above steps, instruct them to click on the submit button to submit, and a data submission dialog box appears to indicate successful submission. The students understood the meaning of "submit" during the experiment. There were many positive responses from students who submitted their data early. Students were also instructed to use the "Clear" button to clear and redraw the graphs if they had been connected incorrectly in the previous and operations.

After the students have completed the operations on the respective platforms, they are guided to freely "connect the dots" to create their favourite shapes. The data is not submitted to the database during the free "connects the dots" session.

As the number of maths toys is limited, students take turns experiencing the maths toys.

Data analysis

A total of 4,112 people participated in the assessment in the four cities due to students' leave of absence. The data was filtered and 3,865 valid data were recorded, with an effective rate of 94%, which is basically the same as the 93% effective rate of the learning strategies.

Distribution of students' cognitive structure types in the four cities

The reduced schema based on student statistics is shown in Table 8.12.

As can be seen from Table 8.12, the study divides them into four main categories: single point schema, combined schema, graphical schema and multi-schema, of which combined schema contains four sub-categories, graphical schema contains three sub-categories and multi-schema contain two sub-categories, as elaborated here. (1) Single point schema means that students are counting by counting points one by one. (2) Combining schema means that students have the concept of sets and are able to combine them using addition. (3) Pictorial schema means that students are able to present geometric patterns on the screen and are able to represent their schema using the corresponding arithmetic. (4) Multi-schema is when students are able to consciously discover complex connections without guidance and use multiplication to count. In sorting the data into categories, the study used the following rules: (1) if both combined and pictorial patterns were present, they were classified among the pictorial pattern types; (2) if both pictorial and multi-schema patterns were present, they were classified among the multi-schema pattern types.

Comparing Table 3.10 with Table 8.12, it can be seen that: the structures in the two tables are similar; the "single point schema" corresponds to the "single structure"; the "combined schema" corresponds to the "multiple structure"; the "graphic schema" corresponds to the "associated structure"; "multi-linked schema" corresponds to the "abstract extension structure"; "combined schema" corresponds to "multiple structure"; "graphic schema" corresponds to "associative structure"; and "multi-schema" corresponds to "abstract expansion structure". The CSV-PDA can be used to assess the cognitive level of learners.

Overall distribution of primary school students' cognitive structures in the four cities

The overall distribution of the four cities according to the primary school students' cognitive structure types in mathematics table is shown in Figure 8.30. From the figure, it can be seen that: the distribution trend is similar in the four cities, which is consistent with the four cities in the learning strategy diagnosis without significant differences; the ranking of the number of all four types is B>C>A>D, which, according to SOLO classification theory, indicates that most of the students in

Table 8.12 Types of cognitive structures in mathematics for primary school students in the four cities

Item	Code	Schema type		Item	Code	Schema type	
		Schema	Algorithmic representation			Schema	Algorithmic representation
Single point schema	A		1+1+1+1 +1+1+1	Graphical schema	C	C₁	5+2
Merged schema	B	B₁	2+3+2			C₂	6+1
		B₂	3+3+1			C₃	3+3+3.2
		B₃	3+4	Multi-schema	D	D₁ Same as combined 1, 2	2*2+3 2*3+1
		B₄	2+2+2+1			D₂	3*3.2=7

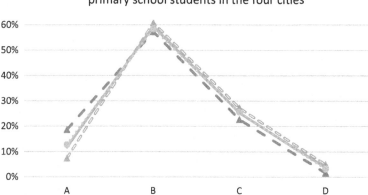

Overall distribution of mathematics cognitive structure of primary school students in the four cities

Figure 8.30 Overall distribution of mathematics cognitive structure of primary school students in the four cities

primary schools in the four cities have not yet reached the level of deep learning; compared with Figure 8.17 and Figure 8.18, type A in city of S is the lowest, and types B, C and D are higher than other cities; city of C has the highest type A and the lowest types B, C and D; the folds in city of W and K tend to overlap, residing between city of S and city of C. This phenomenon is generally consistent with the distribution in the diagnosis.

Gender distribution of the cognitive structure of primary school students in the four cities

The gender distribution of the cognitive structure of primary school students in the four cities is shown in Figure 8.31. Type D, however, does not follow the above trend, and girls are lower than boys. These two points indicate that girls are better learners than boys overall, but there are not as many as boys in terms of the small number of students who have reached a level of deeper learning.

Grade distribution of the cognitive structure of primary school students in the four cities

The grade distribution of the cognitive structure of primary school students in the four cities is shown in Figure 8.32. From the figure, it can be seen that: compared with Figure 8.21 and Figure 8.22, the distribution trend of both figures shows that the type level of the cognitive structure of learners gradually increases as the grade level rises, and the depth learning gradually increases,

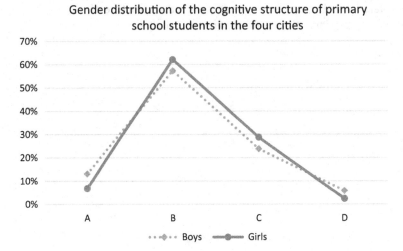

Figure 8.31 Gender distribution of the cognitive structure of primary school students in the four cities

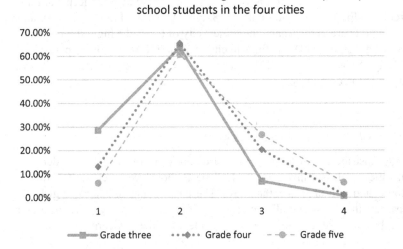

Figure 8.32 Grade distribution of the cognitive structure of primary school students in the four cities

but the increasing trend is not obvious. From grade 3 to grade 5, A and C are the two types with the greatest change, indicating that having type C is the level that most of the top students can achieve, and a small number of top students can achieve type D.

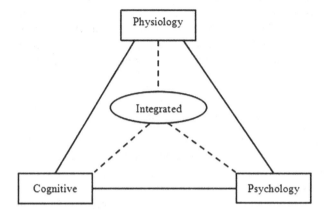

Figure 8.33 The "triangulation" assessment structure for learning

Diagnostic conclusions

In summary, the study can draw the following conclusions: the distribution of learning strategies and cognitive structures basically has a correspondence relationship, and both can reflect the distribution of learners' cognitive levels. The SOLO classification theory can better explain the cognitive level of learners. The empirical data also shows that the SOLO theory is reasonable and feasible, and can be used to quantify learners' cognitive levels. Thinking maps can be used as a concrete form of its operation. The majority of learners are in types B and C, with a low percentage reaching type D deeper learning levels. Deeper learning in classroom techniques is worth investigating.

Research pathways for interaction to brain-machine for effective learning to occur

The "triangulation" assessment structure for learning

The perspective of learning science is about the depth of learning. There is now consensus in four areas: firstly, learners should be active, motivated, critical and constructive. Secondly, learning should be concerned with contextual transfer, problem solving and innovation. Thirdly, learners should have a good emotional experience during the learning process. Fourthly, the learning process is consistent with the social attributes of personalization-based socialization. However, these four areas of understanding are still descriptive representations. It is difficult to quantify and evaluate in practice. Therefore, we have developed a "triangulation" system and methodology to describe the occurrence of learning through a long period of empirical research. We believe that learning can only occur in depth and meaningfully if there is a mutually corroborating relationship between the physical, cognitive and psychological dimensions. Learning is therefore carried out in such a way that the pedagogical elements of the structure of learning content, the representation of learning resources and the implementation of learning activities all contribute effectively to the development of learners in all three of these areas. This is the evaluation criterion and value attributed to brain–computer interaction research and applications.

Interaction to brain-machine and its application in education

Brain–computer interaction is a technology that does not rely on peripheral nerve and muscle tissue to accomplish the exchange of information in a certain interactive way for communication between the brain and the computer. It was in 1929 that the German scientist Hans Berger first detected electroencephalographic signals by means of an instrument. This ground-breaking discovery led scientists to adopt scientific and technical means to detect and analyze brain activity. Brain waves are the rhythm, weak changes in electrical potential that occur when nerve cells and nerve fibres in the brain transmit nerve impulses. These primarily respond to potential changes in the cerebral cortex. Dual electrodes placed on the scalp are used to record such changes in the cerebral cortex, hence its name electroencephalography (EEG). EEG sensors require a great deal of preparation. Electrodes need to be fixed to the experimenter's head with a gel, and brain-wave sensing techniques were previously commonly used in the engineering and medical fields. With the development of technology, it is now possible to use brain–computer interaction to collect brain waves from students, which makes it possible to measure brain waves in the classroom. The continuous optimization of artificial intelligence algorithms has led to an increase in the explanatory power of EEG signals for the learning psychology of humans. As a result, brain–computer interaction is gradually being applied to the fields of physiological or brain science, cognitive psychology and learning science. In the field of learning science and educational technology research, the technology is gradually optimized by observing brain waves in brain–computer interaction. It can become a method and strategy in the design of learning, for example, the characterization, development and application of individual learning resources. At present, brain–computer interaction is mainly used in three ways: firstly, to detect the physiological signals of the brain in individual learners' activities, mainly for research and evaluation of the psychological aspects of learning; secondly, to provide feedback based on brainwave data in intelligent learning systems, and on this basis to continuously adjust the learning path and optimize the learning process, forming an adaptive learning approach to facilitate learners' learning. This is an area that researchers and practitioners in the field of learning science and educational technology are experimenting with; thirdly, we are trying to monitor the condition of brain waves in groups, mainly to monitor the effect of brain synergy, for example, when the synergy between teachers' and learners' brain waves is higher, the better the learning effect will be. This aspect of experimentation can be used in the study of the construction of learning communities and learning cultures.

Possibilities for brain–computer interaction technologies to facilitate effective learning to occur

Brain–computer interaction signals to monitor and represent learning states have now shown some possibilities in focusing on enhancing learners' attention, self-efficacy, attitudes and comprehension; these are precisely the indicators that promote learning towards depth and effectiveness and help to achieve effective alignment between the physiological (brain waves), cognitive (academic performance) and psychological (attention, attitudes and efficacy, etc.) dimensions. They also offer realistic possibilities for the design of pathways and the development of digital resources for effective learning.

Brain–computer interaction technology can reveal to a certain extent the laws of "how people learn". Brain–computer interaction technology can record the signals of brain waves and changes in the whole learning process. Through the collection of signals from the learning population, AI deeper learning algorithms can be strongly correlated with the learning mind, thus revealing a certain degree of "how people learn". For example, one experimenter engaged learners in a multiple number memorization activity and recorded the learners' brain states each time during the process. The study found that when learners summarize the pattern of numbers, the brain state becomes easier compared to the beginning. The EEG signals change. Thus, the physiology of "how people learn" is gradually revealed, providing a scientific basis for the design of learning activities, the characterization of learning resources and the development of intelligent learning systems. It helps to improve the effectiveness and science of teaching design.

Brain–computer interaction technology provides a signal basis for "personalized-collaborative" learning. Brain–computer interaction technology can reflect the learning process of individual learners more accurately. In an intelligent learning system, the individual learner's learning process can be fed back and recorded in real time through brain–computer interaction. This feedback enables the system of intelligent learning to push out appropriate learning resources and adjust learning steps in real time. On the one hand, learning paths are generated to match individual learning styles. On the other hand, individual data can be used to continuously match homogeneous and heterogeneous learners, thus continuously guiding the learning activities of the group and forming an effective collaborative learning path. Learning is an individual-based socialization process. Brain–computer interaction technology can provide a basis of signal for "personalized collaborative" learning.

Pathways for brain–computer interaction technology to facilitate effective learning to occur

The technology of virtual reality is used to create learning environments by integrating brain–computer interaction with the technology of virtual reality. In terms of the creation of learning spaces and environments, there are three main types:

firstly, breaking the constraints of space and time, allowing learners to enter directly from the real world to another time and space, for example, travelling through history, talking to historical , crossing mountains and plains, experiencing and understanding geographic knowledge in real life; secondly, realizing scenarios and spaces that are difficult to reach or touch in reality, for example, satellite orbit observation, cell activity tracking, etc.; thirdly, vocational training with high security requirements, for example, car driving, cell activity tracking, long-distance combat exercises, etc. In the learning environment created by the above-mentioned virtual reality technology, brain–computer interaction technology is integrated to capture the learner's brainwave signals more accurately during the learning process on the one hand, and to interpret these signals through cognitive psychology on the other. This allows for a better understanding of the learner's mental processes and state of mind, which allows for the continuous improvement of the learning environment and facilitates effective learning. The process of training university students' psychological qualities in a virtual reality environment can also be based on brain–computer interaction technology. In this virtual environment, subjects will be exposed to a variety of comfortable, scary and dangerous states. Through brain–computer interaction technology, the researcher observes their brainwave signals and psychological states in order to give interventions.

Integration of brain-machine interaction in AI technology is used to achieve an adaptive learning process. The application of artificial intelligence technology in education is manifested in the brainwave signals of two learning states (good and poor). The adaptive learning path of the learner is continuously and gradually generated according to the learner's cognitive starting point, learning style, stage learning effect and other factors. And what the machine of deeper learning has learned, the accuracy of its data, will directly constrain the science and effectiveness of the learning path. Brain–computer interaction technology is integrated into intelligent learning systems based on artificial intelligence. It can provide valid physiological data for machine deeper learning from the perspective of brain wave signals. It can facilitate the accuracy and effectiveness of machines of deeper learning, thus enhancing the adaptive properties of the learning process.

In brain–computer interaction technology, big data can be used to record and process the entire learning process and behaviour. Brain–computer interaction technology generates 300 individual brainwave values every five minutes, both because of the sheer volume of data and because of the complex learning psychological characteristics of learning that needs to be analyzed. These complex learning psychographics map the behaviour of the whole learning process in reality. It can be seen that a "learning behaviour data chain" is created among the data, the psychological characteristics and the learning behaviour. A number of discrete pieces of data are analyzed by Big Data for Education to reveal the intrinsic psychological characteristics of learners. There is a chain of interactions between these psychological characteristics, which in turn map to the external learning behaviour of the learners. This chain of learning behaviour data will enable teachers to have a more accurate picture of the individual and group learning behaviour trajectories of learners on the one hand, and to identify intervention points in the chain and design intervention methods and strategies on the other.

Brain–computer interaction technologies are applied to intelligent learning systems to enable the "triangulation" of learning. An intelligent learning system is an integration of some or all of the above-mentioned technologies such as virtual reality, artificial intelligence and big data analytics. Based on the above analysis, an intelligent learning system using brain–computer interaction technology will visually reflect the performance of the learner on three levels: physical, cognitive and psychological. If all three have reached the quality of learning thresholds, then the individual or group is considered to have achieved a good level of learning; if one or more of thresholds is not met, then the Data Chain of Learning Behaviour can be used to identify the cause. The learning process is continuously adjusted and modified to achieve effective learning.

Brain–computer interaction technology enhances the intelligence of existing online learning systems

The real-time monitoring and moderation of the learning process in brain–computer interaction better meets the cognitive needs of the learner. Learners are more likely to feel satisfied, more likely to improve their self-efficacy and to achieve better results in such a learning process. This phenomenon suggests that learners are able to adapt to brain–computer interaction interventions in the process of online learning, which can also enhance attention and attitudes to learning. The fact that learners are able to recognize such interventions provides a realistic possibility for the implementation of brain–computer interaction technology in practice.

A dynamic, real-time and accurate adaptive learning path has been created by existing learning systems in an effort to create it. However, the questions of what this concept is based on and how to implement it, how to diagnose the cognitive starting point of learners, how to automate the classification of learning styles and how to intelligently monitor the learning process have been troubling researchers and practitioners of intelligent learning. The involvement of brain–computer interaction technology provides a basis and an object of judgement for solving the above problems to a certain extent. During the experimental operation, multiple adaptive learning paths were generated, which improved the intelligence of the online learning system. All monitoring and intervention processes are based on brain–computer interaction technology, which dynamically monitors the learner's learning state and provides real-time feedback and timely responses and adjustments by the learner.

Physiological, cognitive and psychological dimensions of learning outcomes are improved in brain–computer interaction and illustrated with a range of mutually corroborating data. For example, there is a mapping between brain waves, academic performance, attention and attitude to learning. This is in line with the "triangulation of evidence" requirement in the assessment of learning effectiveness. It goes some way to meeting the need for effective learning to occur, and it provides new ideas for the design and development of effective learning systems.

Notes

1 Mathematical thinking, Baidu Encyclopedia[EB/OL].
    http://baike.baidu.com/view/1872770.htm. 12 December 2016.
2 Website: www.youcubed.org/. 12 June 2015.
3 Website: http://baike.baidu.com/view/1872770.htm. 12 December 2016.

References

Biggs, J.B. (2012). The revised two factor study process questionnaire: R.SPQ.2F. *The British Psychological Society*, *1*, 134–149.

Biggs, J.B. (2014). Learning strategies, student motivation patterns and subjectively perceived success. In J.R. Kirby (Ed.) *Cognitive strategies and educational performance*. Cambridge, MA: Academic Press, INC.

Boaler, J. (2008). *What's math got to do with it?* New York: the Penguin Group. Boaler, J. (2014). China Talk, China Hefei.

Brown, J.S., Collins, A., & Duguid,Q (1989). Situated cognition and the culture of learning. *Educational Researcher*, *18*(1), 32–42.

Carole, A., & Jerrifer, A. (1988). Achievement goals in the classroom: students' learning strategies and motivation processes. *Journal of Educational Psychology*, *88*(3), 260–267.

Carr, M., & Jessup, D. (1997). Gender difference in first.grade mathematics strategy use,social and meta cognitive influences. *Journal of Educational Psychology*, *89*(2), 318–328.

He, J.J., & Liu, H.S.H. (1996). The study on cognitive strategies and development of 10.14 years old under performing students. *Psychological Science*, *19*(3), 189–190.

Lei, L., & Zhang, Q. (2014). Adverse attribution and learning motivation in junior high school students. *Psychological Development and Education*, (4).

Lei, L., Hou, Z.J., & Bai, X.J. (2015). Different grade teachers college students' learning motivation and learning strategies. *Psychological Development and Education*, (4), 17–22.

Liu, A.L., & Shui, R.D. (2002). *Psychology of thinking*. Shanghai: Shanghai Education Press, 5: 35.

Liu, D.Z. (1999). *Study on learning strategies*. Beijing: People's Education Press.

Liu, D.Z., & Huang, X.T. (2005). The application and development characteristics of primary school pupils' math learning strategies. *Psychological Science*, *28*(2), 272–276.

Liu, J.X., Xiu, T., Huang, G.Q., & Shen , J.L. (2014).Middle school students learning motivation, the relationship between learning strategies and academic achievement. *Educational Theory and Practice*, *20*(9), 54–58.

Michael W.E., & Mark, T. (2009). *Keane. Cognitive psychology: A student's handbook* (5th Edition). London: Psychology Press: 526.

Michael, W.E., & Mark T. K. (2015) .*Cognitive psychology: A student's handbook* (7th Edition). London: Psychology Press: 38.

Shen, Z.F. (2013). Shanghai mental health education of primary and secondary schools teachers present situation investigation and countermeasures Research. *Ideological and Theoretical Education*, (3), 71–75.

Siegler, R.S. (1997a). Older and younger adults' strategy choice in multiplication: testing predictions of ASCM using the choice No. choice method. *Journal of Experimental Psychology: General*, *126*, 71–92.

Siegler, R.S. (1997b). Strategy choice in older and younger adult's multiplication. *Journal of Experimental Psychology: Learning, Memory and Cognition, 23,* 71–91.

Tang, Y.J., & Ma, X.Q. (2014). K12 Education in the Internet age: The research and practice in mathematics teaching and learning. *China Educational Technology,* (5), 1–3.

Wan, J.J., & Zheng, X.B. (2014).The investigation on science curriculum's learning motivation and learning strategies of middle school students. *Subject Education,* (10), 41–44.

Wang, X. (2007). Symbols are in mathematics teaching: The understanding of image schema sense. *Chinese Journal of Education,* (1), 63–65.

Wang, Z.H., & Liu,P. (2014a).Motivation factors, learning strategies, the influence of the intelligence level of students' academic achievement. *Journal of Psychology, 32*(1), 65–69.

Wang, Z.H., & Liu, P. (2014b). Theory and research of self on learning motivation. *Shandong Normal University, 47*(2), 89–93.

Zhang, M.L. (2012). *The mathematics learning strategies of junior high school students' and its relationship with strategy consciousness, thinking style, mathematics achievement.* Wenzhou, China: Wenzhou University.

Zhang, Y.L., & Guo, D.J. (2014). Learning strategy teaching research on the influence of learning motivation. *Psychological Science,* (3).

Zhang, Y.L., & Yang, S.L. (2015). Middle school students learning motivation and learning strategies. *Psychological Development and Education,* (4).

Index

Printed in the United States
by Baker & Taylor Publisher Services